HIGHER
EXPECTATIONS

HIGHER EXPECTATIONS

CAN COLLEGES TEACH STUDENTS WHAT THEY NEED TO KNOW IN THE TWENTY-FIRST CENTURY?

———◆———

DEREK BOK

PRINCETON UNIVERSITY PRESS

PRINCETON AND OXFORD

Requests for permission to reproduce material from this work
should be sent to permissions@press.princeton.edu

Published by Princeton University Press
41 William Street, Princeton, New Jersey 08540
99 Banbury Road, Oxford OX2 6JX

press.princeton.edu

First paperback printing, 2022
Paper ISBN 978-0-691-20661-5

The Library of Congress has cataloged the cloth edition as follows:
Names: Bok, Derek Curtis, author.
Title: Higher expectations : can colleges teach students what they need to
    know in the twenty-first century? / Derek Bok.
Description: Princeton, New Jersey : Princeton University Press, 2020. |
    Includes bibliographical references and index.
Identifiers: LCCN 2019056821 | ISBN 9780691205809 (hardcover)
Subjects: LCSH: Education, Higher—Aims and objectives—United States. |
    Education, Higher—Curricula—United States. | College teaching—United States. |
    Educational change—United States. | Education and globalization.
Classification: LCC LA227.4 .B666 2020 | DDC 378.73—dc23
LC record available at https://lccn.loc.gov/2019056821

British Library Cataloging-in-Publication Data is available

Editorial: Peter Dougherty and Alena Chekanov
Production Editorial: Jill Harris
Text Design: Leslie Flis
Jacket/Cover Design: Leslie Flis
Production: Erin Suydam
Publicity: Alyssa Sanford and Kate Farquhar-Thomson
Copyeditor: Cynthia Buck

Jacket/Cover image: Ceiling in entrance hall of Christ Church, Oxford / Alamy

This book has been composed in Sabon LT Std text with Bodoni display

Contents

Preface

Higher Expectations is the culmination of seven decades of engagement with questions of teaching and learning dating back to my undergraduate days in the late 1940s, when I served as a student representative on a curriculum committee at Stanford. At age twenty, my thoughts about education were not always carefully considered. Thus, when a new president, Wallace Sterling, announced in a speech to the students that he was determined to make Stanford "the Harvard of the West," I decided on the following day to write him a letter explaining why Stanford in its present form could never rival Harvard as an academic institution. My point was simply that Stanford could not make up its mind whether it should be a great academic institution, a great athletic power, or a great place for having fun and enjoying a wealth of extracurricular pursuits. Although I had never set foot on Harvard's campus and knew next to nothing about the institution, I proceeded to contrast it with Stanford by describing its unswerving commitment to intellectual excellence. Until Stanford made up its mind to do likewise, I maintained, it could not hope to become "the Harvard of the West."

The very next day, while waiting in line for lunch, I was approached by a member of the staff, who said that President Sterling would like to see me. "Very well," I replied, "I will call and make an appointment." "President Sterling wishes to see you *now*," the emissary replied. Abandoning all thoughts of lunch, I hurried to the president's office and engaged for the next thirty minutes in what the State Department would describe as "a full and frank exchange of views" in which neither of us gave ground to the other.

Decades later, in my twentieth year as Harvard's president, I was asked to contribute a letter for inclusion in a book to celebrate Stanford's first one hundred years. I decided to respond by recalling my encounter with President Sterling. I ended my account with the statement: "History will determine which of us was more nearly correct." I then signed the letter "Derek Bok, Stanford of the East."

After receiving my law degree and spending almost three years in the Army, I continued my interest in education by joining the Harvard

Law School faculty and chairing the curriculum committee, followed by three eventful years as dean. It was no accident, then, that when I came to be president of Harvard in 1971, I chose to make teaching and learning a priority.

I soon realized that undergraduate education occupied a lowly position on the totem pole of faculty concerns. After two decades of basking in the warming sun of continuous growth in federal funding, most professors had become preoccupied with research and graduate (PhD) training. In the mid-1960s, the faculty had made an effort to revise the curriculum but had to abandon it after failing to reach a consensus on how to move forward. That experience left everyone discouraged about the prospects for academic reform. The angry campus protests at the end of the decade over the Vietnam War and other issues had left the faculty with little enthusiasm for spending several more years of effort improving undergraduate education.

Despite these conditions, I was dismayed that such a distinguished faculty seemed unwilling to pay more attention to teaching undergraduates. After all, then as now, Harvard attracted an exceptionally talented and intellectually curious group of students. Surely they deserved the most challenging and stimulating education that their professors could provide.

I therefore decided to devote my first speech before the Faculty of Arts and Sciences to the subject of undergraduate teaching. I worked hard on the speech and felt that it had gone reasonably well until I was visited by Gerald Holton, a professor of physics who had been the youngest member of a committee formed at the end of World War II to review the college curriculum. After expressing appreciation for my choice of topics, he informed me that at least three-quarters of the faculty in the audience had given up on me entirely when I announced the subject of my address.

It is a constant challenge for a university president to try to counter the tendency of professors in the most distinguished universities to value research and publication over teaching. The incentive structure strongly favors the former over the latter. Faculty salaries nationwide also privilege research and publication, and the market compels obedience, else the most accomplished scientists and scholars will soon depart for greener pastures. Even if this imbalance were removed, the outside world would still reward successful researchers with summer stipends, prizes, consulting opportunities, and other benefits that are rarely available even to the most inspiring teachers. Under these conditions, university presidents must summon a lot of ingenuity to create and sustain a lively interest in teaching and educational reform.

Despite these difficulties, I eventually witnessed a few heartening signs of progress. After five years of patient work by my wise and widely trusted dean, Henry Rosovsky, the faculty produced a new and vastly improved curriculum. Henry managed to enlist a number of the most respected teachers and scholars to take the lead in this review. During the ensuing months, the committee made extraordinary efforts to meet with small groups of faculty to discuss its proposals and adapt them where necessary in response to the feedback it received.

As the review reached a critical stage, an unexpected development threatened to derail our efforts. Dean Rosovsky received an offer to become the next president of Yale. When he traveled to New Haven to talk with Yale officials, I feared that all was lost. To my surprise, however, he returned to Cambridge a few days later and informed me that he would stay at Harvard. When I pressed him to explain, he replied: "I thought I ought to finish what I started." Moved by his example, and following some of the most interesting debates that I have ever heard at Harvard, the faculty approved the new curriculum overwhelmingly.

Perhaps the principal lesson I learned from this experience was that the most important accomplishment of the review was to energize the faculty by giving them a clearer common understanding of what the curriculum was meant to achieve. The extensive consultation gave them a sense of ownership of the final product, and, for many professors, an increased interest in contributing to the new program by heavily revising their own undergraduate courses or offering entirely new ones.

A few years later, we were able to take another step toward improving undergraduate education by creating a teaching and learning center, thanks to a handsome grant from the Danforth Foundation. The Harvard-Danforth Center soon began offering various services to instructors such as individual coaching, microteaching, and videotaping. Although interest among the tenured faculty was initially limited, graduate students who served as teaching fellows in large courses soon began coming to the center for assistance. In the years that followed, the center's services expanded to include orientation programs, workshops on pedagogy, and short films depicting difficult moments in teaching that could stimulate discussion on topics such as problems of race and gender arising in the classroom. Over time the clientele for the center gradually increased, more and more representatives visited from other colleges and universities in America and abroad to observe the services it offered, and several of our professional schools started to use the center or develop similar units of their own.

We also carried on a modest program of research on teaching at Harvard in order to discover weaknesses in need of repair. One tactic that proved especially successful was to compare the work of one department with that of another. In the spirit of competition so prevalent in America, few interventions were as effective in bringing about reform as a well-crafted study showing that one department's teaching efforts were clearly inferior in the eyes of students to similar efforts by a neighboring department.

The most striking accomplishment of our research was a study of student writing from the freshman to the senior year. The inquiry revealed that although students majoring in the humanities and social sciences improved their writing substantially, science majors, on average, wrote less well in their fourth year of college than they did when they first entered Harvard. No pleading or cajoling was required to produce corrective action. Once we had distributed the results and explained that science majors regressed because they rarely saw a need to write in complete sentences, the departments quickly introduced more writing assignments. A follow-up test conducted years later revealed that science majors were now making ample improvement in their writing.

Looking back at our efforts to improve teaching and learning, the results, though helpful, seemed modest in comparison with the need. Despite the interest and energy unleashed by the curriculum reform and the growing use of the teaching and learning center, significant weaknesses remained. On one occasion, for example, I managed to insert into the course evaluation forms a question about how much the class had helped to improve students' critical thinking. This question seemed fair enough, since the principal purpose of the courses, according to the faculty's own curriculum committee, was to teach students how to think critically. As the evaluations made clear, however, while students had good things to say about many instructors, only about 10 percent of the courses had helped them to think more critically. The effect of this finding, alas, was not to inspire an immediate effort by the faculty to revise their methods of teaching. Instead, the question was quietly dropped from the following year's evaluation forms.

There were some bright spots, of course. Hundreds of students flocked to courses such as Stephen Jay Gould's lectures on evolution and Michael Sandel's provocative discussions about issues of justice. A small group of professors, almost all of them distinguished scientists, proved to be very interested in teaching and were instant volunteers for several of my educational projects, such as improving the badly outdated premed requirements. One of the most enthusiastic was Dudley Herschbach, a Nobel Prize winner in chemistry, who turned out to have been a freshman football recruit many years before when I was head proctor for the large residence hall that housed all the first-year men at Stanford. Despite these encouraging signs, I ended my twenty-year presidency feeling that I should somehow have accomplished more.

Following my retirement, I began teaching at the Kennedy School of Government, one of my high-priority projects as president. Having been asked to chair a committee at the school on teaching and learning, I helped to initiate an exceptional effort, led by faculty member Dick Light, to assess how much students were learning. His review included studies of the school's programs ranging from the flagship master's degree in public policy to the assortment of one- and two-week sessions for career civil servants and high-level officials, such as newly elected mayors, Red Cross executives, and political leaders from overseas nations. The exercise confirmed my belief in the value of carefully crafted assessments for identifying the strengths and weaknesses of programs of instruction.

In 2006, having retired from teaching, I was happily wintering in Florida when I received an unexpected visit from two members of Harvard's governing board. They brought the startling news that President Lawrence Summers had just resigned and that they would like me to return to take the reins once again until a replacement could be found.

And so it was that after fifteen years I reentered the president's office at age seventy-six for what I soon came to describe as a Rip Van Winkle experience in which much was familiar yet much had changed.

The condition of undergraduate education, as I soon discovered, was a mixture of progress and frustration. Some noteworthy improvements had been made during my fifteen-year absence from the president's office. A small but capable staff had been hired to carry out research on different aspects of undergraduate education. An orientation program focused on teaching had been created for new members of the faculty. The teaching and learning center was larger and serving more graduate students and professors than ever before.

At the same time, a two-year effort to review the undergraduate curriculum was floundering. Unable to agree on real reform, the faculty appeared to be on the verge of settling for a distribution program that would simply require students to obtain a breadth of learning by choosing a stipulated number of courses from existing offerings in the sciences, social sciences, and humanities. In my mind, this proposal gave maximum choice to the students together with complete freedom for the faculty to teach whatever they wanted without establishing any clear objectives to meet the needs of society or the long-term interests of the students.

After some soul-searching buoyed by conversations with several faculty members, I decided to make a fresh start and appoint another committee to create a new curriculum within the fifteen months before my term of office expired. A group of loyal souls agreed to serve and to work through the summer to draft a suitable proposal. They would then undertake the onerous task of conducting extensive consultations with groups of faculty, culminating in a series of full-faculty meetings and an eventual vote at some point in the late spring.

True to their word, the committee worked long and hard over the ensuing months, and the new curriculum was eventually adopted by a huge majority of the faculty. The final product was a great improvement over a simple distribution system and included a set of plausible goals together with a committee to ensure that the courses approved to achieve the goals were aptly designed for the purpose.

I found the review process enlightening—the more so since I had recently published a book on undergraduate education that led me to read a vast amount of research and commentary on the subject. In contrast, while some members of the small review committee, notably cochair Louis Menand and psychologist Stephen Kosslyn, knew a great deal about undergraduate education, the vast majority of the faculty were unacquainted with the literature on the subject. Nevertheless, by the prevailing custom, although I was expected to preside over the faculty meetings on the new curriculum, any effort on my part to enter the discussion, even to call attention to highly relevant research on key points, would have been considered bad form. Members of the staff with special knowledge of undergraduate education also played no role in the faculty deliberations. As a result, the discussion proceeded with little or no awareness of the ample literature on the subject, a practice completely at odds with how the faculty went about their own scholarly work.

I also noticed that the attendance at these faculty meetings, while substantial, still numbered well under half of the eligible tenure-track professors. Apparently, then, although the level of interest in undergraduate education was undoubtedly greater than it was during my first term in office, it still did not extend to anywhere near the entire faculty.

Now that more than a decade has passed, the care and attention given to teaching and learning seem to have increased further, thanks in part to the leadership for more than ten years of a dean of Arts and Sciences, Michael Smith, who was particularly interested in the quality of education in the college. As I point out in the footnote on page 148, faculty are engaged in much more experimentation and innovation than I recall from earlier years. Many eminent professors have devoted much time to creating online versions of their courses. A larger staff is now in place to carry out research and bring new ideas and insights about teaching to the attention of the faculty, and more money is available to cover the cost of experimentation in the classroom. More than one hundred senior professors used the services of the teaching and learning center during the 2018–2019 academic year, and many students have volunteered to listen to trial runs of new courses and teaching methods and give valuable feedback to the instructors.

Only a few weeks ago, I attended a year-end gathering of interested faculty, graduate students, and undergraduates at the center in its new and greatly expanded quarters close to Harvard Yard. The rooms were packed with people, most of them young and highly animated, conversing among themselves about their efforts in the classroom. Being there and watching so many instructors and students talking about teaching left me encouraged by the thought that, given enough time and attention, the smallest seeds can eventually grow into healthy plants and even become large trees.

The growing interest in teaching and learning is not unique to Harvard. In fact, the present moment seems especially propitious for improving the quality of undergraduate education throughout America. As this book will point out, public officials, corporate employers, and commentators of various kinds have all expressed dissatisfaction with the current state of undergraduate education. Meanwhile, psychologists and neuroscientists have discovered intriguing possibilities for nurturing additional skills and qualities of mind that could serve students well in later life. In the face of these demands and opportunities, many academic leaders and faculties are showing an increased willingness to explore new methods for teaching and educating their students. These improving prospects for reform had much to do with my decision to write this book.

HIGHER
EXPECTATIONS

An Overview

America's colleges are facing a challenge of a size and scope they have not encountered since they transformed themselves completely during the decades after the Civil War. In those years, colleges felt compelled to reform in order to meet the demands of a rapidly industrializing nation. Today significant changes in our society have given rise to new pressures that call for fresh thought about the content and instructional methods of undergraduate education.

Since the first great period of transformation, America has grown from an insular nation into a dominant power whose interests are increasingly affected by events in other parts of the world. Our economy has evolved from an industrial base to a knowledge-driven system that puts a growing premium on education and demands more sophisticated skills. Our companies compete in markets that have become more and more global, while using complicated methods that rely increasingly on computers, robots, and artificial intelligence. These trends have helped the economy to grow, but they have also widened the gulf between rich and poor to near-record proportions, created new challenges and risks for the workforce, and depressed the rates of upward mobility in this "land of opportunity" to levels below those of many other advanced countries.

Meanwhile, America has continued to evolve from a nation peopled primarily by whites to one in which a majority of the population will be minorities of color by 2050. Our citizens have become riven by partisan differences, assailed by political rhetoric of unusual hostility, and bombarded by news reports of questionable veracity, all of which have combined to produce exceptional levels of distrust toward government and politicians. Those who study the levels of well-being and satisfaction of entire societies find that Americans, despite their prosperity, have become less happy and less satisfied with their lives than they were in earlier decades.

These developments have produced a daunting list of demands on the nation's colleges. Employers seek graduates who can adapt successfully to rapid changes in the nature of their jobs, solve problems creatively, work adeptly in teams, interact effectively with diverse groups of colleagues, subordinates, and customers, and be resilient enough to overcome the challenges and risks created by constant economic change. Parents want their children to possess the qualities they need to obtain good jobs, pursue successful careers, and, above all, live happy and satisfying lives. Those who worry about the troubled state of democratic politics call for college graduates who are conscientious about voting, think carefully about the issues of the day, and take an active interest in the affairs of their communities. In addition, concerned by growing signs that the basic norms of society are eroding, newspaper columnists and other social commentators are urging colleges to educate young men and women to be sensitive to ethical issues, capable of considering them carefully, and strong enough in character to act according to their principles.

Since colleges fill the largest part of the days and weeks of millions of young Americans during a critical stage in their development, academic leaders and their faculties have a responsibility to consider society's demands with the utmost seriousness. In the past, educators have assumed that many useful qualities of mind and behavior were fixed and immutable long before young people finished high school and hence were beyond the power of colleges to improve. In recent decades, however, psychologists, mental health experts, neuroscientists, and education researchers have found that almost all of the desired capabilities can continue to change at least through early adulthood, and that some actually tend to develop most during the traditional college years. These discoveries, together with the evolving demands of society, create a new world of opportunities for colleges to explore as they seek to respond to the hopes and expectations of society. At the same time, they also give rise to some fundamental questions:

- How successful are colleges today in developing the competencies and qualities their students will need to succeed and flourish in their careers and help our society meet the challenges it faces?

- Do educators know how to develop all of the qualities of mind and spirit that faculties are increasingly called upon to teach—creativity in solving problems; teamwork in carrying out assignments at work; skill in interacting with people; resilience and adaptability in the face of adversity; high ethical standards in public and private life; and wisdom enough to decide how to live purposeful, fulfilling lives?
- What adjustments would colleges need to make in their curriculum and instructional methods to respond to society's demands? Can their faculties be persuaded to make the necessary changes?

These are the questions that this book will explore. Following a brief account of the evolution of the curriculum from the earliest colleges to the present day, chapter 1 summarizes the complaints that have been made in recent decades about the shortcomings of our colleges and closes by describing an exceptionally thorough effort by the Association of American Colleges and Universities (AAC&U) to present a new plan for undergraduate education. This proposal features a set of goals and learning objectives that incorporate the full range of demands that society is making on the educational programs of our colleges.

The next seven chapters consider the feasibility of developing the skills and qualities of mind and behavior that interested groups and the AAC&U would have our colleges teach their students. Some of these objectives are ones that colleges have long had difficulty in achieving, such as preparing students to be active and informed citizens, teaching them not only to understand ethical principles but to live up to them in practice, and helping them to discover a meaningful and fulfilling purpose for their future lives. Other chapters examine the feasibility of teaching undergraduates a number of the so-called noncognitive skills and habits of mind and behavior, such as conscientiousness, creativity, interpersonal relations (including an appreciation and respect for people who differ in race, gender, or sexual orientation), lifelong learning, collaborative skills, and resilience and perseverance (or "grit" as it is sometimes called). Chapter 8 discusses two unorthodox methods of teaching—meditation and positive psychology—that some proponents believe can help students achieve a surprising number of the goals just mentioned.

Chapters 9 and 10 analyze the prospects for persuading colleges to make serious attempts to teach the skills, behaviors, and qualities of mind discussed in the preceding chapters. Chapter 9 examines the arguments that academic leaders and their faculties are likely to make against an effort of this kind and identifies the most serious problems that could impede progress. Chapter 10 presents some practical steps that colleges could take to surmount these obstacles and hasten the process of reform. A brief conclusion to the book explains why a determined effort on the part of colleges to accomplish a more ambitious set of goals could be important not only for students and society but for the future of higher education itself.

———⟫◇⟪———

This book was written several months before the coronavirus plague disrupted our colleges and universities. As I write this postscript, it is still too early to tell what effects this catastrophe will have on the issues and opportunities discussed in these pages. On the one hand, colleges may be forced for a time to set aside all other reforms in their struggle to cope with the financial consequences of closing their campuses. On the other hand, the consequences of living through such a calamity may foster a greater interest in the nurturing qualities such as resilience, empathy, creativity, and teamwork that are discussed in the chapters that follow. The massive effort to create virtual classrooms may also bring a greater willingness to experiment with new ways of teaching students. Though colleges are often slow to embrace major changes in their academic programs, the inequities in our society that the pandemic has exposed may usher in a period of social reform that could envelop higher education as well.

Whatever the future brings, one thing is certain. The underlying conditions that have given rise to the issues discussed in this book are not going away. It is still as important as ever to consider how our colleges and universities should respond.

CHAPTER ONE

A Brief History of the College Curriculum from 1636 to the Present

Until the Civil War, America's colleges embraced a form of education that did not differ fundamentally from the one introduced by the earliest colleges when they were founded many generations before. The standard curriculum at institutions such as Harvard, Yale, and Princeton was heavily prescribed and emphasized the study of ancient writings from Greece and Rome. The students who applied had to demonstrate at least a rudimentary grasp of Greek and Latin merely to gain admission. Once enrolled, they were required to take a series of courses largely devoted to translating and analyzing original texts in painstaking detail. Students were few in number and consisted in the main of young men intending to become preachers, teachers, or leaders in their communities.

As time went on and students aspired to a wider array of occupations, colleges introduced a few elective courses in science, mathematics, and moral or political philosophy. Later, practical subjects such as engineering, soil chemistry, and modern languages began to make an appearance, especially in state universities. Nevertheless, the leading private colleges continued to require most of the courses in the curriculum and to emphasize the study of classical texts, despite growing pressure from outside their walls to introduce more useful subjects.

In 1828, after a Yale trustee openly questioned the value of spending so much time studying "dead languages," the president of the college and members of his faculty issued a report vigorously defending the classical curriculum. They insisted that the detailed analysis of ancient texts in their original language was ideally suited for developing a capacity for rigorous thinking, sound judgment, and discriminating taste.*[1] Armed with this stout defense, most colleges, including the largest and best-known institutions, clung to the traditional curriculum for two generations more.

THE YEARS OF TRANSFORMATION

By the advent of the Civil War, pressure to devote more attention to the practical needs of an industrializing society had grown too intense to be ignored. In the words of one historian of higher education, "The curriculum began to seem like a prison guarding a subject population."[2] When Congress passed the Morrill Act in 1862, donating large tracts of federal land for the support of at least one university for each state, the new law did not prohibit the study of classical languages but stipulated that participating colleges should also "teach such branches of learning as are related to agriculture and the mechanic arts."

Not long thereafter, a wealthy businessman, Ezra Cornell, donated funds to build a new university in New York State "where any person can find instruction in any study." Its founding president, Andrew White, established a curriculum offering classical studies as only one of several options, including vocational programs and a course of study that gave students almost complete freedom to choose whatever subjects they wished. White's curriculum was an immediate success. According to *Harper's Weekly*: "With a grip on the best methods of education which is almost beyond the reach of an institution weighted down with traditions, . . . Cornell University stands in the vantage ground if not at the head of America's educational institutions."[3]

---

*"Those branches of study should be prescribed, and those modes of instruction adopted, which are best calculated to teach the art of fixing the attention, directing the train of thought, analyzing a subject proposed for investigation, following, with accurate discrimination, the course of argument, balancing nicely the evidence presented to the judgment, awakening, elevating, and controlling the imagination; arranging with discrimination the treasures which memory gathers; rousing and guiding the powers of genius." Report of the Committee of the Corporation to the full Corporation of Yale College (1828), p. 7. As one professor put it some years later, "The student who has acquired the habit of never letting go of a puzzling problem—say, a rare Greek verb—until he has analyzed its every element, and understands every point in its etymology, has the habit of mind which will enable him to follow out a legal subtlety with the same accuracy." W. F. Allen, *Essays and Monographs* (1890), p. 141.

In the 1870s, Johns Hopkins University founded a pioneering graduate school that offered a PhD degree with advanced training to college graduates who wished to become faculty members in any of the fields of knowledge or disciplines associated with the liberal arts. Other universities quickly followed suit. From then on, new recruits to college faculties would increasingly consist of PhDs who specialized in teaching and research in physics, philosophy, history, or some other established subject. The instruction they provided no longer emphasized translating and analyzing texts but consisted in the main of lectures and seminars similar to the methods then in use in the much-admired German universities.

Meanwhile, as the demands for practical knowledge in a rapidly industrializing society continued to grow, the pressure on the classical curriculum intensified. The traditional arguments stressing the usefulness of classical learning, so bravely articulated in the Yale report of 1828, suffered a serious blow from the turn-of-the-century findings of noted psychologist Edward Thorndike. Thorndike's experiments revealed that the qualities of intellect mastered in one domain of knowledge (for example, dissecting ancient Greek and Latin texts) were seldom transferable to other fields of intellectual endeavor.[4]

Among the leaders of the older American universities, Charles W. Eliot of Harvard was the first to break sharply with tradition by urging the demise of the heavily prescribed classical curriculum in favor of a course of study consisting almost entirely of electives. Although it took him twenty years, Eliot gradually persuaded his faculty to do away with all requirements except for a mandatory course in expository writing.

Many colleges did not go as far as Eliot did in abandoning virtually all required courses, but almost all moved a long way in that direction. Academic leaders had no other choice if they wished to attract a sufficient number of students. As Frederick Rudolph put it in his history of the college curriculum, offering a wide assortment of electives proved "unavoidable except in colleges with suicidal tendencies."[5]

By the time President Eliot left office in 1909, however, the disadvantages of a largely elective program had already become apparent. Eliot had argued that electives would strengthen teaching by forcing professors to compete for students, while simultaneously encouraging students to work hard at their courses by allowing them to choose the subjects that interested them most. Events proved him wrong on both counts. Many professors turned out to be more interested in research and writing than in teaching undergraduates. Meanwhile, a faculty committee at Harvard found that students were spending only half as many hours per week studying for their classes as their professors had expected. Some 55 percent of Harvard seniors were discovered to have taken virtually nothing but introductory courses, which required less work and left more time for athletics, partying, and other extracurricular pursuits.

Colleges were quick to take corrective measures. To give students the experience of exploring a single subject in depth, faculties began to insist that every undergraduate take at least a minimum number of courses in a single field of knowledge. To avoid overspecialization, they also required students to choose at least a few courses from each of several broad fields of knowledge—typically the humanities, the sciences, and the social sciences. By 1915, most colleges had adopted the tripartite curricular structure that still predominates today, featuring a "major," or field of concentration, a distribution requirement to ensure a breadth of knowledge, and an ample number of courses reserved for student choice.

YEARS OF STABILITY AND GROWTH

After 1915, once the major reforms in the college curriculum were largely in place, little innovation occurred over the next thirty years. Experimental colleges such as Bard, Bennington, St. John's, and Black Mountain were created but failed to attract many followers. Even the most celebrated academic leader of the 1930s, Robert Maynard Hutchins, could not introduce any major reforms that survived for long after his departure. In particular, he failed to persuade his own faculty at the University of Chicago to adopt his vision of a college entirely devoted to the study of Great Books. Once World War II began, colleges shelved any plans for substantial change as many thousands of students left to enter military service.

After the war ended, American higher education began a twenty-year period of unprecedented growth and prosperity. The GI Bill touched off a massive increase in the number of high school graduates enrolling in college. State legislatures provided ample financial support to build the faculties, classrooms, and residence halls to accommodate the continuing surge of students. The great flagship public universities grew in size to enroll tens of thousands of additional undergraduates. New public regional universities were constructed, and community colleges proliferated. One state after another created systems of higher education to coordinate their growing array of colleges and universities.

At the same time, Congress launched a determined effort to make America preeminent in basic research. Lawmakers appropriated a steadily increasing supply of funds to pay for new libraries, laboratories, and equipment for academic scientists and scholars along with generous scholarships for graduate students preparing for careers in the sciences and social sciences. In meeting the growing demand for a college education while building a massive program of scientific inquiry, universities forged a partnership with government that made American higher education the envy of the world.

During this great expansion, many subjects were added to the curriculum, such as vocational majors for new occupations and offerings in international studies to complement America's increasingly prominent role on the world stage. Faculties tried periodically to make their general education offerings more coherent. These initiatives, valuable as they were, neither called for different methods of instruction nor disturbed the tripartite division of undergraduate study into the major, general education, and electives. Most colleges simply offered a growing number of courses, a more and more specialized faculty, and an increasingly fragmented curriculum.

YEARS OF TURMOIL

The years of prosperity came to an abrupt halt in the late 1960s. The steady growth in federal spending ceased as Lyndon Johnson's administration struggled to avoid raising taxes while simultaneously paying for expensive Great Society programs and an escalating conflict in Vietnam. Meanwhile, the baby boom generation arrived on campus, bringing student activists who soon engaged in protests over civil rights, the role of women, and the increasingly unpopular Vietnam War. Male undergraduates were upset by the prospect of being drafted into the armed services and sent to fight in a war that many of them considered unnecessary and unjust. At the same time, black students were demanding that their colleges admit more students of color and hire more minority professors and administrators. Controversies erupted on numerous campuses with angry demonstrations, building occupations, and violent encounters with police. College faculties were badly shaken by these events, and the public's confidence in higher education declined precipitously.

Student unrest dominated the agenda on college campuses for the next several years. Numerous changes took place in response to demands for coeducation in single-sex colleges, the abandonment of parietal rules, the admission of more students of color, and the creation of courses on the history and treatment of minorities and (later) women. Only occasionally, however, did undergraduates seek changes in the basic structure of the curriculum or the accustomed methods of teaching.

Much of the passion and protest disappeared with the ending of the Vietnam War in 1975 and the repeal of compulsory military service in 1973. Free at last from the hectic growth of the 1950s and the angry protests of the late 1960s, colleges seemed ready to renew their interest in matters of education and curriculum. In 1977, Frederick Rudolph ended his widely admired history of the college curriculum on a guardedly optimistic note:

> Amid the growing concerns of critics and society . . . the time may be
> at hand when a reevaluation of academic purpose and philosophy may
> encourage the curricular development that will focus on the lives we
> lead, their quality, the enjoyment they give us, and the wisdom with
> which we lead them. And perhaps, once more, the idea of an educated
> person will have become a usable idea.[6]

As it happened, Rudolph's hopes proved premature. The most notable development in undergraduate education during the mid- to late 1970s arose from a massive shift in the aspirations of undergraduates.

The recession early in the decade followed by rapid inflation and a temporary glut of college graduates turned students' minds to practical concerns. Within the span of a few years, the principal priorities of entering freshmen changed from acquiring a philosophy of life, working for racial justice, and protecting the environment to equipping themselves to get good jobs and make a lot of money. In pursuit of these ambitions, the share of undergraduates majoring in the liberal arts dropped from 60 percent to 35 percent while the number of students entering vocational programs, most notably business majors, rose correspondingly.[7] Once again, however, colleges managed to accommodate these shifts in student interest without altering the basic tripartite structure of the curriculum or the customary methods of instruction.

By the mid-1970s, general education had become "a disaster area," in the words of one foundation report.[8] Although a few colleges introduced more highly structured "core" curricula, most continued to prefer distribution requirements that allowed students to choose any two or three courses from each of the several major divisions of academic study. The average share of the curriculum allocated to general education dropped from 43 to 33 percent to make room for more student electives and more courses and seminars for the majors.

In 1980, the Carnegie Council on Policy Studies in Higher Education completed a comprehensive, multivolume study of American colleges and universities that carefully scrutinized virtually every significant aspect of higher education. In summing up its work, however, the final report devoted very little attention to the curriculum or the quality of undergraduate education.[9] Instead, most of the discussion was devoted to the need for colleges to prepare for an anticipated drop in college enrollments (which never materialized) and the mounting risk of increased government regulation. As events soon proved, however, colleges would encounter pressures of a different kind arising from an unanticipated source.

YEARS OF CRITICISM

In the early 1980s, business leaders, commentators, and public officials began to worry that the United States was losing ground in the increasingly competitive global economy. Europe had largely recovered from the destruction of World War II, while countries such as Japan, South Korea, and later China were growing at unusually rapid rates. The US share of world markets was shrinking, and American corporations in highly visible industries, such as automobiles, steel, and electronic products, were losing market share to companies overseas. Meanwhile, economists emphasized that the prosperity of leading nations now depended more on knowledge than on raw materials and that economic growth rates would be heavily influenced by the skills of the workforce and its ability to innovate. Observing these developments, public officials soon became more interested in the quality of education. State legislators began to ask public colleges and universities for more detailed reports about their performance.[10] Congress ordered accrediting organizations to examine the outcomes of the educational programs in the colleges they visited to determine how much students were actually learning.

In 1983, a federal commission reviewing America's public schools issued a scathing report, *A Nation at Risk*, which warned of "a rising tide of mediocrity" amounting to "unilateral educational disarmament."[11] The report was widely publicized, provoked a great deal of discussion, and quickly lifted the improvement of public education to a prominent position on the list of leading national priorities.

Although *A Nation at Risk* did not touch upon higher education, commentators warned that America's campuses would soon attract critical scrutiny as well. It did not take long. In the late 1980s, a series of books appeared castigating colleges and universities for a variety of sins. Some authors claimed that college faculties had been infiltrated by student radicals from the 1960s who were intent upon furthering their left-wing agendas.[12] Other writers criticized professors for neglecting their students in order to spend more time on research and lucrative consulting assignments.[13]

The most successful of these polemics was Allan Bloom's *The Closing of the American Mind*, which skewered the shallow pretensions of a generation of undergraduates and condemned the faculty and its leaders for failing to uphold proper academic standards.[14] Although much of Bloom's text departed from these themes to engage in a detailed discussion of the evolution of philosophical thought from the Enlightenment to modern times, his book was an instant success, remaining for weeks on the *New York Times* best-seller list. Its popularity signaled a growing dissatisfaction on the part of the educated public with the behavior of academic leaders, faculties, and students.

PROPOSALS FOR REFORM

During the attacks on colleges in the late 1980s, some of the most widely publicized proposals for reforming the undergraduate curriculum came from conservative critics such as William Bennett and Lynne Cheney in their capacity as heads of the National Humanities Center. Both authors began their proposal by deploring the fact that many colleges had so little sense of educational priorities that they allowed students to graduate without taking a single course in American history, English literature, or the ancient civilizations of Athens and Rome, where so many basic values of Western civilization had their roots. Cheney acknowledged that "the matter of what should be taught and learned is hardly one on which we should expect easy agreement." Even so, she argued, "the confusion about it on many campuses has seemed extraordinary in recent years. . . . Because colleges and universities believed they no longer could or should assert the primacy of one fact or one book over another, all knowledge came to be seen as relative in importance."[15]

Bennett, like Cheney, had little doubt about the body of knowledge that students most needed to study. He believed that "the core of the American college—its heart and soul—should be the civilization of the West, source of the most powerful and pervasive influences on America and all its people. It is simply not possible for students to understand their society without studying its intellectual legacy. They will become aliens in their own culture, strangers in their own land." The surest means to acquiring the needed knowledge, he added, was the study of the "great books" of Western civilization, "the best that has been said, thought, written, and otherwise expressed about the human experience."[16]

Literary scholars were quick to condemn Bennett's critique. As Barbara Herrnstein Smith observed, the idea of concentrating on a list of great books "presupposes a national culture which is no longer appropriate in such a diverse country."[17] "Who gets to say which are the works of 'abiding worth'?"[18] added Stanley Fish. Outspoken critics of contemporary American society were even more hostile. According to Professor Henry Giroux, rather than teach the Great Books, liberal education should focus on "challenging the sterile instrumentalism, selfishness, and contempt for democratic community that has become the hallmark of the Reagan-Bush era."[19]

Lost in the clouds of indignant rhetoric were several practical objections to the Great Books idea that have doomed the adoption of such programs ever since the 1930s. Despite the enthusiasm of conservative critics, many undergraduates would undoubtedly resist a requirement that they devote a large portion of their college education to an in-depth study of the Great Books. In the United States, where most colleges compete vigorously for students, either to remain financially viable or to enroll the brightest applicants to enhance their reputation, few faculties will risk the consequences of adopting such an unpopular program.

The second objection to the compulsory study of Great Books is the shortage of instructors who are willing and able to teach the courses. A compulsory Great Books curriculum requires a large faculty, since the teaching needs to take place in groups of approximately thirty students to facilitate lively discussion of the material. Because the vast majority of college professors are specialists in a narrow slice of a single discipline, few feel capable of or interested in teaching courses with the vast scope of the Great Books. Thus, Yale University—which offered a single sequence of courses on the Great Books, taught in groups of eighteen students—was able to staff only enough of these classes to accommodate a minority of its undergraduates. Columbia University, which has long offered a compulsory yearlong Great Books course, has regularly had to recruit many of the instructors from outside the tenure-track faculty. Since the success of such courses depends on the presence of able and enthusiastic teachers for each of the many small groups of students, the problem of finding enough qualified instructors constitutes a serious handicap.

These practical problems have prevented the adoption of the compulsory study of the Great Books in all but a tiny handful of colleges, most of them small, private institutions. Most undergraduates do encounter many of these books in a variety of classes in the humanities and social sciences, and a number of colleges, like Yale and Columbia, even offer one or two courses devoted exclusively to such texts. But the idea of reserving the largest part of the curriculum for a mandatory study of these canonical works seems destined to remain a dream unfulfilled.

Other proposals for reform during the 1980s and '90s were equally unsuccessful. General education received increased attention, and efforts were made to introduce courses in global studies, applied ethics, computer science, and interdisciplinary subjects. Once again, however, the changes were relatively minor and consisted for the most part in adding new courses rather than making any substantial alteration in teaching methods or curricular structure.

Although the books attacking undergraduate education did not elicit much of a response from campus authorities, they were soon followed by some exceptionally severe and sweeping criticisms of the prevailing college curriculum from prominent sources within the higher education establishment itself. One such assessment appeared in a volume authored by Ernest Boyer, a former university president who now headed the Carnegie Foundation for the Advancement of Teaching.[20] Another took the form of a report issued by the Association of American Colleges (AAC), a membership organization of several hundred institutions.[21]

The Boyer book described America's colleges as "a troubled institution" and argued that "many of the nation's colleges are more successful at credentialing than in providing a quality education for their students."[22] The AAC delivered an even harsher indictment:

> There is so much confusion as to the mission of the American college and university that it is no longer possible to be sure why a student would take a particular program of courses. . . . We found at most colleges in our study great difficulty, sometimes to the point of paralysis, in defining purposes and goals. . . . Scrambling for success and driven by marketplace demands, many colleges have lost their sense of mission.[23]

Each of these reports repeated familiar criticisms: the tendency to value research over teaching, the failure to define clear goals for undergraduate education, the fragmentation of the curriculum into ever narrower specialized courses, the emphasis on coverage of subject matter rather than the development of competence and intellectual mastery, and the lack of assessment to measure progress and ensure accountability. Both reports also contained much the same recommendations. Each compiled a similar list of specific goals for undergraduate education. Each affirmed the need to pursue some one subject in depth but argued that college majors ought to be more carefully structured and take students beyond the study of a single field of knowledge to explore its connections to other disciplines together with its limitations, namely, "the questions it cannot answer and the arguments it does not make."[24] Both reports allowed space for electives to permit students to study particular subjects that interested them. However, though each document included numerous suggestions for improvement, neither one challenged the underlying tripartite curricular structure or questioned whether the goals they espoused could be achieved within the space available once the desire of students for electives and the demands of the departments for elaborate majors had been met.

While forthright in their criticisms of academic leaders and their faculties, both documents also failed to probe deeply into the reasons for the shortcomings they deplored or the difficulties involved in overcoming them. The AAC report recognized that the reforms it called for would require "nothing less than the reconstruction of the training of college teachers and a revision of prevailing standards of the recruitment of faculty," but it offered few details about these changes other than a suggestion "to hire more instructors from the world of practical experience."[25] The report did not explain how to persuade colleges to adopt its recommendations beyond exhorting trustees "to ask searching questions about whether academic programs are of high quality" and urging presidents and deans "to lead us away from the declining and devalued bachelor's degree that now prevails to a new core of curricular coherence, intellectual rigor, and humanistic strength."[26]

No careful efforts were made to determine the effect of either document on the nation's colleges. There was little sign, however, of any change remotely equal to the sweeping proposals urged by Boyer and the AAC. In fact, one seasoned observer of curricular debates declared in 1989 that the reform movement had already run out of steam.[27] Another group of experienced authors writing in 2004 found "most curricular changes undertaken during the [1990s] to be modifications to existing general education programs rather than complete revisions or remaking of the courses of study."[28]

THE AAC&U INITIATIVE

By the end of the twentieth century, changes in the economy, the society, and the wider world began to provoke fresh thoughts about the aims and methods of education. The increasing interdependence of nations in coping with problems such as climate change, international trade, financial stability, and migration seemed to require more graduates who were aware of global problems and knowledgeable about differences in the values, habits, and perspectives of other cultures. Disputes about race, gender, sexual orientation, and the distribution of income were rampant in the society, revealing sharp differences of opinion within as well as outside college campuses. Arguments about politics and public policy grew increasingly partisan and gave rise to a growing concern about whether citizens were sufficiently informed and engaged to choose a government capable of dealing with the problems facing the nation.

The nature of the workplace was also shifting in ways that brought new skills and qualities of mind to the fore. More and more employees were no longer working individually according to rules under the supervision of middle managers but were assigned to groups that functioned with greater autonomy to accomplish complex tasks. Workforces became more diverse. Under these conditions, teamwork, creative problem-solving, communication skills, and an ability to collaborate with persons of different backgrounds and talents assumed greater importance. Technological change and global competition helped to bring about more frequent changes in the content and duration of jobs, placing a higher premium on adaptability and a continuing willingness to learn. All of these developments seemed to call for a broader, interdisciplinary education that put greater stress on basic capabilities and qualities of mind and behavior.

Despite these growing challenges and the mounting criticism of undergraduate education, colleges showed little sign of concern. As the incomes of most Americans stagnated for the third consecutive decade, tuitions continued to rise, putting more and more pressure on students and their families to pay the cost of enrolling. Employers complained about the inadequate skills of many recent college graduates they had hired. More and more college students complained of suffering from anxiety, stress, and depression. Yet colleges continued to display little interest in launching serious efforts to alter the curriculum or the methods of instruction.

Finally, as another century dawned, an ambitious effort to reform undergraduate education, referred to as LEAP (Liberal Education and America's Promise), was initiated by the successor to the AAC, now called the Association of American Colleges and Universities, with some 1,400 accredited institutions drawn from every segment of non-profit higher education. Unlike previous reform projects, the AAC&U began by conducting surveys and discussions with campus leaders and faculty members from scores of colleges as well as with employers and representatives of state governments. These consultations lasted for several years and were amply funded by the Carnegie and Pew Foundations. They led the AAC&U to realize that the differences between liberal and vocational education had diminished over the years and that corporate CEOs were now placing a priority on competencies, knowledge, and qualities of mind that were increasingly similar to the aims of liberal education embraced by college leaders and their faculties. The consultative process also persuaded the AAC&U that there was enough consensus and interest in reform among academic leaders and their faculties to warrant a determined effort to redefine the common goals of a contemporary undergraduate education and seek agreement on the methods for achieving them.

As a basis for reform, the AAC&U developed the following list of "essential learning outcomes" to specify the knowledge and the competencies that all colleges should teach and all undergraduates should acquire[29]:

Knowledge of human cultures and the physical and natural world through study in the sciences and mathematics, social sciences, humanities, histories, languages, and the arts

Intellectual and practical skills, including competencies of inquiry and analysis, critical and creative thinking, written and oral communication, quantitative literacy, information literacy, teamwork, and problem-solving practiced extensively across the curriculum, in the context of progressively more challenging problems, projects, and standards of performance

Personal and social responsibility, including civic knowledge and engagement (local and global), intercultural knowledge and competence, ethical reasoning and action, and foundations and skills for lifelong learning anchored through active involvement with diverse communities and real-world challenges

Integrative and applied learning, including synthesis and advanced accomplishment across general and specialized studies demonstrated through the application of knowledge, skills, and responsibilities to new settings and complex problems

A close reading of these outcomes reveals a number of skills and behaviors that are not commonly included as goals of a college education but are numbered among the attributes that employers, commentators, and other interested parties consider desirable for college graduates to possess. Among these capabilities are "teamwork," "ethical action" (not just ethical reasoning), "intercultural competence," and "foundations and skills for lifelong learning." Another document from the AAC&U, providing more detailed definitions of the essential outcomes, lists additional qualities such as skills in conflict resolution, leadership, a capacity to interpret "intercultural experience from [one's] own and more than one world view," and "an ability . . . to understand and develop individual purpose, values, and ethics."[30]

To give more concrete meaning to these goals, the AAC&U endorsed a Degree Qualifications Profile (DQP), developed with the support of the Lumina Foundation and the participation of hundreds of faculty members. The DQP described with unusual specificity what a college degree should represent in terms of the knowledge, skills, and other qualities included in the essential learning outcomes. The final product took the form of rubrics describing in detail the stages of intellectual growth through which undergraduates needed to pass to master each of the recommended learning outcomes.[31] These rubrics provided a common framework for colleges to use in evaluating the work of students and their progress toward the desired goals.

In addition to the goals and rubrics, the association produced a series of reports to help colleges achieve the essential outcomes. One report provided "guided pathways": suggested sequences of studies that, buttressed by good advising, could help students choose the courses and activities needed to achieve their desired goals.[32] These pathways were accompanied by brief descriptions of the steps that exemplary colleges were already taking to provide the necessary sequences of courses and appropriate guidance.

The association also endorsed a group of high-impact educational practices (HIPs) developed with the aid of George Kuh of Indiana University, who drew upon research on student learning to specify methods of instruction that were particularly effective.[33] These practices included first-year seminars, learning communities, undergraduate research opportunities, service learning (combining a course for credit with a related community service program), and "capstone projects" in the senior year that required students to integrate knowledge and methods of analysis from several fields of inquiry to explore a real-world problem.

Finally, the association paid attention to the practical problem of securing faculty approval for its ambitious reforms. It published a separate paper offering specific suggestions for gaining the necessary faculty support, complete with an extensive list of common mistakes, or "potholes," that had derailed previous efforts at curricular reform, along with suggestions for how to avoid them.[34]

The measures just described represent a remarkably comprehensive effort to reform undergraduate education in America. The amount of study and consultation by the association to ascertain the views of college leaders, faculty members, students, employers, and public officials was unprecedented. The proposals themselves and the learning outcomes toward which they are directed are more detailed by far than those of previous reform efforts, and the accompanying reports devote much more attention than has customarily been given to questions of implementation.

In short, the AAC&U initiative is the most ambitious attempt in over one hundred years to reform American undergraduate education. Based on extensive consultation with interested parties, the goals described by the association provide the nearest approximation ever produced of a consensus among academic leaders, reform-minded professors, employers, and public officials on the aims that will best serve the interests of students and society at this juncture in the nation's history. The recommended changes to implement the plan are comprehensive in scope and require new subjects, widespread redesign of existing courses, and innovative methods of instruction.

The threshold question raised by these reports is whether colleges and their faculties know how to teach their students to achieve the array of goals enumerated in the essential learning outcomes and described in great detail in its rubrics. The goals themselves are extremely ambitious, involving capabilities that are undoubtedly important but could be very difficult to nurture. For example, do academic leaders and faculties know how to teach the multitude of cynical, apathetic, and apolitical freshmen who arrive on campus today and transform them into active and informed citizens? Although philosophy professors may be able to help students analyze ethical issues, does anyone know how to teach them to *act* ethically? Are instructors aware of how to teach their students to interact more easily and effectively with persons from different cultures, economic backgrounds, ethnic groups, or political orientations? Are they capable of assisting undergraduates in their search for a purpose and a set of values that give meaning to their lives? Do they know how to teach students to collaborate effectively by using such skills as "address[ing] conflict directly and constructively to manage/resolve it in a way that strengthens overall team cohesiveness and future effectiveness"? Can they train students to think creatively "in new, unique, or atypical recombinations, uncovering or critically perceiving new syntheses, and using or recognizing creative risk-taking to achieve solutions"?[35] These are the kinds of questions that the next seven chapters will try to answer.

CHAPTER TWO

Educating Citizens

The presidential election of 2016 prompted many academic leaders and faculty members to ponder the implications for their own institution. Much of the conversation has dwelt on what the current administration is doing or seems likely to do about research funding, the enrollment of foreign students, affirmative action, and financial aid. Yet mounting concern over the deep divisions of opinion in the body politic, hyperpartisanship in all three branches of government, and the pervasive distrust of public officials has also led some educators to wonder whether more should be done to prepare young people to be responsible citizens in a democratic society.

The 2016 election gave ample reason to devote fresh thought to this subject. After many months of primary campaigns, multiple televised debates, and millions of ballots cast, the nominating process produced the two candidates with the highest disapproval ratings of all the contenders seeking the nomination of their party. The media coverage of the race for the White House was marked far more by a persistent emphasis on scandal rather than substance. The campaigns themselves were noteworthy not only for the unusual amounts of exaggeration and misrepresentation but for blatantly false stories planted in the social media by sources here and abroad.

In the end, the election produced another modest turnout despite all the money spent on elaborate "ground games" to get supporters to the polls and the high stakes resulting from the wide differences in the policies of the two candidates. The outcome was the election of a president possessing the least governmental experience, the lowest public approval ratings, and the skimpiest knowledge of public affairs of any newly elected chief executive in living memory. The whole experience, coupled with the rise of authoritarian governments in several other countries, sounded a wake-up call that Americans must not take their democracy for granted but should regard our form of government as a system perpetually in need of an active, informed, and vigilant citizenry.

THE DECLINE OF CIVIC ENGAGEMENT

There were plenty of reasons for concern long before 2016 about the political apathy and limited knowledge of government among American citizens and the reluctance of so many to participate in elections and civic affairs. By the year 2000, voting rates in presidential elections by eligible voters, including young college graduates, had already declined by at least ten percentage points since the early 1970s, leaving the United States with one of the lowest levels of electoral participation among the more prosperous nations of the world. Researchers reported that young Americans had remarkably little knowledge about our system of government or about current political issues.[1] Fewer than one-quarter of high school students were "proficient" in civics according to tests administered in 2010, while the percentage scoring "below basic" climbed to 36 percent.[2] Interest in politics and newspaper readership among young people had diminished substantially over the preceding decades. Responding to these trends, an American Political Science Association task force declared more than a decade before 2016 that it was "axiomatic that current levels of political knowledge, political engagement, and political enthusiasm are so low as to threaten the vitality of democratic politics of the United States."[3]

The election of Barack Obama in 2008 kindled hopes that political engagement among young Americans might be rising again. But the turnout in that year proved to be only a small, momentary shift in direction. More recent writings on college-age students suggest an even less encouraging picture. According to one such study based on extensive interviews with young people: "The extent of public disengagement among the vast majority of emerging adults (18–23 years of age) is astonishing . . . almost all emerging adults are either apathetically uninformed, distrustful, disempowered, or at most only marginally interested in politics and public life."[4] The percentages of twelfth-graders who trust public officials, believe that government is run for the people, or are confident that political leaders are honest have sunk to the lowest levels since statistics for these opinions were first compiled in 1976.[5]

Trends such as these have disturbing consequences for the health of our democracy. Political apathy is not evenly distributed throughout the population. Ultraconservative and ultraliberal voters tend to be more involved in politics and to vote at higher rates than moderates, thus intensifying the divisions in Congress that have repeatedly blocked bipartisan collaboration. Well-to-do Americans go to the polls much more regularly than their poorer fellow citizens (and provide the bulk of the campaign contributions), causing lawmakers to be disproportionately responsive to the concerns of affluent constituents and well-organized interest groups. The ease with which uninformed voters can be manipulated tempts politicians and other purveyors of political information to resort to misleading or even blatantly false assertions.

Civic education cannot cure these ills by itself. But it might help to bring about higher levels of voting, a more knowledgeable electorate, and a more accountable government, while encouraging more citizens to become active in politics and public affairs at the national, state, and local levels. Over the years, this possibility has inspired a series of authors and commissions to publish books and reports urging educators to mount a vigorous effort to prepare their students to be active and informed citizens. And yet, one looks in vain on most college campuses for signs of a well-considered program of civic education. Rarely does a college catalog contain a mandatory set of courses to inform students about their government and the importance of an engaged citizenry. Faculties seldom even engage in a serious discussion of the topic. Why colleges devote so little attention to a subject that seems so urgent and so necessary is the threshold question in a chapter on the role of civic education.

WHAT DO WE MEAN BY CIVIC EDUCATION?

Commentators who write about civic education usually have several objectives in mind. First, students should be made aware of the important role of citizen participation under our system of government.

Second, they should acquire the basic information that helps them to understand how the government works and to grasp the most important and enduring issues of public policy. Third, civic education should give students an understanding of the rights and protections provided for individuals and the fundamental principles of justice and fairness that will help them evaluate many government policies and actions. Finally, civic education should motivate students to take an interest in politics and civic affairs and teach them the basic skills and qualities of mind required for responsible civic participation, such as analytic ability, proficiency in written and oral communication, respect for the rights of others, and the capacity to work with fellow citizens effectively and collaboratively toward common goals.

CAN PUBLIC SCHOOLS DO THE JOB?

Schools rather than colleges have long been the primary source of civic education in America. As that early champion of public education, Horace Mann, pointed out more than 150 years ago: "One of the highest and most valuable objects to which the influence of a school can be made conducive consists of training our children for self-government."[6] Since public schools enroll the vast majority of America's youth, they would seem to be the most obvious locus for preparing young people for their future role as citizens.

No serious observer, however, has argued that public schools can take care of providing civic education by themselves. Many studies have pointed to the difficulties that beset our K–12 education, especially in schools in lower-income neighborhoods. A series of problems hamper existing efforts, including ineffective teaching, inadequate funding, and conflicting pressures from school boards, parents, politicians, and textbook publishers.[7] Moreover, most states place surprisingly little emphasis on civic education in schools. Ten do not require any high school courses in civics, thirty-one merely require a single course lasting one semester, and only sixteen require periodic assessments of civic knowledge. A mere 24 percent of twelfth-graders performed at or above the proficiency level in civics according to the national assessment conducted by the US Department of Education in 2010.[8]

Colleges can never fully compensate for the weaknesses of public schools. Not everyone goes to college, and only two-thirds of those who do ever graduate. Still, at least 85 percent of today's high school graduates enroll in a college at some point in their lives. Moreover, college graduates make up a disproportionate share of American voters and a very high percentage of political officeholders and persons active in civic organizations. Professors are also much freer from outside partisan pressures than public school teachers in choosing the content of their courses and the materials they assign their students. There are good reasons, then, for calling on colleges to play a substantial role in the preparation of active, informed citizens.

SHOULD COLLEGES EMBRACE CIVIC EDUCATION?

Not all educators believe that colleges *should* undertake the responsibilities just described, and a few have expressed outright opposition. The noted educator Robert Maynard Hutchins once flatly declared that "education for citizenship has no place in the university."[9] More recently, professor and onetime dean Stanley Fish has argued in the *Chronicle of Higher Education* that "promoting virtuous citizenship is no doubt a worthy goal, but it is not an academic goal, because . . . it is a political goal," and hence an inappropriate aim for colleges to pursue.[10] Such skepticism is not unusual. Carol Schneider, the recent president of the American Association of Colleges and Universities, concluded not long ago that after "five years of active discussion on dozens of campuses . . . I have been persuaded that there is not just a neglect of but a resistance to college-level study of United States democratic principles."[11]

The Argument of Stanley Fish

Some of the resistance from faculty members may result from a worry that civic education could either degenerate into shallow appeals to patriotism or become a vehicle for promoting the partisan political views of the instructor. For example, Professor Fish correctly points out that aims such as "virtuous citizenship" can be taken to mean almost anything from unquestioning patriotism to a commitment to some liberal vision of social justice. Both of these alternatives could amount to indoctrination and come in conflict with the overriding aim of colleges to seek truth and understanding. Yet trying to avoid any subject matter that could compromise the pursuit of truth and understanding seems extreme, much like the now widely discredited quest for entirely "value-free" scholarship. Adopting such a policy would make it difficult, if not impossible, to prepare students to contribute to the kind of democratic society on which universities depend for their very existence.

Certain basic principles of government seem so widely accepted as worthwhile by our society that they may appropriately form the basis for a deliberate program of civic education. Almost everyone will agree that America is a democracy that should be responsive to the will of its citizens. If such a government is to function well, citizens should be willing to express their preferences by voting and try to be reasonably informed and cognizant of arguments for and against important policy questions. To do so, they require the freedom to express their opinions without restraint, except for the most compelling reasons. They also need encouragement to participate in the affairs of their community and to play a part in the political process when the opportunity presents itself.

Goals of this kind do not presuppose any particular government policies. Nor do they imply that America has the best government in the world, deny the many problems that remain to be solved, or prohibit a faculty member or student from pointing out the virtues of alternative political systems. They do reflect a widely shared belief that democracy is the best form of government yet conceived for fulfilling the needs and hopes of its citizens and enabling universities to pursue their goal of increasing truth and understanding. As representatives of educational institutions dependent upon a healthy and successful democracy, academic leaders have a duty to themselves, their students, and their society to try to preserve and strengthen the basic principles and civic responsibilities that are essential to our system of government.

Many professors who accept these propositions may still shrink from embracing civic education out of concern that such an undertaking could degenerate into the kind of shallow patriotic exercise that should have no place in a college or university. Others may worry that civics teachers could be biased, since very large majorities of political science faculties describe themselves as liberal. By this logic, however, political science departments would have to give up teaching courses on American government, while economics departments could be asked to cease teaching basic economics on the grounds that some instructors might promote an unquestioning faith in the virtues of the free market system. A great many subjects may be taught in biased or dogmatic ways; the proper response is to discourage such teaching when it occurs, not to prohibit entire subjects from being taught.

The Argument of Moral Psychologists

A very different form of skepticism about the value of civic education has emerged in recent years from the research of moral psychologists such as Jonathan Haidt of New York University's Stern School of Business. Haidt has launched a frontal attack on the assumption that colleges can educate their students to reach informed, reasoned conclusions about issues of public policy and the choices to be made among rival candidates for public office.[12] The traditional view has been that informed voters will compare the policy positions of rival candidates, along with other information about their background and behavior, and then make up their minds about which one to support. Colleges are assumed to improve this process by giving students more knowledge and greater skill with which to evaluate the views of opposing parties and their candidates.

Professor Haidt, however, denies that most people engage in such a rational process. Instead, he argues, individuals tend to reach immediate conclusions about which candidates and policies to support based on instinctive preferences that are partly inherited and partly shaped by experiences beginning in childhood. Most people, he claims, tend to be either liberals or conservatives. Liberals are chiefly concerned with alleviating distress and avoiding unfairness; they are against unjustified and needless suffering. Conservatives usually share these concerns, but not as keenly as liberals, because they also care about maintaining order, traditional values, and respect for authority in order to avoid a breakdown of social stability.

Animated by these differences, some people are predisposed to favor liberal politicians, while others instinctively favor conservatives. Once these instincts are in play, Haidt maintains, voters pay attention to the facts and arguments for and against each candidate, not to make up their minds about whom to support but simply to find additional reasons to confirm their initial preference.

Haidt's conclusions are not mere supposition; he cites evidence from his own psychological experiments and from the findings of anthropologists, psychologists, and neuroscientists to support his argument. Even so, while many people may arrive at political decisions in the way that Haidt describes, there are reasons not to write off civic education entirely. Not all candidates can be easily classified according to Haidt's dichotomy. They are not so clearly and reliably liberal or conservative on all political issues. Some voters also change their minds and their political orientation over the course of their adult lives in the light of experience and reflection; for example, Haidt mentions that he himself shifted during his research from identifying as a self-proclaimed liberal to declaring himself as an independent.

Today a large and growing percentage of adults do not classify themselves as Democrats or Republicans but as independents. Others may acknowledge some tendency to support one party or the other but still vote for candidates from the opposing party when they consider them to be stronger. It is reasonable to suppose that many of these people do not jump quickly to conclusions but rather weigh the evidence about rival candidates and arrive at decisions that are guided, at least to a significant extent, by the information and arguments they have received. This assumption has received support from several philosophers and neuroscientists who point to experimental evidence that initial reactions are frequently shaped by previous rational deliberation or are eventually modified after subsequent reflection and analysis.[13]

There is also reason to question Haidt's belief that education can do little to change the way people think about questions of politics and public policy. Haidt explains his views on how individuals think about political issues by likening them to lawyers who hunt for evidence to vindicate their client rather than behaving as judges do by analyzing the facts with an open mind to discover the truth. This analogy seems flawed. Lawyers would be poor counselors for their clients if they lacked the ability to consider arguments on both sides of the issue in describing the legal risks and likely legality of a proposed course of action. For this reason, much of legal education consists of efforts by instructors to instill these habits of thinking in their students. As a law school graduate, I believe, as do all of the lawyers I know, that professors who use the Socratic method to develop the habit of critical thinking about legal problems succeed in teaching most students to search for the arguments on each side of every issue and to weigh them carefully and dispassionately before coming to a conclusion about the probable legal outcome. In college, as in law school, there is reason to believe that courses on critical thinking, properly taught, can improve the way students think about political questions along with other practical problems. Studies by researchers have consistently shown that courses on critical thinking do manage to improve students' reasoning significantly.[14]

In short, Haidt may be correct in describing how *some* people make decisions involving politics and public policy. He is less convincing, however, in suggesting that almost everyone thinks in this way and that attempts to teach students to undertake a more careful, open-minded search for their conclusions can do little to alter this tendency.

HOW EFFECTIVE IS CIVIC EDUCATION
IN OUR COLLEGES?

Few academic leaders will agree with critics who dismiss civic education as either a hopeless or an inappropriate task for their institution to undertake. Indeed, college mission statements usually include an explicit affirmation of their commitment to preparing citizens. In most colleges, however, it is hard to find any reference to this purpose in course catalogs or faculty discussions about the curriculum.

If pressed to explain, campus leaders will undoubtedly point out that many of the skills and qualities of mind that are emphasized in college—critical thinking, problem-solving, empathy, global awareness, and respect for other races, religions, and points of view, merely to mention some obvious examples—are important for enlightened citizenship. Many undergraduate courses also convey valuable knowledge about issues of domestic and foreign policy. Community service projects, student government, and other extracurricular activities offer practical experience in civic engagement, teamwork, and the exercise of leadership skills.

These efforts appear to have positive results. In their massive study of research on higher education, Ernest Pascarella and Patrick Terenzini report that most college seniors have made significant gains, on average, in critical thinking and problem-solving and become more interested in politics and public policy. According to these authors, "Studies indicate that education produces substantially greater understanding of the principles of democratic government, . . . more knowledge of current political facts, stronger socio-political orientation, and increased social activism."[15] Once college students have graduated, research consistently shows that they vote more frequently than citizens with only a high school education and are much more likely to participate in civic affairs. The effects appear to last long after students have completed college.

Although these findings are encouraging, they are not entirely convincing. Various college courses may be useful to citizens, but many students do not take them. A substantial fraction do not complete a single course in economics, and fewer than one-third enroll in a class on American politics and government. Fewer still take a course in political philosophy or international affairs. Although most colleges report that solid majorities of their students engage in some form of community service during college, only one-third link students' service work with a course that encourages them to reflect on their experience and explore its connection to issues of politics or public policy.[16] Not surprisingly, many students appear to look upon community service as an alternative to politics rather than a stimulus to participate in the political process.

With respect to helping students think critically, investigators have discovered that even though most undergraduates do improve their ability to think critically, the average amount of improvement is not terribly impressive and has declined by almost half in recent decades. Entering freshmen who rank at the exact middle of their class in their ability to think critically tend to get better over the next four years, but only by enough, on average, to rise from the fiftieth to the sixty-seventh percentile if they were to take the test again with a similar group of beginning freshmen. Up to one-third of undergraduates seem to make little, if any, progress.[17]

As for political participation, it is true that college graduates go to the polls and engage in civic affairs more often than citizens with only a high school education. Still, only 48 percent of college graduates under the age of twenty-five voted in the presidential election of 2016.[18] Moreover, although the weight of the evidence suggests that college increases political and civic involvement, a growing body of recent research has raised doubts about this conclusion. Two professors conducted a study of monozygotic twins, one of whom went to college and graduated while the other did not. After investigating the later-life civic involvement of the twins in the study, the authors found no significant difference in the civic behavior of those who graduated from college and those who did not.[19] Other investigators have come to the same conclusion about the higher voting rates of college graduates.[20] These findings suggest that the increased levels of civic engagement among college graduates may result from dispositions acquired *before* entering college, not from the college experience itself. This conclusion has gained support from other studies showing that high school seniors who plan to go to college are much more inclined to express an intention to vote and to volunteer to help their communities than classmates who do not plan to enter college.[21]

Still other researchers have found that some students may even become *less* civically engaged by attending college. Popular undergraduate majors such as those in business, science, and engineering appear to *diminish* civic involvement; the more courses students take in these subjects, the less likely they are to vote or engage in community service after they graduate.[22]

If going to college truly encouraged voting, one would expect that the vast increase in the share of young Americans with BA degrees since the 1950s would have caused election turnouts to rise. In fact, however, voting rates in presidential elections declined after 1960, from over 60 percent to little more than 50 percent today. Moreover, if colleges were actually providing effective civic education, one would assume that the massive growth in the percentage of Americans under age twenty-five who have entered college and earned a degree would have improved the political knowledge of young people. Yet researchers find that the level of political knowledge among recent college graduates today is no greater than that of high school seniors in the late 1940s.[23]

Finally, however successful academic leaders may *think* their colleges are in preparing citizens, students and staff appear to be much less confident. A recent survey of twenty-four thousand students, professors, and campus professionals from a diverse set of colleges conducted by the University of Michigan revealed a large gap between what students and professionals believed that college *should* do about civic education and what they felt *actually* took place.[24] Fifty-eight percent of students and 74 percent of college professionals agreed, either strongly or somewhat, that preparing students to contribute to society should be an essential goal of college education, but only 41.5 percent of students and 43 percent of campus professionals agreed that contributing to the larger society was a major focus of their own institution.[25] Moreover, the percentage of students strongly agreeing that "the campus actively promotes awareness of US social, political and economic issues" declined, from 44.2 to 34.1 percent, from the freshman to the senior year.[26] Only 36.4 percent of the students strongly agreed that their commitment to contributing to the greater good through community involvement had increased during college, and only 31 percent strongly agreed that their college had helped them learn the skills necessary to change society for the better.[27]

WHAT MORE CAN COLLEGES DO?

These findings suggest that more should be done to prepare engaged and active citizens. However, the numerous studies and commission reports on civic education are often vague when it comes to making specific recommendations on what colleges should do to improve matters. A common suggestion is to have more departments and programs in the college demonstrate the relevance of their subject to current civic problems and engage their students in discussions of these issues. Although efforts of this kind might inspire some students to become engaged with public questions, getting faculties to cooperate is difficult. By long tradition, professors enjoy great autonomy in deciding on the content of their courses and their methods of instruction. Most of them feel hard-pressed already to cover all of the material that needs attention. Moreover, many may not feel qualified to teach about matters of public policy. As a result, exhortations to faculty members to conduct discussions of this kind in their classes are likely to go unheeded.

Requiring Courses on Civics

Although colleges offer many classes and activities that could help prepare their students to be citizens, very few *require* any courses aimed at achieving this result. Instead, learning to become a citizen appears to be treated as an option rather than a responsibility, much like preparing to be a doctor or a lawyer or a business executive, even though citizenship is not a choice but a status acquired automatically by the vast majority of undergraduates. Many undergraduates do not take even basic courses on subjects such as economics or American government. Thus, one may legitimately ask whether colleges should mandate that all students take certain classes that are designed to prepare them to be active and informed citizens.

On closer analysis, there are reasons why few colleges have instituted such requirements. A serious effort to instill a sense of civic responsibility and equip students with the knowledge they need to be active, informed citizens would call for a formidable array of courses. As a practical matter, however, amid the many other demands on the college curriculum, faculties would find it difficult to set aside more than three or four required courses for this purpose. It is no simple matter to decide which subjects should be included. A course on American government and politics? On basic economics? American history? Sociology? Political theory? International relations? Comparative systems of government? Should colleges offer a class to teach all students civic skills? Although many professors could supply their own choice of three or four mandated courses, it is far more difficult to obtain agreement from an entire faculty representing a wide variety of disciplines and educational philosophies.

In addition, many students dislike requirements and would almost certainly prefer to have the faculty refrain from adding new ones. Colleges can disregard such sentiments, but teaching young people who resent having to listen is seldom appealing or even successful. Doing so could even turn students against politics and civic engagement, exactly the opposite of what is needed.

It might be possible to lessen these difficulties to some extent by requiring students to complete a minimum number of courses that will help to prepare them for citizenship, but allowing them more choice about which subjects to study. All undergraduates could be required to take a single introductory course on government in the United States covering a variety of subjects ranging from the reasons for our system of checks and balances and other important provisions of the Constitution to the actual process of selecting and electing candidates, the role of citizens and civic organizations (along with other interest groups) in influencing policy, and the relations between federal, state, and local governments. Comparative material could be included to describe how other countries have dealt with problems of democratic governance similar to ours. In addition to this one required class, students could be asked to choose at least two or three courses from a variety of offerings in such subjects as economics and economic policy, international relations and foreign policy, and social welfare legislation and other efforts to combat poverty and inequality.

A scheme of this sort might make it easier for a faculty to reach agreement while providing some freedom of choice for students. Even so, one can still question how much good such courses would do. Students have a notoriously short memory for information they receive from their professors. Even when tested immediately after listening to a lecture, most members of the class can recall no more than half of what they heard.[28] After a week, they remember even less. In light of these findings, one wonders whether a small cluster of required courses would contribute much of lasting value that would help graduates take an active part in political and civic affairs or make more enlightened decisions about political candidates and government policies. Because issues constantly change, the knowledge that might seem highly relevant to young citizens in college will often be much less so twenty or even ten years after they graduate. For these reasons, despite the importance in principle of preparing students to be citizens, colleges may hesitate to devote several required courses to this purpose.

It is much harder to justify the unwillingness of most colleges to include a single required course on the basic principles of American government—how it functions, its strengths and weaknesses, the role of citizens and their effect on public policy, and the reasons why the government behaves as it does. Such a course might help students understand why voting is important, why our government and constitution are constructed as they are, what problems exist in the way the government functions, and why some of these difficulties are harder to fix than others. Even the most cynical students might emerge from such a course with a deeper, more informed understanding of our government and its importance. Some of them might at least come to appreciate the wisdom in Winston Churchill's famous remark: "Democracy is the worst form of Government except for all those other forms that have been tried from time to time."[29]

In addition to a required course, there is much to be said for trying to do a better job of developing competencies colleges already teach that can help students participate effectively both as voters and as citizens engaged in political and civic activities. Skills such as critical thinking and problem solving are much more likely than facts and information to remain with students for long periods of time and to retain their value even as the issues facing government continuously change.

Critical Thinking

Virtually every professor in America claims that "critical thinking" is a "very important" or "essential" goal of undergraduate education. No wonder. In their massive analysis of student learning in college, Professors Pascarella and Terenzini define this skill as a "capability to . . . identify central issues and assumptions in an argument, recognize important relationships, make correct inferences from data . . . interpret whether conclusions are warranted based on data, [and] evaluate evidence or authority."[30] This definition seems quite apt for describing the way one would like citizens to go about choosing among candidates or considering ways to solve problems arising in their communities.

Despite the importance that faculties place on critical thinking, there are ample reasons for concern about the way most professors teach their students to develop this capability. As previously mentioned, while undergraduates tend to increase their proficiency in college, the average gains are fairly modest. It is not hard to discover why. Many instructors do not emphasize this skill in the courses they teach. A recent study from California has found that "only 9 percent of professors were able to explicate how they taught to encourage critical thinking."[31] The same study reports that 70 percent of instructors at nonselective colleges relied on multiple-choice tests supplied by textbook publishers, even though short-answer exams almost always assess recall rather than careful reasoning. An earlier analysis of examinations given at prominent research universities discovered that fewer than 20 percent of the test questions called for critical thinking, with most simply requiring recall of information or comprehension of relevant material.[32] Even today, at least half of college faculty continue to lecture extensively, especially in large college courses, despite persuasive evidence that active forms of problem-solving are more effective at helping students learn to think carefully and reason well.[33] In short, there is plenty of room for improving the way colleges teach this important skill.

Media Literacy

The election of 2016 highlighted an additional challenge in preparing students to inform themselves about politics and government. The campaign for the presidency drew attention to the appearance of "fake news" deliberately planted by various sources to sway voters. Now that many people rely on social media to keep informed about the news, the harm that may be done by false or misleading material has greatly increased. Surveys of public opinion have revealed that alarming percentages of Americans believe that President Obama is a Muslim and was born outside the United States, that the 9/11 attack on the World Trade Center was a CIA plot, and that scientists are sharply divided on whether climate change is occurring and whether human beings are responsible.

In response to these developments, scores of colleges are now providing a course to teach students how to evaluate the stories they encounter in newspapers, on television, or through social media.[34] These courses encourage students to be open to views and information that conflict with their own beliefs, but not to believe all the news accounts they read. Much of the instruction is devoted to teaching students how to evaluate the stories they receive by checking their sources and seeking independent verification of their accuracy.

As yet, there are few rigorous studies to ascertain the effectiveness of these courses.[35] Surveys reveal that students who have taken them think that they are now more aware of the need to question news stories and seek independent verification of their content. But few studies have attempted to discover how much student behavior has actually changed and how long the changes last. The few findings that do exist are mixed. Common sense would suggest that there are limits to the amount of time and effort people will devote to checking sources for news stories and verifying the contents. Courses on media literacy could turn out to help. But major improvement in guarding against false and misleading information may ultimately depend on regulating social media and developing new technology that will prevent material that is clearly false and simplify the task of discovering the sources of information and evaluating its accuracy.

Capitalizing on Diversity

In today's diverse and highly partisan society, it is also important to encourage undergraduates to open their minds to contrary opinions and arguments and to discuss the differences respectfully. Most campuses are well positioned to encourage these habits. Merely by assembling a student body of widely varying backgrounds and political orientations, colleges can help undergraduates learn to engage constructively with political opinions that differ from their own.

Many colleges have introduced courses and workshops specifically aimed at developing tolerance and understanding of different points of view, and much research suggests that they are helpful. However, these offerings typically concentrate on increasing understanding of differences of race, gender, and sexual orientation rather than learning to respect opposing political opinions. The polarized state of political discourse today has led a number of college instructors to create opportunities to engage in discussions about divisive issues that encourage students with conflicting views to participate in a civil and respectful way. More colleges could follow this example.

Colleges could also do more to promote civil discourse outside of class. Obviously, there are limits to what campus authorities can do or even be aware of. But when officials learn of efforts to intimidate, harass, or insult those with different views, they can certainly express their disapproval and explain to the perpetrators why their behavior is inappropriate and at odds with the kind of civil discourse that the college is trying to promote.

Unlike their student bodies, almost all college faculties are predominantly liberal in their political orientation, especially in the social sciences, which account for most of the courses on politics and public policy. In departments of sociology and political science, liberals typically outnumber conservatives by ratios of ten-, fifteen-, or even twenty-to-one. The meager representation of conservative professors is not deliberate, nor is there much evidence that the political orientation of students changes significantly during college. Still, the liberal orientation of most college faculties creates a risk that students will hear few thoughtful expositions of conservative points of view unless colleges make a deliberate effort to bring visiting lecturers and speakers to campus to present their ideas.

Community Service

A majority of undergraduates on many campuses practice civic engagement by participating in some form of community service during college.[36] Many colleges also help students obtain internships in government agencies and nonprofit organizations where they can gain experience by practicing civic skills and develop a taste for public service. The growth of these opportunities in recent decades represents a substantial achievement by the nation's colleges. As previously mentioned, however, many fewer students can enroll in classes that allow them to combine community service with an opportunity to reflect on their experience and learn more about the economic and social problems they encounter and their connection with government and public policy. Colleges could offer more courses of this kind, since research suggests that such classes do more than community service by itself to encourage students to engage in civic and political activity after they graduate.*

Making More of Elections

There are other, smaller ways in which colleges could demonstrate the importance of the political process and the need for every student to take part. Federal and state elections provide a valuable occasion for such efforts. Colleges can establish polling places on campus instead of leaving students to hunt for a place to vote in the surrounding town or city. They can encourage students to launch registration drives or serve as volunteer poll watchers on election day. They can organize debates, bring candidates to the campus for speeches, and hold mock conventions. At the very least, campus officials can comply with the provision in the 1965 Higher Education Act that *requires* universities receiving benefits under the act to obtain voter registration forms well in advance of federal elections and distribute them to students. (A 2004 national survey found that one-third of all colleges and universities subject to the law had not even obtained registration forms and that another 19 percent were "not sure."[37]) Vigorous efforts by colleges to interest students in elections will carry an important message about the importance of voting in our democracy, just as a minimal effort will convey the opposite message.

---

* See, for example, Ashley Finley, "Civic Learning and Democratic Engagements: A Review of the Literature on Civic Engagement in Post-Secondary Education," paper prepared for the US Department of Education (May 24, 2011), p. 19; Matthew J. Mayhew et al., *How College Affects Students*, vol. 3, *21st Century Evidence That College Works* (2016), p. 552. Some faculty members look upon service learning courses with suspicion, fearing that they can easily become a forum for persuading students to dedicate themselves to the vision of social justice favored by the instructor; see, for example, Stanley Fish, "Citizen Formation Is Not Our Job," *Chronicle of Higher Education* (January 17, 2017). If indoctrination of this kind does occur, it is inappropriate and should be resisted. Yet this problem is not unique to community service. It can arise in teaching economics, sociology, political science, and many other subjects. Once again, the proper response is surely to discourage indoctrination wherever it occurs rather than do away with entire categories of instruction simply because it *might* happen.

Student Government

Participation in student government offers other valuable opportunities for students to learn the skills of politics and community leadership. Researchers have found that such experience in college and high school frequently leads to greater civic engagement in later life.[38] Although almost every campus already has some form of student government, it is often regarded by undergraduates as unimportant and ineffective. Many colleges could do more to raise its status and encourage participation by giving elected student representatives greater opportunities to have input into decisions that affect their lives.

HOW MUCH CAN CIVIC EDUCATION ACCOMPLISH?

Despite the many ways in which efforts to prepare citizens might be strengthened, most colleges have done much less than they could to implement these practices. Again and again, civic leaders and educators have authored books and signed commission reports deploring student apathy and urging a more robust commitment to civic education. These writings have repeatedly called attention to the ignorance of young people about politics and public affairs and higher education's lack of emphasis on preparing active and enlightened citizens. Apart from encouraging more community service, however, the response from most campuses has been minimal.

One possible justification for not doing more is the persistent doubt about whether attempts to improve civic engagement will make any difference. Even if one rejects the views of Stanley Fish and the sweeping conclusions of psychologists such as Jonathan Haidt, there are grounds for questioning how much colleges can accomplish to prepare students to be thoughtful and engaged citizens.[39] As pointed out earlier, recent empirical studies have challenged the belief that going to college increases the inclination to vote and take part in civic activities by arguing that the higher voting rates and increased participation in politics displayed by graduates merely reflect the greater civic interest among entering freshmen compared with that of high school graduates who do not go to college.

Universities should encourage research to resolve these doubts. Such efforts, however, could take a long time to arrive at definitive results. What, then, should colleges do in the interim?

This question is easily answered. Almost all of the steps suggested in this chapter have been shown to have a variety of positive results. Improving current methods for teaching critical thinking will benefit students in all kinds of ways, both at work and in their private lives. Community service and service learning have been found by researchers to enhance empathy, self-knowledge, leadership, and social skills in addition to whatever positive impact they have on the subsequent civic activities of college graduates.[40] Class discussions among students of diverse backgrounds and political opinions appear to achieve a variety of useful outcomes, including increasing mutual respect, tolerance, and interpersonal skills. Participation in student government helps to develop leadership as well as speaking and writing skills and competence in working with others.

In short, most of the ways to strengthen civic education that have been mentioned in these pages will further important aims of undergraduate education whether or not they succeed in developing active and enlightened citizens. The only exception is the introduction of a compulsory course on American government and politics. Even this modest step seems justifiable as a worthwhile experiment to try to combat the prevailing apathy, cynicism, and civic ignorance among many college students today.

There are many steps, therefore, that colleges can take to improve civic education without waiting for definitive proof of their impact on the subsequent behavior of their graduates. Having benefited so greatly from existing in a democratic society, colleges can surely do this much in the hope of strengthening the political system that sustains them.

CHAPTER THREE

Preparing Students for an Interdependent World

We hear much discussion today of an interdependent world, a global economy, a clash between rival cultures. What these terms all help to describe is a condition in which our lives are affected more and more by nations, problems, and crises beyond our borders. Hostile and dysfunctional governments; trends in rates of global fertility, poverty, and fossil fuel consumption; fluctuations in overseas economies; terrorists and computer hackers from far-off lands—all affect the lives of Americans in significant, often threatening ways. At the same time, distant countries offer new markets for American companies, valuable allies for the United States in resisting its enemies, new ideas for solving common problems, and cultural achievements that enrich our lives.

Students recognize the need to prepare themselves for living in a more interdependent world. In 2016, a study by the Council on Foreign Relations found that 63 percent of college graduates considered it "essential," or at least "very important," to be knowledgeable about international relations, 81 percent felt the same way about keeping up with world events, and 56 percent recognized the need to have some understanding of foreign cultures.[1] Faculties shared these opinions. Well over half of college professors believed either "strongly" or "somewhat strongly" that all undergraduates should be required to take international courses and that faculty members had a responsibility to help students become more aware of foreign affairs and foreign cultures.[2]

Universities paid little attention to international studies prior to World War II, but they started to take a greater interest in the subject after 1945, when America began to play a much more active role in world affairs. Over the next decades their international activities rapidly increased. By 1980, at least twenty research universities *each* employed more professors of international subjects than the total number of such scholars throughout the entire United States only four decades earlier.[3] Today most colleges offer a wide variety of courses on global subjects and foreign languages along with programs to enable undergraduates to study abroad and to bring more students from other countries to study in the United States.

In seeking to determine the appropriate place of international studies in the undergraduate curriculum, however, colleges immediately confront a problem. How can they prepare their students adequately for a global environment composed of hundreds of different countries, languages, and cultures and beset by problems that are constantly emerging and evolving, often in sudden, unexpected ways? How can anyone predict what undergraduates will eventually need to know about foreign nations and global problems after they have graduated from college? These questions pose a more difficult challenge for educators than most other issues involving the undergraduate curriculum.

THE PURPOSE OF INTERNATIONAL STUDIES

Although most four-year colleges now claim to be engaged in internationalizing their curriculum, there is no consensus yet on what the principal aim of such an effort should be. At least four different rationales have attracted a following.

The earliest proposals for expanding international studies reflected a strong sense that Americans were much too ignorant of world affairs and that steps needed to be taken to overcome their parochialism. Those who expressed this point of view often cited the poor showing of young people on tests about world affairs and the large percentages who were unable to answer questions such as how to locate Iraq on a map of the world. In response, some professors and academic leaders recommended that colleges adopt a program of "comprehensive internationalization" consisting of foreign language requirements, overseas study programs, and courses on other countries and cultures in a concerted effort to add an international component to every facet of the undergraduate program where such enhancement seemed plausible.[4] For those who still favor this strategy, any addition to a college's international offerings is a welcome step in the right direction.

A second reason sometimes given for emphasizing international studies is a need to maintain America's position as the predominant world power and the preeminent actor in the new global economy. In 2012, the College Board described this rationale in the following terms:

> As other countries become increasingly competitive through rising levels of interaction in the global economy, the US is faced with the challenge of retaining the competitive advantage it has built through decades of economic growth. In order to achieve this goal, the US must possess a citizenry who demonstrate sufficient levels of global competency— that is, they have the right skills, aptitudes, and dispositions to navigate and excel in a highly fluid, globalized, and increasingly competitive environment.[5]

This purpose has found greatest acceptance among faculties offering programs to prepare students for professional careers in fields, such as business and engineering, whose graduates are likely to find jobs in companies and firms that have extensive trade with foreign countries or maintain branch offices or facilities overseas.

A third rationale for international studies stresses the need to educate what some advocates refer to as "global citizens." This approach emphasizes the importance of curricula that help all undergraduates to appreciate the importance of major problems that affect everyone in an interdependent world, such as climate change, massive immigration, the risk of nuclear war, and worldwide poverty. Proponents usually favor the creation of interdisciplinary courses on important global problems reinforced by efforts from instructors throughout the curriculum to incorporate material on these issues wherever possible into their readings and class discussions. The most persuasive justification for such a curriculum is the need to prepare students to be informed citizens who understand the increasing importance of problems that affect the lives and welfare of Americans and other populations throughout the world.

Finally, a prominent variant of the global citizenship rationale views the world through the lens of social justice. Those who favor this approach emphasize the importance of creating change to end social injustice wherever it occurs by working for "full and equal participation of all groups in a society that is mutually shaped to meet their needs."[6] Proponents believe in having colleges make a conscious effort to inspire their students to contribute to building societies throughout the world that are equitable and in which "all members are physically and psychologically safe and secure."[7]

Advocates for any of the several competing rationales for international studies seldom give reasons why the version they prefer is superior to the alternative models. Instead, proponents typically proceed, like ships in the night, to promote their vision without acknowledging the existence of other rationales. As a result, the literature is lacking in the kind of informed debate that might eventually bring about a consensus on a suitable curriculum.

INTERCULTURAL COMPETENCE

Notwithstanding the differing views about the purpose of international education, there is wide agreement on the need to prepare students to take appropriate account of the distinctive values, meanings, customs, and other behavioral characteristics of different cultures. Companies doing business in foreign markets, employees of nongovernmental organizations grappling with global problems, and citizens seeking to understand major international issues all need to be aware of cultural differences and understand how they can affect the behavior of other populations.

Various definitions have been offered to describe this capability. The American Council on Education has declared that interculturally competent individuals "understand how other people think, how other cultures work, and how other societies are likely to respond to American actions."[8] Darla Deardorff, a frequent commentator on international education, used the Delphi technique to synthesize the views of a panel of experienced international practitioners and define intercultural competence as "having an open mind while actively seeking to understand cultural norms and expectations of others, and leverage this gained knowledge to interact, communicate, and work effectively outside one's own environment."[9]

Scholars who write about intercultural competence recognize that it has several components: enough self-knowledge to appreciate how one's own assumptions and values affect one's thinking and behavior; a recognition that people in other cultures often think differently; a curiosity to explore these differences with a nonjudgmental, open-minded attitude; and an appreciation of how these differences can affect a conversation, a negotiation, or the choice of an appropriate course of action. The writings on the subject do not offer much enlightenment on how to develop these capabilities. Language teachers often assert that teaching foreign languages can help students understand other cultures, but attempts to test the validity of this claim have not yielded strong support.[10] Study abroad is often said to be useful, and many students have found the experience to be enlightening, even transformative, by opening their eyes to different cultures and the lives and behaviors of different peoples. Yet many of these programs seem undemanding rather than carefully designed experiences to promote foreign language learning and intercultural competence. Research into the effects on student learning of typical semester-long study abroad programs has reached conflicting conclusions about their lasting value.[11]

Instructors in courses on intercultural competence encounter another practical problem. There are innumerable separate cultures throughout the world, and a single nation will often have several. In the United States, for example, rural Appalachians presumably have a culture quite different from that of "Little Korea" in Los Angeles or that of affluent professionals residing in Westchester County, New York. In the limited space available in a crowded curriculum, however, it is seldom possible to familiarize students with more than one or two different cultures.

In view of this difficulty, it may be necessary to settle for a course that simply offers a preliminary preparation for living in a multicultural world by making students aware of the importance of cultural differences, with the aid of materials that demonstrate how to discover such differences, reflect upon them, and take them into account when encountering them in later life. Such a course can build upon attitudes and habits of perception, reflection, and adaptation already developed through classes and workshops that most colleges provide to help students understand and appreciate the differences within their own student body in outlook and opinion associated with gender, race, socioeconomic background, and sexual orientation. In this way, instructors seeking to develop intercultural competence can regard their efforts as part of a continuum. It begins with the natural tendency of college students to become more sensitive to differences within their own circle of acquaintances, proceeds through attempts by the university to encourage understanding and appreciation of the differences within our own society, and culminates in efforts to teach students how to identify, reflect upon, and adapt to differences in norms, values, and other cultural features in other parts of the world.

Although a course of this kind seems promising, courses on how to adapt to foreign cultures suffer from a lack of solid research to determine their effectiveness. According to a report from the Educational Testing Service in 2016, "the psychometric properties of existing measures leave much room for improvement."[12] Many of the existing studies are based on self-reports of questionable reliability in which students describe their attitudes toward international affairs and different cultures. Other studies involve excessively small samples or fail to account for preexisting differences between students who participate in international programs and students who do not. For the time being, therefore, it is not possible to state with any confidence how successful efforts to teach intercultural competence can be.

PROBLEMS IN CONSTRUCTING AN
INTERNATIONAL STUDIES PROGRAM

Although colleges often speak confidently about having internationalized their curriculum, the reality is quite different. As one thoughtful observer put it after examining the subject:

> While language about "global interdependence," "global awareness," and "global responsibility" was widely used in institutional mission statements and strategic plans, there was a profound disconnect between these rhetorical commitments and actual campus practice. . . . In most cases, responsibility for global learning was relegated to study abroad

offices, language departments, or programs that focused on international relations or on comparative culture, history, or politics. . . . As a result, the current situation calls for a new approach to organizing the curriculum, institutional structures, and faculty-staff development—one that brings new coherence to undergraduate education.[13]

The desired coherence will not come easily. Certainly, it will not be achieved by simply adding an international component wherever it can be introduced. This "comprehensive" approach may do something to overcome parochialism among students, but if the only aim is to add more and more international courses and programs with no objective other than to "internationalize," the result will surely be more confusion rather than less. Besides, each of the typical component parts of internationalization, such as foreign language requirements, study abroad, and the increased enrollment of foreign students, raises serious questions that need to be addressed.

- Do foreign language requirements provide lasting value? At least 60 percent of the colleges that mandate such courses have requirements lasting too short a time (one year or in some cases only one semester) to serve any useful purpose.[14] Such brief encounters, in the words of one skeptical observer, "teach students only enough to order dinner from the menu but not enough to compliment the chef." Not surprisingly, a comprehensive study of student development in college found that only 8 percent of seniors believed that their language skills had grown "much stronger."[15] Even if students are required to take the extra time to master a foreign language, their efforts will have little value if the language they learned turns out not to be one they need in later life.
- How useful is study abroad? Such experiences will rarely have enduring value unless the length of the stay is at least a semester and the housing arrangements and the program of study are designed to put students in constant contact with natives of the host country. Shorter programs can sometimes accomplish lasting results, but only if they are narrowly focused and carefully planned to achieve a specific objective. Many programs do not meet these criteria; they seem designed more as added attractions to persuade prospective students to enroll than as experiences that will enable them to perfect another

language or to acquire genuine intercultural understanding. A recent
review of research on such programs concluded that earlier studies
showing significant gains from study abroad did not adequately control for differences in the values of students prior to entering college
and that these differences, not the study programs themselves, probably accounted for many of the benefits claimed.[16]

- How much value derives from the presence of foreign students
  on campus? Such students are unlikely to add much to the "global
  competence" of their American classmates unless vigorous steps
  are taken to promote frequent contact between the two groups. Yet
  many colleges have not met this challenge successfully.[17] All too
  often, the real reason for recruiting overseas applicants is to ease
  severe financial pressures by enrolling more students who can pay
  full tuition.

- Above all, measuring progress and success merely by how many foreign students are enrolled or how many undergraduates study abroad
  has little meaning without a prior agreement on what the overall international program is meant to accomplish.

Those who advocate international studies to help America compete
successfully in global markets also need to answer several questions.

- Are the courses designed for this purpose useful for all students or
  only for those who major in business, engineering, or some other field
  with extensive international involvement?

- Do the courses provided for this purpose succeed in improving the
  ability of graduates to help businesses perform better in their international operations?

- Is global competence important enough to require that all business
  students acquire it when fewer than 25 percent of employers in some
  surveys regard "awareness and experience with other cultures"
  or "proficiency in foreign languages" or "staying current with global
  developments and trends" as important qualities for the graduates
  they hire?[18]

Educators who emphasize the need to prepare all students to address large global problems are seldom interested merely in conveying
knowledge about international affairs, and they are moved still less

by a desire to help America compete more effectively in foreign markets. Instead, they are animated by a conviction that problems such as climate change, inequality, and mass migration will be among the most critical issues facing the United States and the world over the next two or three generations, and that colleges should therefore prepare their students to play an active and constructive role in addressing them. Faculties can presumably design courses for this purpose that will convey a lot of knowledge about global problems and the existing international organizations and methods for coping with them. Nevertheless, difficult questions remain, not only about how to teach students the skills they will need to address these complex issues effectively, but also about whether it is appropriate for colleges to make this effort the overriding reason for their international program.

- Do college faculties know how to teach students all of the capabilities that active global citizenship of this kind is often said to require, such as intercultural competence or the ability to design creative solutions to complex global problems?
- Is it possible to teach all of the necessary knowledge and competencies without requiring more courses than colleges can allocate in view of the many other demands on the curriculum?
- Given a choice between attempting to resolve a domestic (American) problem and trying to solve a global problem, a vast majority of Americans favor attending to issues here at home. In view of this marked preference, should colleges give the effort to address major global problems priority over working to resolve domestic issues?

The issue raised by the last question becomes particularly acute for those who advocate a social justice rationale for requiring international study.

- Since many students may never engage actively in addressing large global problems during their lifetime, is it appropriate to *require* them to prepare for such a role?
- How can proponents respond to the charge that many critics are likely to make—that by prioritizing efforts to combat injustice around the world, liberal professors are imposing their own values on their students? Should colleges even adopt such a priority or should they

leave it to students to decide how to apportion their efforts among local, national, and international subjects?

- Advocates of the social justice rationale often seem to assume that global trade is a modern form of imperialism that inevitably works to the disadvantage of poorer nations. Since this point of view is not universally shared, is there a risk that the social justice approach will involve a kind of indoctrination? (By the same token, are international programs to help maintain America's lead in global competition open to similar criticism by taking for granted that free trade among nations led by American business will be beneficial?)

Despite the torrent of words on the subject of international studies, few of its proponents attempt to answer these questions. Instead, most essays arguing for one rationale or another offer ambitious descriptions of what their preferred approach will achieve without paying much attention to legitimate questions about its appropriateness or feasibility.

CREATING A VIABLE PROGRAM OF INTERNATIONAL STUDIES

In view of these competing visions and unanswered questions, college leaders and their faculties face formidable problems in trying to agree on a convincing plan for including international studies in the curriculum. Resolving all of these issues is beyond the scope of this study. It may be helpful, however, to begin with the following general criteria, which are applicable to all proposals for an undergraduate curriculum. These criteria will then suggest some more specific observations on the choice of an appropriate rationale and a suitable set of requirements for international studies.

General Criteria

1. In devising the undergraduate curriculum, colleges should not impose a curricular *requirement* on all students unless there is good reason to believe that most of those who complete the requirement successfully will acquire knowledge, skills, or qualities of mind that will help

them live more satisfying lives, fulfill their civic, ethical, or vocational responsibilities after they graduate, or achieve some other purpose of substantial value. To put it more succinctly, a curriculum should not impose requirements that promise to be of little or no value to a substantial fraction of the students involved.

2. It is inappropriate to establish a goal for the curriculum if the number of courses required to achieve the purpose exceeds the number of courses that the college can demand of its students without sacrificing other equally desirable objectives.

3. It is unreasonable to choose a goal for the curriculum and specify requirements to fulfill the purpose unless members of the faculty have reason to be confident that they know how the aim can be achieved through their teaching alone or in combination with other courses or extracurricular activities.*

4. It is normally inappropriate to establish, still less require, courses or programs that assume value propositions that are subject to serious, credible differences of opinion. Such disagreements should be acknowledged and discussed by instructors fairly, carefully, and preferably without taking sides in order to allow students to make up their own minds on the issues involved. To do otherwise threatens to impose a kind of indoctrination that violates basic norms of instruction in a university.

---

*This principle is often violated in practice. To take but one prominent example, most distribution requirements compel students to acquire "breadth" by taking two or three courses from each of several broad categories of knowledge—typically, humanities, social science, and science. The assumption that any eligible course that students choose will broaden their minds in some valuable way seems implausible on its face, since most of the courses involved will have been created with other purposes in mind. Thus, countless nonscientists must enroll in one of their college's introductory science courses even though there is no reliable evidence that courses designed as an introduction to one of the scientific disciplines, such as chemistry or biology, teach the average nonscientist much of lasting value about the nature of science or its importance to society. It is likely that most nonscientists simply choose the introductory science course that is reported to be the easiest in order to satisfy the requirement.

In the late 1970s, when Harvard's Arts and Sciences faculty was overhauling its undergraduate curriculum, a spirited debate took place on the subject of whether it was even possible in one or two courses to teach anything of lasting value about "science" to nonscientists. The biologist E. O. Wilson argued that such a goal was possible and important because the sciences were converging to yield important common truths. Members of the Physics Department expressed the opposite view and denied that any such convergence was taking place. No consensus emerged from this discussion.

Specific Guidelines

With the foregoing principles in mind, one can derive several guidelines for use in evaluating proposals to include international studies in the curriculum.

1. No college should try to "internationalize" its curriculum without first identifying the educational outcomes that the suggested courses, activities, and programs are meant to achieve. Without such a rationale, there is no convincing way to test the appropriateness of the undertaking or evaluate its success. Moreover, there is a serious risk that many of the courses and activities prescribed will not receive enough space in the curriculum or be sufficiently related to each other to achieve any useful objective or provide enough lasting value to justify the time and effort expended by students and faculty.

2. While students should have ample *opportunity* to learn other languages, foreign language *requirements* for all undergraduates should normally be avoided (except when necessary as reasonable prerequisites for a particular course or program). Few undergraduates can anticipate which foreign language they will need in later life. Moreover, experience has shown that the amount of study specified by most colleges to fulfill their language requirement is insufficient to enable most beginners to acquire the competence needed to achieve any meaningful purpose.

3. Similar objections can be raised against the effort in a number of colleges to teach students global or international competence by simply requiring them to take one or two of the college's courses on another country or culture.

4. The vast majority of undergraduates will either be or become American citizens and should therefore receive preparation to fulfill that role. In pursuit of this goal, it may be appropriate to require a study of major global problems that promise to remain important during students' lives, including material concerning the policies, procedures, and institutions through which these problems can be addressed. As with other curricular requirements, however, the number of required courses allocated for this purpose must be sufficiently limited to leave room for other equally legitimate claims on the undergraduate curriculum.

5. It is normally inappropriate to require all undergraduates to take courses designed to prepare them to live their lives in a certain way, such as becoming "active participants in individual or collective efforts to promote social justice throughout the world," or working to "advance equity and justice at home or abroad." Since many graduates may be informed and conscientious citizens of good character but choose other ways to live useful and meaningful lives, there is no compelling justification for requiring them to prepare themselves for these specific purposes. The hope that the requirement will persuade *some* students to pursue a certain kind of career is ordinarily not a sufficient justification for requiring *all* students to take a particular course or group of courses.

6. It is likewise neither necessary nor wise to require courses aimed at maintaining America's competitive edge in the global marketplace if large numbers of students subject to the requirement are not likely to be significantly engaged during their lives in activities related to that goal. Thus, while it may be appropriate to require such courses as part of a business major, it would not be proper to impose such requirements on the entire student body.

7. As with all instruction that touches on controversial problems, programs that focus on competing successfully in doing business with other countries should not simply assume that international trade and global competition are beneficial but should make students aware of the arguments and evidence concerning both their benefits and their disadvantages. Similarly, courses that seek to prepare students to promote social justice should not simply assume without discussion that international trade is a form of modern colonialism and a means of exploiting the people of less developed countries.

One may agree or disagree with the preceding observations. Even so, adopting some set of general guidelines for constructing college curricula can be a fruitful way to facilitate deliberations over the purpose and content of international studies. Basic principles of the kind suggested here can at least provide a framework for analyzing alternative proposals in order to arrive at a set of programs and requirements that can accommodate the large and important subject of global learning within the overall undergraduate course of study in fair and feasible ways.

At present, we still seem far from reaching this result. There is little sign of a lively debate, let alone a consensus, about the appropriate goals for international study.[19] Each of the alternative formulations proposed thus far raises important questions about its ends as well as its means. Several of the ends envisaged seem hard to achieve within the space in the curriculum that colleges are likely to make available. Meanwhile, continuing disagreement over the appropriate aims of international studies complicates the effort to agree on appropriate methods for evaluating the success of existing programs.

In conclusion, we are left with the question posed at the beginning of this chapter: how can colleges prepare their students for an increasingly interdependent world when the body of relevant knowledge is so vast and continually changing? At present, the international field comprises at least five different bodies of knowledge: global problems, such as climate change and population/migration; international relations, including American foreign policy and the growing number of supranational regimes such as the United Nations, the World Trade Organization, and the European Union; foreign languages and literature; comparative studies of various kinds; and finally, regional studies, such as programs on South Asia, sub-Saharan Africa, or Western Europe. Most research universities typically *offer* courses in all or most of the categories just listed, but few, if any, colleges *require* their students to study all five. Although there is some overlap between the different categories, the knowledge needed for each constituent segment is sufficiently different from the others that it would be very difficult, if not impossible, to devise one or even two or three courses that would constitute a suitable introduction to the entire international field. Instead, colleges may have to choose a narrower goal for any course requirement.

If any one of the categories can justify a mandatory course for all students, the most promising candidate would be an offering devoted to pressing global problems, since these issues seem destined to affect the lives and thoughts of most of today's students and preoccupy our government during the next several decades. Yet even a course on global problems may not be the best alternative for every student. Undergraduates who aspire to join the US Foreign Service may prefer a course on American foreign policy. Others may see the center of gravity in world affairs moving toward Asia and desire to learn more about China or India. A budding writer may wish to study comparative literature.

As a practical matter, therefore, many colleges may choose not to require a course on major global problems. They may plausibly conclude that the best alternative is to offer a variety of international courses and simply require students to choose the ones that will best serve what they think are most likely to be their future needs. If a college desires more depth of study, it can require all students to select three or four courses within a single category of international studies, such as one region of the world, one foreign language, or a review of major global problems. Given the lack of consensus on the best approach to international studies and the varying interests and ambitions of undergraduates, allowing students to choose which aspect of international studies to emphasize may well be the best and perhaps the only way to proceed.

Character: Can Colleges Help Students Acquire Higher Standards of Ethical Behavior and Personal Responsibility?

No one has expressed the importance of good character more succinctly than Immanuel Kant in his *Groundwork of the Metaphysics of Morals*. At the beginning of section 1, he observes that virtues such as courage, resolution, and perseverance "are undoubtedly good and desirable for many purposes." But, he adds, "they can also be extremely evil and harmful if the will which makes use of these gifts of nature [and] is called *character*, is not good."[1]

WHY COLLEGES SHOULD CARE ABOUT THE CHARACTER OF THEIR STUDENTS

Colleges share a responsibility to do what they can to help students build their character. College, after all, fills the lives of undergraduates during a period of years in which they have an unusual capacity for growth in personal responsibility and habits of self-control while living in an environment that offers them exceptional opportunities to discover, clarify, and apply the values they wish to live by. Everyone benefits from successful efforts to improve ethical standards. In the world of business, more than 80 percent of CEOs consider ethical judgment an important factor in hiring employees, one of only five qualities to receive such widespread recognition.[2] In society, honesty increases people's trust in one another, contributes to well-being, and raises our confidence in government.

There is ample evidence to suggest that colleges have a lot of work to do to help their students acquire a strong set of ethical principles and the will to live up to them in practice. Most freshmen come to college largely free of parental supervision and without clear moral standards or enough self-discipline to adhere to them. In a survey of high school students in 2002, 98 percent of the respondents claimed to recognize the importance of possessing a good character, but 82 percent acknowledged that they had lied to their parents about something important during the preceding year; 62 percent admitted to having lied to a teacher and cheated on an exam; 22 percent acknowledged stealing something from a relative; and 27 percent disclosed that they had pilfered something from a store.[3]

In a more recent study of a nationally representative sample of young adults (aged eighteen to twenty-three), investigators found that most respondents had very primitive views about ethics.[4] True, only one in six of the respondents believed that "it is okay to break moral rules if it works to your advantage and you can get away with it." And only one in three "believed that morality is *entirely* a matter of individual decision." But almost half replied that "morals are relative; there are no definite rights and wrongs for everybody." The dominant view appeared to be that moral principles are matters of personal opinion and that one cannot judge the morality of others. Asked how people can know the right thing to do, a large majority replied that their conscience would tell them, while 39 percent opined that doing the right thing is "doing what would make you feel happy." On the basis of these findings, the authors were moved to observe that "the adult world that has socialized these youth has done an awful job when it comes to moral education and formation."[5]

Critics within and outside of academia have chastised colleges for doing much less than they should to improve upon this situation. According to Professor David Hoekema, a study of more than one hundred college catalogs revealed that, "when we look closely at the content of the curriculum, we find very little that directly addresses the question of how to discern right and wrong."[6] *New York Times* columnist David Brooks has observed that "highly educated young people are tutored, taught, and monitored in all aspects of their lives except the most important, which is character building. When it comes to this, most universities leave them alone."[7]

These are sweeping criticisms. But are they justified?

TEACHING MORAL REASONING

One prominent method that many colleges employ to help undergrad
uates recognize their ethical responsibilities is to offer courses in
moral reasoning that will enable them to perceive ethical problems
when they arise, take account of the relevant arguments involved, and
reach a thoughtful and reasoned judgment on how to respond. After
many decades of neglect, teaching of this kind enjoyed a renaissance of
sorts beginning in the late 1960s, fueled by the widespread public attention given to controversial moral questions such as those involving
abortion, civil disobedience, racial justice, and women's rights. Today
hundreds of courses on moral reasoning are taught to undergraduates,
although only a minority of colleges *require* students to take one.

Opposition within the Faculty

Despite the growth of moral reasoning courses, faculty members have
long been ambivalent about the place of such instruction in a college.
For most of the twentieth century, teaching students what Henry Sidg-
wick described as "practical ethics" disappeared completely from all
but a few, mainly religiously affiliated colleges.[8] Most philosophers directed their attention to other subjects, while some dismissed ethics
entirely because it had to do with mental states and hence was not a
proper subject for objective study.* Today the tide has definitely turned.
More than 80 percent of faculty members either agree or agree strongly
that it is their role to "develop students' moral character and help them
develop personal values."[9] Yet even now, some prominent scholars,
such as John Mearshimer of the University of Chicago, believe that
colleges have no business offering courses "where you discuss ethics
or morality in any detail."[10]

---

*This tendency represented a clear break from the attitudes of earlier philosophers who
emphasized the importance of putting ethics "to the use of life." As Aristotle declared in his
Nicomachean Ethics, "what other reason could there be to study virtue if not to learn how
to become good." Epictetus also asserted that the most essential part of philosophy was
"the application of principles as, for instance, the principle not to speak falsely." *The
Enchiridion*, trans. W. A. Oldfather (Loeb Classical Library, 1928), p. 536. I am indebted to
Sissela Bok for calling my attention to these statements.

One reason for a lingering ambivalence may be a fear that instruction in practical ethics will become a form of indoctrination. After all, the purpose of most moral reasoning courses is to help people decide how they *should* behave. In trying to achieve this goal, it is quite possible that some professors will be tempted to impose their own ethical beliefs on their students.

Instructors can easily avoid this hazard. The main purpose in teaching moral reasoning courses is not to insist on particular answers to ethical issues but to help students recognize ethical questions when they arise and be able to raise and thoroughly discuss all the relevant arguments in light of the assigned readings. It is possible that a few instructors will not use this approach but will insist instead on the correctness of their own ethical opinions. Even so, similar risks are present in teaching economics, political science, and many other traditional subjects. Just as in teaching civics, the appropriate response is surely to discourage indoctrination whenever it occurs rather than abandon all teaching of subjects in which it *might* occur.

However, instructors who scrupulously avoid taking sides on highly controversial issues, such as abortion or conscientious objection in time of war, can encounter another problem. The discussions they conduct may lead some members of the class to conclude that ethical questions have no convincing answers but simply give rise to endless arguments and exchanges of opinion. Such beliefs can easily lead students to adopt a moral relativism that discourages careful thought.

Fortunately, this problem too can be overcome. Certain basic ethical propositions, such as the importance of telling the truth, living up to one's promises, and refraining from acts of violence against others, have been accepted widely enough in a variety of societies and cultures to be considered *presumptively* correct, although subject to exceptions in certain circumstances.[11] In the course of class discussions about ethical dilemmas, without any effort by instructors to impose their views, these shared presumptions will often lead students to agree that some answers to moral dilemmas are convincing, while other moral conflicts can be avoided entirely by devising an alternative course of action that raises no ethical problems yet seems fair and satisfactory to both sides. A number of studies have found that classes featuring vigorous discussions of challenging moral dilemmas do have a positive effect in helping students to perceive ethical issues when they arise, take account of the arguments on all sides of the issue, and reach a conclusion on an appropriate course of action.[12]

Is Moral Reasoning Useful?

Several moral psychologists, however, have recently questioned the value of ethical reasoning, using arguments very similar to those advanced by Jonathan Haidt to dispute the utility of trying to teach students how to be thoughtful citizens.[13] Haidt has conducted experiments to observe the responses of people to rather bizarre ethical situations, such as that of a man who buys a chicken in a market, goes home, and has sexual intercourse with the dead chicken (whatever that means) before cooking and eating it. He finds that most people are divided between those (mostly conservatives) who find such behavior immoral because it is so disgusting and those (mainly liberals) who agree that the behavior is disgusting but do not consider it immoral since no one has been harmed or treated unjustly. Haidt then draws upon the findings of other social scientists to conclude that any subsequent reasoning is not an open-minded search for the correct answer but merely an effort to discover reasons to support one's initial reaction.

Although Haidt's examples are cleverly contrived to support his point, most ethical problems that occur in real life do not elicit such strong, immediate emotional responses.[14] Granted, some people may not choose to take the time to think about their decisions. Others may trust their "gut reactions" and see no need for further thought. Even Haidt would agree, however, that some people do find moral reasoning helpful. Were this not so, the *New York Times* would hardly print a weekly column by Anthony Appiah on how to think about and resolve ethical problems of everyday life, and Sissela Bok's book *Lying: Moral Choice in Public and Private Life* would not have sold hundreds of thousands of copies. What courses on moral reasoning can do is increase the number of people who find that thinking carefully about ethical problems helps them to perceive such issues when they arise and to take better account of all the arguments and facts that bear on their resolution.

Many studies have been carried out to examine the overall effects of a college education on students' moral reasoning. The results reveal significant gains, although the amount of improvement seems to have declined in recent decades. Prior to 1990, meta-analyses of this body of research found an average increase of approximately one standard deviation—enough to enable students who entered college with average ability compared to their classmates to reach the eighty-fourth percentile as seniors if they were to take a test of moral reasoning again with a comparable group of entering freshmen.[15] In the 1990s, however, the average gain slipped to 0.77 of a standard deviation.[16] It dropped again from 2002 to 2012, to a gain of only 0.57 of a standard deviation, or little more than half the improvement recorded during the 1970s and '80s.[17] The reasons for this decline are not yet clear.

MORAL BEHAVIOR

The public undoubtedly cares much more about what colleges do to help students *act* more ethically and responsibly than about how much undergraduates improve their ability to perceive ethical issues and analyze them carefully. Professors who teach moral reasoning appear to be divided on whether they can teach students to behave more ethically.[18] Yet it seems plausible that students who have improved their ability to perceive ethical problems when they arise and think about them carefully would at least be *somewhat* more likely to behave in a principled manner. Although not everyone is convinced, the authors of a comprehensive review of educational research over the past twenty years have concluded that "there is extensive evidence of a positive relationship between the level of principled moral reasoning and the likelihood of principled behavior."[19]

The Role of Empathy

One important factor in the decision to act ethically is empathy—the ability to appreciate the feelings of other people and the desire to help them avoid or alleviate suffering. It seems likely that someone who is strongly motivated to avoid causing harm to others will try especially hard not to behave unethically. Interestingly, people with greater empathy also appear to make friends more easily, experience greater happiness, and suffer less depression.

Until quite recently, empathy, like other qualities of mind discussed in subsequent chapters, was thought to be largely determined by one's genes and to become fixed and immutable early in life. Psychologists continue to agree that genes are important and estimate that they account for roughly 50 percent of the variation in people's capacity to appreciate the feelings of others. But recent research has shown that empathy, along with other qualities such as creativity, resilience, and sociability, can change significantly, at least through early adulthood. This discovery has prompted a growing body of research to explore what kinds of experiences or deliberate interventions can increase concern for others.[20]

Psychologists have identified several activities that may develop empathy. Learning to be an actor, which involves understanding the feelings and behavior of the characters one plays onstage, is thought to have this effect. In the hands of a skillful teacher, literature may arguably increase empathy through exposure to compelling descriptions of people and their inner feelings. Portrayals of suffering on television or in films and videos may conceivably produce similar effects. Some reformers have achieved promising results from programs designed to help police officers appreciate the feelings of residents of high-crime neighborhoods. Others claim to have increased empathy by training students to engage in "loving kindness" meditation.

A substantial number of colleges offer courses to help students manage the transition from high school to college, and more than one-third of these classes claim to include efforts to foster empathy as one of their major aims.[21] Some of these offerings are mandatory, at least for particular groups of entering students, while the rest are optional. I could not find any rigorous studies measuring the effects of such instruction on the empathy of participants.

Efforts to help individuals become more empathetic and understanding of the feelings of others are complicated by the fact that people can have *too much* sensitivity. Nurses, doctors, and clergy who are continuously exposed to suffering can experience burnout or become callous, resulting in poorer diagnoses, inadequate treatment, and, for the caregiver, sleeplessness and alcoholism. Some police officials believe that officers who have too much empathy can fail to take appropriate steps to defend themselves when confronted by genuine threats to their safety or the safety of others. Such findings suggest that those who seek to increase the empathy of others must not only find methods that work but also try to discover how much empathy is valuable and when it threatens to become excessive or even harmful.

Notwithstanding these complications and the need for further study and experimentation, the recent findings by psychologists suggest the exciting possibility that educators may someday learn how to help students build "empathic concern" that will strengthen their desire to act more ethically and help others in need. Since experimenters have found that empathy among young people has been declining for several decades, such discoveries could hardly be more timely.[22]

There is some evidence that college already has a positive effect. One study comparing self-reports from freshmen when they enter and again at the end of their junior year found a large gain (from 14 percent to 27 percent) in the percentage of students scoring high in the desire to help others who are in difficulty, to reduce pain and suffering, and to increase social justice.[23] Interestingly, while students in this study who majored in political science and history were especially likely to show an increase in these attitudes, those majoring in statistics, engineering, and mathematics tended to suffer a decline by the end of their junior year.[24] More work is needed, however, to build a solid body of knowledge about the effects of college on empathy.

As yet, there is no reliable way to measure the overall effect of undergraduate education on the moral behavior of students in their everyday lives. It is hard enough to measure the change in one specific type of behavior without attempting to estimate the development of students' character as a whole over the course of their four years of college. When one team of investigators asked seniors whether they had developed an "increased sense of personal integrity" during their years at college, most respondents answered affirmatively.[25] Self-reports of this kind, however, are not reliable enough to place much weight on the results. For the time being at least, the best one can do is examine how colleges have performed in taking the kinds of actions that seem especially likely to have a positive effect on the character of their students.

SETTING A GOOD EXAMPLE

Colleges can presumably affect the ethical conduct of students in many other ways besides offering courses in empathy or moral reasoning. Surveys of students suggest that participation in community service can have a positive effect, as can engaging in conversations with faculty or counselors outside of class and taking courses that foster awareness of the feelings of others through discussions of controversial issues with students of differing opinions and backgrounds.[26]

Another way in which colleges may have a significant impact on their students' character is through the example set by the institution and its staff. Principled athletic coaches can provide their players with valuable lessons about the importance of competing fairly (instead of indicating by their behavior that winning is all that matters). University officials can carefully explain their reasons for taking controversial actions and thereby set an example of moral seriousness for the entire student body, including those who disagree with their decisions. Above all, campus leaders can work to hold the college itself to high ethical standards and to avoid acting irresponsibly, such as by ignoring complaints of sexual harassment or failing to deal with immoral behavior by professors or members of the staff. There is no surer way for campus officials to foster cynicism and undermine respect for the institution and its attempts to improve ethical standards than to refuse to act when students or staff members behave in morally indefensible ways.

The Problem of Cheating and Plagiarism

The most extensively studied subject involving the example set by colleges is the creation and enforcement of rules involving academic honesty, such as cheating on exams or plagiarism in writing papers. Such rules tend to be much more effective when they are clearly expressed, carefully explained and justified, and administered fairly. Research also demonstrates quite consistently that violations decline when a college employs an honor code, especially if the students acquire a sense of "ownership" and personal responsibility toward the code by having an opportunity to discuss it, make suggestions for improvement, and ultimately endorse the code by voting to affirm it.[27]

Although every college and university condemns cheating and plagiarism by its students, the efforts on most campuses to deal with these infractions are discouraging. In a series of studies of undergraduates nationwide, the percentages of students who admit to having cheated at least once during college are consistently well above 50 percent.[28] A recent survey covering 110 colleges conducted by the University of Michigan at the request of the AAC&U found that barely 20 percent of undergraduates "strongly agreed" that "students on this campus are academically honest" and that the percentage declined steadily from 25 to 15 percent from the freshman to the senior year.[29] Only 35 percent of students strongly agreed that "academic honesty policies on this campus help stop cheating," and the percentages of faculty and administrators answering in the affirmative were even lower.[30]

Studies of the way rules on academic honesty are administered throw some light on why the incidence of cheating is so high. Many colleges make surprisingly little effort to explain the reasons for existing rules or even to clarify the meaning of vague terms such as "plagiarism." The Michigan survey found that only 44 percent of students strongly agreed that they had gained a better understanding of academic integrity since coming to college.[31] Fewer than 60 percent of academic administrators, faculty, and student affairs professionals could even agree strongly that "faculty understand academic honesty policies."[32]

Professors may not only be uncertain about campus policies and procedures for upholding standards of honesty; they also seem to have little inclination to follow them. According to one study, only 9 percent of faculty members who catch students cheating penalize them for doing so.[33] In another survey by Donald McCabe covering some eight hundred professors at twelve universities, 40 percent of the respondents admitted that they had *never* reported an incident of cheating in their class, while an even larger percentage—54 percent—said that they had *seldom* reported a case of cheating to campus officials, preferring either to ignore such incidents or to deal with them by imposing their own penalties. Only 6 percent claimed that they "often" reported cheating.[34]

When asked why they do not cooperate in reporting misconduct, professors give a variety of answers.[35] Some blame the administration for having reversed findings of cheating that the instructors involved were sure had occurred. Others point to the amount of time it can take to determine that cheating took place and the further delays that often occur while the case works its way through the appeals process.

Researchers report that the incidence of cheating may be significantly reduced by taking seemingly simple precautions. As previously mentioned, honor codes appear to have this effect if properly designed and implemented. One author estimates that stern warnings about cheating can reduce violations by over 10 percent, as can the use of more proctors to monitor exams.[36] Having a tenure-track professor teach the course instead of a graduate student allegedly lowers violations by as much 25 percent. Nevertheless, many campuses continue to lack preventive measures of this kind.

Enforcing Other Rules

Most colleges seem to approach other regulations involving student behavior on campus in much the same casual manner. Rules of conduct are often expressed in very general terms or left completely undefined. One survey of 110 liberal arts colleges found that only 56 percent of them had issued materials explaining the reasons for their rules and that "these statements were often expressed in vague constructs such as 'honor for its own sake.'"[37] Only 30 percent of the colleges published rules describing unacceptable *non*-academic behavior.

There is also ample evidence of universities' failure to set a good example themselves by behaving in accordance with appropriate ethical standards. Familiar examples include improper recruitment and treatment of varsity athletes, lack of compliance with laws requiring the disclosure of crimes on campus, and reluctance to investigate cases of sexual assaults. The pressure to raise money and protect the university's reputation from adverse publicity probably accounts for most of these unfortunate behaviors and for the frequent failure to acknowledge them properly.

CONSCIENTIOUSNESS

Character includes more than understanding and observing high ethical standards. Ideally, students should also learn to be conscientious by regularly preparing for class, completing course assignments, and meeting deadlines for dropping courses and handing in papers. The consistent ability to fulfill one's responsibilities and commitments is not only beneficial for others but is also an important quality for success in most of life's endeavors.[38] Employers consider a strong "work ethic," or conscientiousness, to be among the most important qualities in evaluating employees and applicants for employment. Some researchers have even found that conscientiousness, together with other so-called noncognitive skills, has almost as great an effect on future earnings and career success as cognitive ability.[39]

Conscientiousness has other positive effects both during college and thereafter. It has an important influence on whether students complete their studies or drop out before earning a degree. Several studies have found that regular attendance in classes and the time undergraduates devote to their courses are the most important factors under the control of students that affect their grades and the amount they learn.[40] Researchers have also discovered that adults who ranked high in living up to their commitments tend to have better health, longer lives, greater happiness and satisfaction with life, and even more stable marriages.[41]

Can Conscientiousness Be Taught?

Conscientiousness, like empathy, was long thought to be hereditary and largely immutable. However, recent studies have found that it tends to increase substantially during the years immediately following adolescence. According to one leading authority on the subject, "conscientiousness is particularly interesting because it does not show systematic changes until young adulthood [including the college years], at which it appears to accelerate upwards for most populations."[42] Another student of the subject explains that "one part of the brain that has been recently shown to change during early adulthood is the prefrontal cortex, which controls executive functions, including planning and time management, that give students the self-regulatory maturity to plan their time by trading the spontaneity of the moment for longer-term educational benefits and delayed gratification."[43] Much of the increase in conscientiousness during early adulthood comes about because of the prospect of having to assume the adult responsibilities of embarking on a career and getting married. Even so, the college years would appear to offer abundant opportunities to reinforce the tendency of young adults to develop habits of conscientiousness.

Unfortunately, little research yet exists on how a college can capitalize on this opportunity. Investigators have discovered interventions to diminish specific mental blocks that tend to inhibit conscientiousness, such as persuading students that intelligence is not immutable but can be improved by hard work, or reducing the "stereotype vulnerability" that causes minorities to fear that they will underperform on tests and thus confirm impressions that members of their race are intellectually inferior.[44] But more work is needed to discover and test other steps that colleges can take to motivate students to carry out faithfully the tasks assigned to them. According to Brent Roberts, a leading researcher in the field, "Now that we know what conscientiousness can do, we must progress toward a better understanding of what it is and where it comes from [through] well-informed longitudinal studies tracing the development of conscientiousness and its formative antecedents from childhood to adulthood."[45]

How College Affects Conscientiousness

Even without confirming evidence, one would suppose that faculty members can exert at least *some* influence over the conscientiousness of undergraduates by the amount of work they require and the way they grade student papers and enforce deadlines for completing assignments. Such efforts should help prepare students for their adult responsibilities by strengthening their resolve to complete their work on time, be meticulous in the preparation of term papers, and prepare carefully for examinations. By most accounts, however, academic standards have become *less* demanding and *less* strictly enforced over the past several decades.

The most detailed study yet of the hours per week that students report spending on homework found that the total has dropped by an alarming 40 percent since the early 1960s.[46] This decline cannot be attributed to the growing number of students who have to work long hours in order to pay for college, since the study included only undergraduates who were enrolled full-time. Nor is the trend a result of social media, since most of the decline occurred before the internet came into widespread use. Because the number of hours spent studying varies widely from one college to another, the average on many campuses would appear to be far below what it could be.

Evidence about the use of social media suggests that the time students do spend on their courses may have deteriorated in quality as well as quantity. Surveys indicate that large and growing percentages of undergraduates "multitask" while studying by checking for email, using Facebook, texting, tweeting, and engaging in other forms of social networking. Annual findings from the National Survey of Student Engagement (NSSE) on several hundred college campuses indicate that two-thirds of students sometimes use social media even while sitting in lectures, and that 39 percent of freshmen and 31 percent of seniors do so "frequently."[47] Studies to determine the effects of multitasking regularly find that the amount of learning diminishes significantly.[48]

The response of the faculty to this apparent deterioration in the quantity and quality of student effort seems to have been weak on the majority of campuses. By most accounts, amounts of required reading and paper writing have declined. Course grades, far from dropping due to declining student effort, have actually risen.[49] As one might expect, the effect of easier grading is to diminish the care taken by students with their assignments and the time they spend studying once they become aware that less work will still allow them to achieve the grade they desire.[50]

There is only anecdotal evidence of the strictness with which instructors enforce such rules as deadlines for handing in assignments and dropping courses or rescheduling exams and attending classes.

Surveys suggest that the vast majority of colleges now allow students to take courses again to improve their grade.[51] In addition, it is widely believed that faculties have become less willing to impose requirements and that professors have tended to become more permissive in enforcing those that do exist. As Roger Geiger observes in his recently published book *American Higher Education since World War II*:

> Pedagogy evolved from the late 1960s to accommodate laxity. What were once standard coercive practices—homework, pop quizzes, strict attendance policies, grading curves—became rare outside of STEM fields. Classes with no examinations could tolerate superficial discussions and group projects invited free riders.[52]

During the past several decades, parietal rules have also disappeared, and laws against underage drinking are weakly enforced on most campuses. Although there are plausible reasons for these developments, the diminishing number of rules and the greater lenience in enforcing those that remain threaten to undermine conscientiousness. Graduates may thus be poorly prepared to enter the world of work, where most employers are less forgiving.

SUMMING UP

What does the preceding discussion tell us about the effect of college on the character and conduct of students? We do know that the moral reasoning of most undergraduates improves, at least moderately. But no reliable evidence exists for measuring the overall effect of college on the moral behavior and conscientiousness of students. There are only impressions gleaned from a variety of sources. Some 60 percent of college seniors believe that their college experience has contributed "very much" or "quite a bit" to their development of a systematic code of ethics, according to the National Survey of Student Engagement, conducted each year on several hundred college campuses.[53] But self-reports are known to be unreliable. For example, whereas 62 percent of graduating seniors considered themselves well prepared in ethical judgment for employment, according to a survey conducted by Hart

Research Associates in 2015, only 30 percent of employers agreed.[54] Moreover, as noted earlier, substantial majorities of students have consistently admitted cheating during college according to a series of surveys conducted over the past several decades.

In the Michigan study previously mentioned, 48 percent of students strongly agreed that "I believe that I have gained an increased sense of personal responsibility since I have been in college."[55] However, only 28.2 percent of students strongly agreed that "this campus helps students develop their ethical and moral reasoning abilities, including the ability to express and act upon personal values responsibly."[56] Only 21.5 percent of the students in the same survey strongly agreed that "students on this campus are academically honest," and only 26.6 percent agreed that "students on this campus conduct themselves with respect for others."[57] Academic administrators, faculty, and student affairs professionals all shared similar or even worse impressions of the academic honesty of students and their respect for others on campus. Moreover, while 70.6 percent of students in the Michigan survey and 86.9 percent of student affairs professionals strongly believed that personal and academic integrity *should* be an important institutional focus of their college, only slightly more than 40 percent of each of these groups agreed strongly that these goals *are* an important focus on their campus.[58]

What Colleges Can Do

There are several steps that educators could take that might help students develop a stronger character. To begin with, many colleges could and should consider requiring students to take at least one course in moral reasoning. Not only is this subject important to the lives of every student; it also provides a useful supplement to wider efforts in the curriculum to teach critical thinking and problem-solving.

Many undergraduates seem to regard courses on moral reasoning as an unnecessary and unwelcome requirement, yet there are practical ways to make the subject more interesting and relevant to students. One promising approach is to offer several courses, each of which studies challenging ethical problems that frequently occur in a major profession, such as law, medicine, engineering, or business. Undergraduates considering a career in one of these callings will naturally be interested in such a class. In any university with professional schools, faculty members can be recruited to teach these offerings, since almost all such schools now offer courses in ethics taught by professors well versed in the subject.

Another step that colleges can take is to supplement a mandatory course in moral reasoning by embedding ethics problems in other classes. Since suitable problems can be devised for a wide variety of courses, it may be possible to persuade several professors to participate in such an effort. A member of the philosophy department or a graduate student in philosophy might be willing to act as an adviser to participating instructors. Discussions of this kind would do more than simply reinforce the lessons learned in a required moral reasoning course. By illustrating the ubiquitous nature of ethical issues, they would also convey a message that ethics is a subject of pervasive importance rather than an isolated topic with little apparent connection to the lives of undergraduates.

Still another useful step in helping to build character is to address the weak and haphazard enforcement of rules against plagiarism and cheating. Colleges without honor codes could consider adopting one, since research clearly indicates that well-constructed codes adopted with the support and participation of students reduce cheating significantly. Much more, however, is needed. On most campuses, including some with honor codes, professors appear to pay no heed to the established rules and procedures for dealing with infractions, preferring instead to respond as they see fit. Efforts to address this problem will require a determined effort to gain the confidence and participation of the faculty by working with them to devise appropriate standards and procedures.* Although success will not come easily, the prevailing situation seems sufficiently unsatisfactory to warrant an attempt to

---

*To gain the cooperation of the faculty, college leaders may need to revise and simplify their procedures, since one reason why professors fail to report violations is that they hold current methods for enforcing rules of academic honesty in low esteem and fear becoming embroiled in time-consuming appeals, which may never arrive at a definitive conclusion. Other safeguards against violations, such as improved communication between faculty and administration about the rules and their application, can also help reduce violations.

enlist the cooperation of professors and administrators in trying to do better. On the many campuses where the consequences of violating the rules vary from one instructor to another and the chances that violators will be apprehended and penalized are extremely low, it should be difficult for any conscientious faculty member to refuse to join in a serious effort to improve matters.

Many colleges could also review their other rules governing student behavior to make sure that they are worded with sufficient clarity and that the reasons for adopting them are adequately explained. In the process of review, college authorities might consult widely with students and solicit their views in order to gain acceptance of the rules and increase the likelihood of compliance. Although these steps may seem obvious, there is evidence that many colleges have yet to take them.

Finally, campus leaders could take greater pains to ensure that their own administration adheres to a high ethical standard. To be sure, embarrassing incidents are bound to occur occasionally in universities, as in any large organization. But leaders can at least acknowledge such cases when they occur and hold the perpetrators accountable instead of ignoring the problem in the hope of protecting the reputation of the institution. They can also take care to explain in detail the reasons for any controversial decisions they make so that even those who disagree with their decisions can recognize that the college values ethical standards enough to make a serious effort to take them into account. The very act of considering how to justify controversial decisions can often persuade campus leaders that the course of action they are contemplating is inadvisable, thus sparing the college later embarrassment and conflict.

There are many other ways in which campus authorities can enhance the moral education of students.*[59] Disciplinary proceedings

* Efforts by campus leaders to increase the conscientiousness of their students are likely to be more difficult. Colleges can presumably do something to halt grade inflation by working closely with their faculties to develop a normal distribution of grades while making sure that the system is explained well enough to employers and admission committees in graduate and professional schools to minimize the risk of penalizing students unfairly when they are competing with graduates of institutions where grading is more generous. Even here, however, problems will arise in deciding how to provide appropriate flexibility for grading students in small classes and seminars and how to gain the cooperation of recalcitrant

can be administered not merely to enforce rules but as occasions for teaching student offenders to appreciate the harm they have done to others and thereby feel genuine contrition for their behavior. Athletics can provide abundant opportunities for coaches to teach students the importance of sportsmanship and obeying the rules instead of seeking to win by any means available. Residence halls are ideal places to teach undergraduates why it is important to respect the interests of others and to discuss how that goal can best be achieved. Since many students come to college without knowing anyone to whom they can turn to talk about the moral dilemmas and temptations they encounter, it is important to try to prepare as many members of the staff as possible— student affairs professionals, graduate teaching assistants in ethics courses, residence officers—to respond helpfully to students who come to them for advice.

Last but not least, research universities could play an active role in encouraging and supporting research by psychologists on ways to nurture empathy and conscientiousness. Now that investigators have determined that these traits continue to change throughout early adult-hood, it would surely be worthwhile to try to discover whether there are feasible ways to help students develop these qualities.

The Difficulty of Attempts to Improve Character

Before passing judgment on college leaders or assessing the prospects for improvement, critics must recognize that the nature of academic institutions makes it difficult to do as much as one might like to strengthen ethical standards and encourage conscientious behavior. To begin with, there is much less top-down authority in a university than in most other kinds of institutions. The individuals in the best position to influence students—faculty members and student affairs personnel— are professionals who require and receive much independence and discretion in how they carry out their duties. Professors in particular

---

professors. Policies to counter excessive lenience in turning in papers on time or to increase homework assignments to encourage greater student effort are even more difficult to ad-minister. Although the underlying problem may deserve periodic discussion with the fac-ulty, the distaste of most instructors for rules of this kind could discourage college leaders from embarking on a serious effort to change existing practice.

are almost completely free to decide how they conduct their teaching and deal with their students. Such loyalties as they do possess are chiefly to peers in their discipline and colleagues in their departments, not to their deans and presidents.

In this environment, it may be difficult for college leaders to do very much to improve the character of students or even set a good example by maintaining consistently high standards throughout the institution. Deans and presidents may persuade their faculties to require courses in moral reasoning, but they cannot order the instructors who give these courses to teach them in ways that actually help students develop their ability to analyze ethical questions carefully. Presidents can set a good example by directing their university to take principled positions in managing its investments or in its relations with neighboring communities, but they cannot control how the campus newspaper interprets such decisions and explains them to the student body. It is also much harder for a president or a dean to induce members of the faculty to enforce the rules on matters such as cheating on exams, grading, and respecting deadlines for papers than it is to gain compliance in more hierarchical institutions, such as corporations or military units.*

Enforcing standards for the extracurricular behavior of undergraduates is equally difficult. Even in the eighteenth century and much of the nineteenth, when colleges put character-building among their highest priorities and strenuously enforced extremely detailed rules of conduct, presidents achieved only limited success in taming the exuberant spirits of their students. Riots occurred periodically, bombs were exploded, fires were set, and undergraduates often drank to excess and consistently sought to evade the rules and escape detection. Eventu-

---

* Most college teachers today are not protected by tenure but work on short-term contracts and thus might seem more subject to administrative control. For many of them, however, decisions on whether to renew their appointment depend heavily on student evaluations of their teaching. Without repeated reassurance from the administration, these instructors are likely to worry that strict enforcement of rules and a reputation as a tough grader could easily lead to unfavorable student ratings and cause them to lose their jobs. Moreover, now that grade inflation has become widespread, even the most conscientious instructors will feel pressure to adopt more lenient standards of grading in order not to put their students at an unfair disadvantage compared to students at other institutions, with whom they will eventually compete for jobs and admission to graduate schools.

ally, academic leaders and faculties capitulated rather than continue bearing the burden of reporting cases of student misbehavior and meting out appropriate discipline.

Under these conditions, it is not surprising that the attempts by most colleges to improve the character of their students seem weak. The amount of effort and cooperation that is needed from faculty and staff is often impossible for even the most respected leader to elicit. Not all professors agree that character-building is even an appropriate goal for colleges to pursue, and many will not cooperate in enforcing basic rules against cheating. Campus leaders may refrain from trying to strictly enforce rules of conduct, such as those regarding the sexual activity of students in college dorms or laws against underage drinking, on the grounds that their limited power to enforce such prohibitions makes the effort impractical. After all, officials can hardly peer through keyholes or install surveillance cameras in residence halls. Even a seemingly straightforward action, such as requiring all students to take a course in moral reasoning, may prove impossible to implement properly in a large university if the faculty cannot assemble enough qualified instructors to staff the numerous small sections that are needed to provide the lively discussion so essential to teaching the subject effectively.

A Balanced View of Moral Education

In light of this discussion, what can we make of David Brooks's comment at the beginning of the chapter that "highly educated young people are tutored, taught, and monitored in all aspects of their lives except the most important, which is character building. When it comes to this, most universities leave them alone." On the one hand, as Brooks points out, character is surely one of the most important qualities for a college to nurture, since it not only affects the well-being of the students and the respect they receive from others but also has beneficial effects on everyone with whom students interact and on levels of trust within society as a whole. It is also true that most colleges could try to do more to help their undergraduates develop a stronger character. At the same time, efforts of this kind must surely rank among the most difficult tasks that a college can undertake, since they require the commitment and cooperation of the entire faculty and staff; a tall order for an organization in which the leaders have so little power to enforce the existing standards and policies. Under these conditions, while one can appreciate the importance that Brooks attaches to the development of character and agree that most colleges should be doing more, critics need to recognize that in most universities, especially those of substantial size, there are limits to what even the most dedicated campus leaders can accomplish.

CHAPTER FIVE

Helping Students Find Purpose and Meaning in Life

Among the aims of a college education, helping students find greater meaning and purpose in their lives—a personal philosophy, if you will—is surely one of the more difficult for educators to describe. The most frequently quoted definition is that of William Damon, who speaks of the desire "to accomplish something that is at the same time meaningful to the self and consequential for the world beyond the self."[1] What "meaning" and "purpose" seem to imply is a life consciously shaped by worthwhile goals that matter to oneself together with a way of pursuing them that reflects one's personal interests and values—a life, in short, that one can look back upon eventually with approval and satisfaction.

Helping students develop their own definition of a meaningful and purposeful life is accepted in principle as an appropriate goal of college by many professors and students. According to a faculty survey in 2010 conducted by the Higher Education Research Institute at UCLA, more than 80 percent of college professors considered developing a philosophy of life either an "essential" or a "very important" aim of a college education.[2] In the latest national survey of college faculty conducted in 2017, 85 percent "agreed" or "strongly agreed" that helping students develop personal values was part of their role as professors.[3] Although barely 40 percent of entering freshmen think it "essential" to acquire a philosophy of life—a figure far below what it was in the 1960s—the proportion appears to grow during college by an average of more than ten percentage points by the end of the junior year.[4]

Researchers have found that a meaningful and achievable purpose brings multiple benefits. It is normally accompanied by a greater satisfaction with life along with better health and greater longevity.[5] Purpose also helps to reduce boredom and increase resilience by giving meaning to one's efforts and increasing one's motivation to overcome setbacks and surmount obstacles. There are ample reasons, then, why colleges should try to do what they can to help their students make wise choices about the future course of their lives and the values to guide their journey.

HOW MUCH HELP DO STUDENTS RECEIVE FROM COLLEGE?

Despite the support of many faculty and students, a noted scholar in the field of undergraduate education, Alexander Astin, describes with some dismay how little attention faculties pay to the subject of *how* to help students acquire a philosophy of life.[6] Colleges affiliated with a religious body do tend to take the subject seriously, but in most colleges and universities one would have to look long and hard to find a faculty meeting devoted to a serious discussion of the subject.

On most campuses, the principal organized effort to help students think about their future lives (apart from graduation speeches) is the career services office. Almost every college has one. Years ago, their chief activity was to provide routine information about different careers and arrange job fairs and visits from company representatives to put students in contact with prospective employers. Over time they have added more counseling to help students make informed choices about their vocation. By now, most of them can test students to ascertain their backgrounds, interests, and aptitudes and help them use this information to select a career that is suited to their abilities as well as their ambitions. Roughly one-third of these offices offer career planning courses, some of which provide opportunities for students to consider in greater depth the connection between their career and their personal values and desires about the kind of life they wish to lead.[7]

Although some students benefit from the advice they receive from career offices, surveys find that fewer than 20 percent seek such assistance.[8] Most undergraduates claim to have found their first job through the advice of parents or friends. If colleges are serious about helping students think about how they wish to lead their lives, they must do more than merely offer career assistance.

In some colleges, staff members from the student affairs office offer a course to help undergraduates think about their future. Rather than giving lectures, most of these teachers rely on classroom discussions in which they ask thought-provoking questions that challenge students to think about the kind of person they hope to become and the sort of life they wish to lead. Such discussions can be valuable simply by encouraging students to reflect more deeply about their future lives and discuss their thoughts with classmates. Instructors who teach these classes and write about the experience seem to believe strongly in their value.[9] However, no one knows for sure how many colleges offer such instruction. Nor is there solid evidence of their lasting value that colleges can rely upon in deciding whether to offer similar courses on their own campus. It would be difficult, in any case, to ascertain their usefulness without questioning students years after they graduate to discover what significance they attach to such instruction and how their satisfaction with their chosen career compares with that of a similar group of college graduates who did not take such a course. I could find no rigorous studies of that kind while writing this chapter.

Rather than offering courses specifically designed to help students define a fulfilling life, many faculties seem content to hope that a well-rounded undergraduate education coupled with an active job placement office will do enough to help students find the answers they seek. The variety of courses and subjects the curriculum offers, the ability to change majors and add minor fields of study, the diversity of students who live, study, and talk together, and the wealth of extracurricular activities on many campuses are assumed to provide an environment that is stimulating enough to enable students to explore a number of different interests and develop a clearer sense of the life they wish to lead.

How valid is this hope? How much does the experience of going to college give students the stimulus, the ideas, and the information they need to develop their own purpose and philosophy of life? Such questions hardly lend themselves to exact answers. At best, one can find only scraps of evidence that throw some light on the question.

Student surveys suggest that many seniors *believe* that they have come to understand themselves better during college and have acquired a clearer idea about the kind of life they wish to pursue.[10] Even if one accepts these self-evaluations as accurate, however, the findings do not reveal how much these reported gains result from experiences at college or simply from changes that could occur anywhere as young adults mature and the need to decide what to do next approaches. Nor have I found longitudinal studies that reveal how well the values and purposes acquired during college hold up under the challenges and vicissitudes of adult life.

There is abundant evidence that students' values change significantly during college. Most longitudinal studies find that seniors tend to become more tolerant, more egalitarian (for example, with respect to relations between men and women), less inclined to value the importance of earning a lot of money, more interested in serving their communities, and more altruistic and willing to help others.[11] A variety of college experiences are thought to play a part in bringing about these changes. Among the most important are interactions with a diverse group of students, studying abroad, and community service activities combined with the service learning courses that often accompany them. These findings are encouraging. Taken alone, however, they do not do enough to help students form a coherent view of the life they wish to lead.

SHOULD COLLEGES BE DOING MORE?

There are signs of increasing concern that colleges should be doing more to help students find their way. One professor, Tim Clydesdale, who has advised a great many undergraduates, has concluded that the great majority "drift into careers without much conscious thought about how they wish to live their lives."[12] After interviewing large numbers of college students, Professor Damon discovered that only 20 percent had long-term goals and were working to achieve them; 25 percent were disengaged, had no purpose in life, and were making no effort to find one; 25 percent were "dreamers" who had a purpose but were making no effort to achieve it; and 31 percent were "dabblers" who had flirted with several goals but made no real commitment to any of them.[13]

Many recent studies of college students find that today's undergraduates have been sobered by growing up during a recession and devote more thought to preparing for employment. But choosing a career is a far narrower task than finding a philosophy of life. What most entering freshmen today claim to value most about a job is making a lot of money.[14] Such findings suggest that students will need to broaden their thinking considerably before they can make a wise choice of career, let alone conceive of a meaningful and fulfilling life.

In recent years, the presidents of several highly selective colleges have given speeches expressing regret that so many recent graduates flock to investment banks and consulting firms whose chief appeal appears to be the size of their starting salaries. A former college teacher, William Deresiewicz, makes much the same point in his book *Excellent Sheep*.[15] A page 1 study published in the *New York Times Sunday Review* describes the creation of several programs and even two or three experimental colleges in response to what the author describes as "a growing movement of students, teachers, and reformers who are trying to compensate for mainstream higher education's failure to help young people find a calling to figure out what life is for."[16]

There is also persuasive evidence that recent graduates are taking longer to make basic decisions about their future lives. In his widely read study of the passage from adolescence to adulthood, Professor Damon observes that "only a few decades ago, almost all young people knew by the end of adolescence where they would live, what their occupation would be and whom they were going to marry. . . . A large portion of today's young people are hesitating to make commitments to any of the roles that define adult life, such as parent, worker, spouse or citizen."[17] Elaborating on this point, a *New York Times Magazine* cover story asserted that young college graduates increasingly "move back in with their parents, they delay beginning career paths, they put off commitments."[18] According to the authors of this article, only 28 percent of young male college graduates and 39 percent of young female BAs have managed by age thirty to complete all five of the traditional accomplishments of adulthood—leaving home, finishing their education, getting married, having a child, and becoming financially independent. In 1960, the article claims, two-thirds of thirty-year-old men and 77 percent of young women had achieved all five of these goals.*

Several professors who share a concern over the difficulty that many young people have in making decisions about their lives have written at length on the importance of teaching undergraduates to achieve "self-authorship," that is, the ability to "act on [their] own purposes, values, feelings, and meanings rather than those [they] have assimilated from others."[19] Self-authorship does not mean relying only on one's own instincts and opinions, a habit that would surely be pigheaded and result in numerous mistakes. Rather, what the term signifies is a willingness to accept responsibility for making decisions after weighing the available evidence and the views of others in light of one's own values, ideas, and opinions, while being ready to adjust one's beliefs when new evidence and arguments require it.

Accepting such responsibility is doubtless an important step in becoming a mature adult. By itself, however, it does not provide much assurance that students will have sufficient knowledge to decide what kind of person they wish to become and what kind of life they hope to lead. Many undergraduates require more information and ideas and more opportunities to reflect on what they have learned in order to arrive at sound and satisfying conclusions. In response, a number of colleges have experimented with different ways to satisfy this need.

THE LILLY FOUNDATION PROGRAM

In 2002, the Lilly Foundation announced a plan for awarding grants of $2 million each to eighty-eight colleges to design and implement programs for this purpose.[20] The hope that inspired this project was that the undergraduates involved would engage in study and reflection in order to conceive of their lives as a vocation, linking their search

---

*It is possible that the growing burden of educational debt on those who go to college has contributed to these tendencies. But debt does not seem to be the only cause, or even the most important one, since similar trends have been observed throughout Western Europe, Japan, South Africa, and Australia.

for an appropriate career to a larger quest for a life of purpose and meaning.

Almost all of the colleges receiving grants were affiliated with a Christian denomination, but the range of denominations was very wide. Participating colleges enjoyed considerable latitude in deciding how best to fulfill the underlying purpose. Most of them offered freshman seminars devoted to discussions about the meaning of vocation and how an undergraduate education could help students imagine such a journey. Thereafter, colleges provided additional courses, conversations with mentors from the faculty and staff, and other opportunities to experiment with different possible vocations through community service projects, study abroad, and internships with corporations, government agencies, or nonprofit organizations. Some colleges invited outside speakers to talk about their careers and created capstone projects that required students to draw upon their experiences in college to present their own ideas about a meaningful vocation.

Once these programs were firmly in place, the foundation hired a professor to evaluate their effects, including comparing the experience of participants with that of undergraduates possessing similar background characteristics, either at the same college or a different one.[21] These comparisons showed that students in the program made greater progress than nonparticipants in clarifying their plans for a career and linking them to a larger sense of purpose in their lives. Two-thirds of the participating students who responded to a survey credited the program with helping them identify their "skills and talents," and one-third said that the program had led them to alter their life plans. After graduation, over 70 percent of participants agreed with the statement: "I have drawn upon vocational discernment and reflection to guide my decisions."[22]

Respondents also claimed to have developed a clearer understanding of why they were in college and how their education could contribute to their future lives. They remained enrolled and eventually graduated at significantly higher rates than students in the comparison groups. A year or so after leaving college, they tended to express much greater satisfaction with their lives than other graduates, although it is not possible to discern to what extent these results were attributable to the program rather than to preexisting characteristics of the graduates who chose to enter the program and respond to the survey.[23] Overall, the Lilly project seems to have had considerable success in achieving its objectives.

ALTERNATIVE APPROACHES

Great Books Courses

Various colleges have experimented with other ways to encourage students to think together about the lives they wish to lead. One of these initiatives is a hardy perennial, a "Great Books" course devoted to discussion of a list of enduring classics from ancient times to the present. While classes of this kind can be designed and taught to serve several different aims, many teachers and students have found them ideally suited to provoking discussion and fruitful thought about how to live one's life.

Two authors have written at length about the experience of taking or teaching such a class. One of these is David Denby, a regular contributor to *The New Yorker* who decided in middle age—in response to either "a midlife crisis or a crisis of identity"—to enroll in Columbia University's fabled yearlong Great Books course, "Literary Humanities," which he had taken years before as an undergraduate.[24] Denby's teacher, a professor of English named Edward Tayler, announced to his students on the first day of class: "You're here for very selfish reasons. You're here to build a self."

In the months that followed, students met and discussed a series of books from Homer to Virginia Woolf. Reflecting on the experience, Denby concluded that

> these books—or any such representative selection—speak most powerfully of what a human being can be. They dramatize the utmost any of us is capable of in love, suffering, and knowledge. They offer the most direct representation of the possibilities of civil existence and the disaster of its dissolution. The courses in the Western classics force us to ask all those questions about self and society we no longer address without embarrassment.[25]

The second author, Anthony Kronman, is a professor and former dean of the law school at Yale University.[26] Inspired by a course on existentialism he had taken years before at Williams College (where he "discovered that the meaning of life is a subject that can be studied at school"), he elected to teach a section in the Yale Great Books Program in Directed Studies. This program enrolled some 120 undergraduates divided into discussion groups of approximately 18 students who met twice a week to discuss a series of classic texts on literature, politics, history, and philosophy. As in the Columbia courses, "at the heart of the program is the question of what living is for." According to Kronman, student interest in the program was high enough that the applications far outnumbered the quota of 120 places that was imposed because of the limited number of faculty volunteering to teach the sections. His book is an extended account of the reasons why such courses have become rare and why undergraduate education has been impoverished as a result. His own enthusiasm for teaching such a course and for its beneficial effects remains undiminished.

Courses on Happiness

An entirely different way to help students think about the purpose and values to guide their lives is to offer a course devoted to the findings of empirical research over the past forty years on the effects of all kinds of experiences and events on the happiness of individuals and their satisfaction with the lives they are leading.* Most of this work does not seek to prescribe how individuals should live. What it does provide is a substantial body of evidence on how large numbers of people have reacted to the multiple events and circumstances of their lives.[27] Some of the results may not seem remarkable. Few people will be surprised to learn that commuting to work is one of the most disagreeable parts of a normal day, while socializing with friends is among the most enjoyable. But other findings may not seem so obvious. For example, most people revert surprisingly quickly to a state quite close to

---

*Teachers of this subject may also want to consider including material on the effects of biological factors on happiness, such as serotonin and dopamine; exercise, diet, sleep; and Buddhist meditation. For a succinct and provocative analysis of these alternative approaches, see Yuval Noah Hariri, *Sapiens: A Brief History of Mankind* (2014), p. 176.

their preexisting level of well-being after such fortunate events as winning the lottery or getting a raise in pay. Conversely, individuals who have suffered a grievous injury, such as the loss of an arm or leg, recover much of their previous state of well-being within a few months. Some other common events, however, such as the death of a loved one or being laid off from work, often result in longer-lasting unhappiness.

Perhaps the most striking conclusion by many happiness scholars is that people with the strongest ambition to become rich tend to be less and that those earning more than a relatively modest income—say $75,000 per year—gain diminishing levels of happiness from receiving additional increments of money. This conclusion is still controversial, but most researchers agree that levels of happiness in the United States and many other prosperous countries have not risen in the past several decades despite substantial increases in real per capita income.[28]

One survey of Canadians reached the surprising conclusion that some of the poorest provinces enjoyed among the highest average levels of happiness and well-being, while the richest provinces, Ontario and British Columbia, were among the least happy. A breakdown of the figures revealed that higher incomes did boost average levels of happiness for residents of the prosperous provinces, but that these gains were more than counterbalanced by the much higher percentages of people in some of the poorer provinces who claimed to have at least two or more individuals they could count on in a time of need. This finding, along with others, suggests that after a threshold of income is reached, happiness depends more on human relationships than it does on money.

Trends in the overall happiness of Americans relative to other advanced nations tell a somewhat similar story. The average level of happiness in the United States lags well behind that of all the Nordic countries despite the fact that our gross domestic product per capita is just as high or higher.[29] Over the past several years, the average level of happiness reported by Americans has actually declined significantly. According to Columbia University economist Jeffrey Sachs, this decline is not the consequence of low economic growth but results primarily from a sharp drop in people's confidence in government, their increased perceptions of corruption, deficiencies in our social support system, and diminished levels of trust in one another. These findings suggest that many Americans attach excessive weight to wealth as the most important source of greater happiness and underemphasize the social factors that often have a greater effect on their overall levels of contentment and satisfaction.

Such conclusions will hardly provide a blueprint for students in thinking about the kind of lives they wish to lead. However, surveys show that achieving happiness is one of the most important goals, if not *the* most important goal, for more than 80 percent of entering freshmen when they are asked to indicate why they are going to college.[30] At the same time, more than 70 percent believe that making a lot of money is also very important. Under these conditions, there is much to be said for a course on what psychologists and other empirical researchers can tell us about the experiences in life that contribute most to well-being. Few students can discuss this body of research without thinking about the relevance of the findings to their own beliefs and to the choices they must make once they graduate. Thus, the greatest value of such courses may again be the stimulus they give students to engage in more reflection and conversation with others about their future lives.

Designing a Life

At Stanford University, two professors have invented a course that applies design thinking—a method originally developed for discovering new or improved consumer products—to the process of considering how to create a satisfying life.[31] (Design thinking is considered further in a section in chapter 7.) "Designing Your Life" is an elective open not only to undergraduates but to others as well, including individuals who are not Stanford students.

The course begins by asking participants to reflect upon the lives they are living or planning to live and to consider the effects on their health, work, play, and love. They are then asked to take the time to imagine alternative lives that would be better, taking care not to become bogged down in imagining a single "one best possible life" that would be virtually impossible to achieve, such as earning millions of dollars as a professional basketball star. Instead, they are urged to use their imaginations to conceive of multiple plausible alternatives that would improve upon the life they are leading. When students have thought up as many possible lives as they can, they are asked to choose the three to five most attractive alternatives, since they may find it harder to reach a final decision if they have too many choices to consider.

After reducing the number of possible lives, students "prototype" their preferred choices by gathering relevant information about each one and asking people who are living one of the preferred alternatives to talk with them about their experience. After collecting enough information, members of the class are instructed to gather a small group of good friends and relatives to discuss which alternative seems most promising. In choosing among the possibilities, they are advised to seek the solution that best satisfies both their deliberative mind and their "gut" feelings, since meeting both will yield the most satisfactory results. Once they make their choice, students are urged to devote all their energies to implementing their decision and not look back to reconsider their conclusion and agonize over whether another choice might have been even better.

The course just described and the thinking process it recommends may not appeal to everyone. Some may recoil from the notion that one's life should be treated like a commercial product and dismiss the recommended process as superficial and banal. Others may ask whether someone going through such an elaborate search for a satisfying life might become too self-absorbed. One must also wonder what the world would be like if all those who feel dissatisfied with their lives began to approach strangers and assemble groups of friends to talk about choosing a happier existence, especially if, as the instructors claim, the choice of a happy life is never final but should be revisited every few years. Socrates may be correct that the unexamined life is not worth living, but the examined life the instructors suggest could require a good deal more time and effort than most people and their relatives and acquaintances wish to devote to the subject.

Despite these reservations, "Designing Your Life" has been a popular course for Stanford undergraduates and for all those from outside the university welcomed into the class by the instructors. One can readily imagine how this systematic approach could appeal to many people. At the same time, although some of the steps the instructors recommend are supported by psychological research, I am not aware of any rigorous, independent inquiry to determine the lasting effects of these classes on a representative group of individuals who have taken them.*

What use should colleges make of offerings such as the three alternatives just discussed? Since students who already have firm ideas about their goals and values may have no desire to take classes of this kind, while others may not feel ready to begin a serious quest for direction in their lives, colleges would be ill advised to *require* such courses. Students who have no interest in this subject are unlikely to benefit much from being made to study it against their will. Nor do colleges have sufficiently compelling evidence about the value of such instruction to make it a requirement.

On the other hand, the number of students who do take these courses offers powerful reasons for offering them on an elective basis. As previously mentioned, the Yale Great Books Program in Directed Studies in which Professor Kronman taught cannot accommodate all the students who seek to enroll. A course at Harvard on happiness research drew some eight hundred students each year, making it the largest course in the college. In 2018, a similar course at Yale attracted twelve hundred students, occasioning feverish efforts to find a large enough hall to accommodate the audience and to hire enough teaching fellows to staff dozens of small discussion sections. The Stanford course also seems to enjoy an enthusiastic reception.

Rather than simply offer such instruction, however, colleges would be well advised to do what they rarely do and survey students after the course is over and again some years later to ascertain what effect

---

*The alternatives described in the preceding pages do not exhaust the possibilities for helping students think about how to live. College courses can acquaint undergraduates with the teachings of various philosophers who have written on "the good life." Biographies and autobiographies can create opportunities for fruitful discussions on the same subject, and carefully selected works of fiction can do likewise. The value of such alternatives derives not so much from the reputation of the works selected as from their capacity to provoke thought and a lively interchange among students about questions of meaning and purpose.

it may have had on helping them arrive at a clearer sense of how they wished to live their lives. According to Professor Kronman,

> Too many graduates today view their college years—the most leisurely years of their lives . . . as a wasted opportunity squandered in pursuit of a disorganized and idiosyncratic program of study. They view it with regret, as a lost chance to explore the question of what living is for before the demands of life take hold and they become too busy to ask it.[32]

Surely it would be useful to put Kronman's statement to the test by surveying alumni to determine whether courses such as those considered here actually help substantial numbers of students to find a greater purpose and direction for their lives.

SUMMING UP

In conclusion, what can one say about the current efforts of higher education to help students ponder the most important questions they face as they prepare to graduate? Just as in the case of moral and civic education, most faculties seem satisfied to continue as they are in the hope that students will choose the kind of life they wish to lead simply by sampling the vast smorgasbord of courses, readings, conversations, and cocurricular activities that colleges typically provide. Once again, there is little reason to believe that this approach will suffice to meet the need.

Although a substantial number of seniors claim to have acquired a clearer purpose as a result of their years at college, it is hard to determine whether these respondents fully understand what is meant by "how to live" or whether they see the question as merely asking about their ability to choose what career to pursue after leaving college. We also do not know how many students would stand by their statement a decade or so after they graduate. According to scholars who study adolescence, such as Professor Damon, the fraction of students who actually acquire a larger purpose during college is distressingly small. Researchers studying self-authorship add that one-half to two-thirds of American adults have not even acquired the confidence to rely on their own values and beliefs in making such choices.[33]

While many colleges with ties to a religious faith are making serious efforts to help students choose a direction for their lives, others
could surely do more to help students find their way. In addition to
the value of such efforts for undergraduates in thinking about the
future, those who do acquire meaningful goals and who are able to
perceive their connection with courses and extracurricular activities
appear to enjoy college more and feel more motivated to work at their
studies and eventually earn a degree. This finding alone provides good
reason for colleges to consider experimenting with courses and programs such as those described in these pages and questioning their
alumni years after they graduate to discover whether these experiences
helped them gain a clearer and more fruitful sense of how to live.
Armed with such findings, college leaders and their faculties could
eventually become much better informed to decide how to prepare
their students to make these critically important choices.

CHAPTER SIX

Improving Interpersonal Skills

The various capabilities often referred to misleadingly as "soft" or "noncognitive" skills have attracted a lot of attention in recent years. Employers frequently complain that too few college graduates possess these skills. Nobel economist James Heckman has shown how much they matter to productivity, while professor of education David Deming has documented their growing influence on employee earnings.*[1] According to Patrick Kyllonen from the Educational Testing Service, "The 21st century is becoming the era in which we recognize the importance of soft skills, the role education plays in developing these skills, and the way they evolve throughout the life cycle."[2]

What *are* these skills? Are many colleges teaching them? Do educators even know how to help students acquire them?

Commentators have identified more than forty of the competencies in question. This jumble of frequently overlapping and redundant behaviors includes some familiar capabilities, such as critical thinking, writing, and oral communication, that have long been central to the teaching of colleges and universities. Most of them, however, are qualities that have traditionally received less attention in college classrooms, such as teamwork, resilience, and creativity.

Despite all the talk about the importance of these skills, some educators question whether colleges should even try to teach them. One argument for not doing so is that training of this sort is best left to the employers that will benefit from it. This reason is surely unpersuasive. Some larger corporations do provide such training, but many others

---

*The so-called soft skills apparently have an influence on earnings comparable to that of cognitive skills, but cognitive skills appear to be more important for jobs requiring above-average levels of compensation. James J. Heckman and Tim Kautz, "Hard Evidence on Soft Skills," *Labour Economics* 19 (2012), p. 451.

are reluctant to do so, fearing that after employees are trained, they may leave at any time and take their capabilities with them to benefit another company, perhaps even a competitor. Smaller enterprises often lack the funds to engage in formal training. Thus, if the economy is to benefit fully from the development of these competencies, colleges will have to play an important part.

Other faculty members argue that teaching these skills will compromise the traditional mission of colleges to provide a liberal education. But colleges have long since crossed this line by creating vocational majors (which now attract some 60 percent of all undergraduates). Since preparing for a career is the most important reason for attending college in the eyes of both students and legislators, colleges should presumably try to address vocational needs insofar as they are capable of doing so. Besides, almost all of the skills in question (such as creativity and resilience) provide important benefits for graduates outside the workplace, either as citizens or simply as human beings seeking a full and satisfying life.

Colleges cannot be faulted for overlooking these skills if it is not possible to teach them. For a long time, this argument seemed convincing. However, as this chapter and the next will seek to explain, recent findings by psychologists suggest that these behaviors may be teachable after all by knowledgeable college instructors.

It is impossible in a short book to pay separate attention to all or nearly all of the many capabilities that are numbered among the so-called soft or noncognitive skills. In the following pages, therefore, I discuss only six of the most important ones (in addition to conscientiousness, which was considered in chapter 4). Three of the skills examined here are primarily *inter*-personal: a talent for getting along well with other people, be they customers and supervisors or friends and colleagues; an ability to collaborate effectively as a member of a team; and a respectful understanding of racial differences and other forms of diversity. The other three capabilities are mainly *intra*-personal and are discussed in chapter 7: creativity in solving practical problems and perceiving new opportunities; a willingness to engage in lifelong learning; and resilience and perseverance (sometimes called "grit") in the face of adversity.

PEOPLE SKILLS

The ability to interact successfully with other people is valuable in all sorts of ways. In the fourth century BC, Epicurus observed that "of all the means which are procured by wisdom to ensure happiness throughout the whole of life, by far the most important is the acquisition of friends."[3] Empirical studies on the sources of happiness have confirmed his conclusion that human relationships matter more than money, success, or virtually anything else in the lives of most people. In our predominantly service economy, where more and more employees engage with customers and work is increasingly done by teams, employers attach great importance to interpersonal skills in evaluating applicants for employment. Recent research by Professor Deming has found that over the past two decades, jobs requiring "people skills" have grown more rapidly in numbers and compensation than jobs that call only for math and other cognitive abilities, while jobs requiring *both* people and quantitative skills have grown more rapidly still.[4]

According to surveys, 70 percent or more of graduating seniors say that their ability to interact with others has increased during college.[5] Although self-reports of this kind are not very reliable, more sophisticated studies tend to confirm that students do make significant gains in social self-confidence during their college years.[6] However, the evidence is thin when it comes to determining exactly what kinds of activities and experiences contribute most to interpersonal relations, or whether going to college accomplishes more than serving in the armed forces, working in a department store, or other kinds of practical experience.

Students seldom learn much about getting along with their fellows by listening to lectures. Any improvement in human interaction brought about by college is likely to result less from formal instruction in "interpersonal relations" than from the multiple opportunities that undergraduate life provides for eating, playing, working, and studying with other students. If this is true, the contribution made by colleges to the development of people skills presumably varies depending on the nature of the college. Residential campuses can do a lot to improve confidence and skill in relating to others, since students interact constantly with classmates throughout their waking hours, not only in classes but also in their dormitory, in their social activities, and during other extracurricular pursuits. On the other hand, an undergraduate who lives by himself in an apartment, commutes to a nearby metropolitan college, and comes home alone each evening may benefit less.

Most colleges try to enhance interpersonal skills by creating abundant opportunities for students to interact with one another. Extracurricular activities, such as community service, student government, and intramural sports, can bring together students with common interests under conditions that encourage them to work effectively with one another. In commuter colleges, however, efforts to improve these skills may have to rely more on opportunities within the curriculum, such as learning communities, group projects, and frequent discussions among members of a class.

Recent findings by psychologists have suggested new possibilities for developing interpersonal skills. Prior to this century, investigators believed that the traits making up one's personality are largely inherited and unlikely to change after adolescence. In particular, people skills, which are largely a product of two of the "Big Five" personality traits—extroversion and, to a lesser extent, agreeableness—were thought to be fixed by the time students reach college. In the past twenty years, however, a large body of evidence has accumulated showing that personality traits, including extroversion and agreeableness, are not as immutable as psychologists had thought and can continue to change throughout almost the entire life span.[7]

Subsequent research has revealed that more than 60 percent and even up to 70 percent of college students would like to change their personality—often by becoming more extroverted and hence more outgoing and sociable.[8] Recent studies have gone further and found that individuals can actually change their personality to a small or moderate degree and become more extroverted by engaging in deliberate and repeated efforts to reach out to people and overcome the shyness that has inhibited them in the past.[9]

As yet, research on this subject is very new and much has still to be learned. Existing studies tend to rely on self-reports by students, which are known to be unreliable. Thus, one cannot yet be sure whether the exercises performed by students actually *cause* them to be more sociable or whether they merely *think* they are more outgoing. Nor is it known how long these effects last once the training ends.[10] Teaching shy undergraduates to become more outgoing and confident in interacting with other people remains an intriguing possibility rather than a proven method of instruction.

The discovery that personality traits are malleable and may be altered by deliberate effort raises thorny questions that colleges will need to answer. Should colleges venture beyond training the minds of their students to helping them to change their personalities? Even if instruction for personality change is optional (as it surely must be), are eighteen-year-olds competent to make such choices? And finally, should all personality changes be treated the same? Some people who would gladly endorse efforts to help students become more conscientious might balk at attempting to help them become less shy and more extroverted.*

Meanwhile, colleges have already had some success in developing methods of classroom instruction that help students perform better in specific kinds of interpersonal relations. One such method is the use of collaborative projects in which students work together on challenging problems and learn how to improve their teamwork skills. Another method takes the form of courses and workshops to increase understanding and overcome prejudice toward people from different races, backgrounds, and ethnic groups.†

Teamwork Skills

In 1906, President Charles W. Eliot of Harvard tried unsuccessfully to abolish ice hockey. "It requires teamwork," he declared, "and I must say that I have no use for a game that requires that."[11] Since then, times have definitely changed. More and more work in business and the professions is now being done by groups of people.[12] As a result, employers and professional organizations are attaching increased importance

---

* Perhaps this difference results from the fact that conscientiousness often affects other people in direct and obvious ways, while extroversion has less significant effects on others. It is also possible that efforts to help students become more extroverted seem problematic because of a fear that they might simply make students more clumsy and boorish.

†A third classroom method used successful in professional schools (law, business, government) is teaching students how to negotiate.

to teamwork skills. For example, in its 2004 report *The Engineer of 2020*, the National Academy of Engineering declared that "the engineering profession recognizes that engineers need to work in teams" and that "the challenge of working effectively in teams will continue to grow."[13] A survey sponsored by the Association of American Colleges and Universities found that more than 80 percent of CEOs listed collaborative skill as a "very important" quality for the college graduates they employed.[14] Some companies even have job applicants participate in games that are monitored with the aid of artificial intelligence technology to evaluate their performance in terms of leadership potential, contributions to the team, skill in presenting ideas to teammates, and ingenuity in devising strategies and solutions.

For many years, professors tended to discourage collaboration in their classes on the grounds that group work made it hard for them to grade the performance of each student. More recently, however, instructors have been deliberately creating opportunities for students to work together on problems, since such exercises can elicit greater effort and enthusiasm from students and promote deeper learning and longer retention of the material involved.

Using group projects to solve problems can be an exceptionally valuable form of teaching because it develops several different competencies not easily nurtured by having individuals work alone. Group members can help the team in various ways—by supplying leadership, listening attentively to team members, contributing creative ideas, engaging in trust-building behaviors, and resolving conflicts. Another benefit of group learning is the opportunity it provides for peer teaching, since fellow students are often better than instructors at figuring out why their classmates are encountering difficulty. Underlying all these qualities as "the essential heart of cooperative efforts is positive interdependence, the perception that one's success is not possible unless others succeed (and vice versa) and that group members' work benefits one's own and one's work benefits them."[15]

Hundreds of studies have been carried out on collaborative learning. A strong consensus has emerged that teamwork usually produces better results than those achieved even by the most talented team members working separately.[16] Apparently, if "two heads are better than one," several heads can be better still.

Researchers have also discovered, however, that teaching teamwork by forming groups of students to solve problems is a more complicated task than one might imagine. To succeed, instructors need to exercise skills quite different from those commonly used in teaching courses and seminars. They must know:

- how to form student groups that are diverse enough to bring a range of skills and perspectives to the collaborative process;
- how to create problems for the group to solve that are challenging enough to elicit real effort without being beyond the capacity of the group;
- how to make each member of the group feel accountable for preparing adequately and contributing usefully to the collective deliberations;
- how to provide frequent, immediate, and helpful feedback to the group without diminishing the team's responsibility to arrive at its own solution;
- how to utilize appropriate methods and criteria both for judging the group's work as a whole and for evaluating the contributions of each of its members; and
- how to teach additional skills that may be needed to engage successfully in the increasingly common practice of collaborating with groups whose members are located in different cities or even different countries.[17]

Analysts who study the use of groups frequently remark that results are more likely to be disappointing when instructors fail to manage the process properly than when team members are incompetent or unmotivated.[18]

The challenge of using group projects successfully may be complicated enough to warrant prior training for instructors. In one study evaluating a yearlong program to prepare teachers to use this method, students in groups taught by faculty who had received the training learned more, not only about how to solve the problems addressed in class but about nurturing the collaborative skills that improved the performance of the group.[19] If colleges require special training, however, they may have difficulty persuading busy professors to use this method of teaching.

Whether or not instructors are properly prepared for the task, collaborative student work is gradually becoming more common. According to the faculty surveys conducted every few years by the Higher Education Research Institute, the percentage of professors claiming to make use of such methods increased from 31.6 to 45.5 percent from 1991–1995 to 2013–2014.[20] However, it is hard to know just what this trend implies for teaching collaborative skills, since many professors who use group work do so mainly to help students understand complex material rather than to improve teamwork.

Enough is already known about how to conduct group problem-solving and the benefits that result to justify its growing use. The capability that technology gives instructors to examine the contributions of each participant in the collaborative process could yield further insights about how to use the method effectively. In view of the variety of interpersonal skills that can be developed in this way, colleges have good reason to continue searching for ways to bring about an even more extensive and skillful use of this promising form of instruction.

Relations among the Races

When colleges in the late 1960s began to make deliberate efforts to admit a more racially diverse student body, many campus officials felt that all they needed to do was locate promising minority students, persuade them to apply, and find the money that would allow them to afford the cost of earning a degree. They soon discovered, however, that enrolling minority applicants was only the first in a series of problems to be overcome.

One of the most challenging tasks has been to create a welcoming environment with abundant opportunities to bring students of every race together in positive interactions that will help everyone gain a greater understanding of classmates with different backgrounds, attitudes, and life experiences. The importance of this effort is obvious. By 2045, more than half of all Americans are projected to be members of a minority group. Social commentators and employers agree that harmonious relations among the races will be increasingly important not only for individuals but for the workplace and society as a whole. Colleges have an important role to play in fostering such understanding, the more so since large percentages of both minority and white students have grown up in predominantly segregated schools and neighborhoods and consequently come to college with little or no experience of living in a racially diverse environment.

Experts in the field of race relations have long since found that prejudice and misunderstanding tend to dissipate with repeated positive contact among members of different races and ethnic groups and that the beneficial effects can persist for fifteen years or more.[21] Such interactions do not occur automatically, however; the natural tendency of most students is to socialize with members of their own race, and colleges need to seek ways to encourage positive and fruitful interracial encounters. According to Gordon Allport, a pioneer in the study of prejudice, such interaction tends to be most effective when blacks and whites are equal in status, working together to achieve a common goal in an activity sanctioned by the institution.[22] More recent research, however, has found that the conditions leading to fruitful interaction are more complicated than Allport's formula suggests, especially for changing the attitudes of minorities.[23]

Colleges have labored with some success to create an inclusive environment. In one large survey in 2016, 91 percent of students of all races claimed that their institution "promotes an appreciation of cultural differences," while 85 percent believed that their campus "has a longstanding commitment to diversity."[24] Part of this effort is the provision of courses on race that focus on the history and culture of minority groups in the United States or discuss present-day relations among different races in America and the steps still needed to achieve greater racial equality. Many classes on other subjects supplement this effort by making a point of including relevant material involving race. Surveys suggest that more than two-thirds of undergraduates enroll in one or more classes that address racial issues.[25] In addition, many colleges arrange noncredit, one- or two-day workshops for students that deal explicitly with issues of unintended discrimination and other common problems and misunderstandings involving relations between whites and minorities.

Teaching students about race presents unusual challenges. Classroom materials about systemic discrimination or the advantages that whites derive from social injustice can provoke angry discussions that may be difficult for teachers to deal with successfully. According to one observer,

> many faculty members of all backgrounds are struggling to help students participate in the difficult dialogues occurring across higher education. They report walking on eggshells in their classrooms, unsure of how to facilitate rigorous discussions about institutional racism, microaggression, and freedom of speech. They worry about "coddling" their students with trigger warnings . . . and they wonder if higher education is preparing students for the harsh real world.[26]

When instructors react instinctively to avoid conflict by terminating discussions that seem to be getting heated or by ignoring students with strong views, they can inhibit learning, just as a deft response to such incipient problems can result in interchanges that provoke useful thought and lead to greater understanding.

Despite the difficulties encountered by teachers, students tend to be quite positive in their reflections on courses and workshops about race. More than 90 percent of undergraduates in one national survey reported that they had recognized biases in their own thinking as a result of these classes.[27] Seventy-seven percent of these students claimed to have subsequently challenged other individuals "at least occasionally" on issues arising from conversations about race (31 percent reported having done so "frequently").[28] More than half of the respondents said that they had applied lessons derived from diversity courses in real-life situations.*[29]

Efforts to measure the effects of such instruction on student attitudes toward race have come to mixed conclusions, as one would expect given the difficulty of the task. Overall, however, according to most evaluations of the existing evidence, the net effects of both courses

---

* Courses on diversity and race relations can be especially valuable for the many white undergraduates who have attended all-white public schools and lived in predominantly white neighborhoods. Some investigators have found that such classes have their greatest effect on students of this kind, especially those from low- and moderate-income families. Conversely, the views of black students about their interaction with persons of other races appear to be less affected than those of whites by courses on relations between the races. On the other hand, black students report being more affected than whites by courses dealing with racial inequality in America and policies to overcome it.

and workshops tend to be positive for openness to diversity, cultural awareness, commitment to racial understanding, and acceptance of other races and cultures.[30]

Findings on the *size* of these effects vary considerably. Many of the studies are based on self-reports, which are known to be subject to bias and wishful thinking. Evidence of this kind tends to show greater improvement than research that employs more rigorous methods. Most scholars who have analyzed the entire body of work on these subjects conclude that the results on the whole are positive but that the effects are generally small or moderate in size.[31]

Various college experiences outside of class can also contribute to healthy race relations, among them living in residence halls, participating in athletics, engaging in community service programs, and a host of other extracurricular activities. Some researchers find that these experiences are more effective than courses in diminishing prejudice and racial bias, and many colleges try hard to promote them.[32]

Increasing the opportunities to mix with members of other races is not enough, however; the interactions need to be positive, and it is not always easy to bring about this result. Colleges cannot control students' behavior outside of class. Fraternities and sororities with predominantly white members can actually have negative effects on the attitudes of students. A few irresponsible individuals can do a lot of damage to the racial climate, and even well-intentioned undergraduates can say things that give unwitting offense. Surveys show that black and Latino students continue to experience racial slurs and social exclusion far more often than their white classmates.[33] Still, the weight of the evidence indicates that the net effect of college on racial attitudes is usually positive.

The limited research that exists also suggests that many colleges have become more effective over time in improving race relations and racial understanding. One detailed survey of two cohorts, each with several thousand students who entered twenty-eight selective colleges in 1976 and 1989 (with exceptionally high response rates of over 80 percent), found that positive attitudes toward race increased from the earlier to the later cohort on every question asked.[34] The percentage of white graduates claiming that "getting along with people from different races and cultures" was "very important" rose from 44 to 55 percent and for black graduates from 72 to 76 percent.[35] The percentage of graduates claiming that college had helped "a great deal" in their ability to work effectively and get along well with people of different races and cultures also rose substantially, from 36 to 46 percent among whites and from 18 to 34 percent among blacks.[36] The percentage of white students who "knew well" at least two or more black students rose to 56 percent in the later cohort, even though black students made up less than 10 percent of the student body in all but one of the twenty-eight colleges.[37] The percentage of black students claiming to "know well" two or more white students reached 88 percent in the later cohort.

Looking back, black and white alumni from the more recent class expressed great appreciation for their college years. More than 60 percent of both groups of graduates from the cohort entering in 1989 reported being "very satisfied" with their college experience, and over 90 percent were either "very" or "somewhat" satisfied.[38] Only 6 to 7 percent of students of either race felt that they would attend another college if they had to choose again.[39] The various findings from this study, including graduation rates, subsequent earnings, and appreciation of the undergraduate experience, strongly contradict the frequent claim that preferential admissions hurt the very minority students they are intended to help by forcing them to compete against better-qualified white classmates.

There is undoubtedly room for further efforts to improve racial attitudes and experiences in college. Graduation rates for black and Latino students continue to fall below those of whites in all but the most selective colleges. Black students tend to perform less well in selective colleges than their high school grades and test scores predict (although the average earnings premium that black graduates receive compared with blacks who only attended high school is greater than that of whites).[40] Protests continue to occur at one campus or another, and the response of college authorities is not always as effective as it might be. Overall, however, it is fair to conclude that the efforts of colleges to improve racial attitudes and interactions rank among their greatest accomplishments of the past few decades.

Encouraging Tolerance and Respect for Other Kinds of Differences

Race is only one form of diversity being addressed in college classrooms; others include differences of gender, sexual orientation, age, religion, and physical handicaps. Tolerance and understanding among such groups are obviously valuable as a matter of simple decency. Corporate employers whose operations involve contact with diverse customers and workers of every kind, both in America and around the world, need employees who are sensitive to the beliefs, life experiences, and needs of everyone they encounter, whatever their differences.

Preparing students for such a diverse world creates a problem for colleges not unlike the challenge of trying to help them become "globally competent." Just as it is impossible for colleges to acquaint their students with every culture in the world, it is also hard to teach them to understand and respect the distinctive backgrounds, feelings, and experiences of all the different groups they will encounter in later life. Some colleges address this difficulty with courses that only try to increase students' understanding of one or two groups, hoping that these classes will prepare students to respond to other differences they encounter with greater insight and appreciation. Other courses seek to acquaint students with all of the most significant differences, despite having to treat each group superficially.

However colleges choose to proceed, they are bound to encounter problems of execution. Teaching about diversity requires vigorous class discussions rather than simply lecturing or including materials about gender, sexual orientation, or some other grouping into one's course materials. Discussions about differences can easily go awry, just as in classes on race, leaving some students feeling misunderstood, resentful, or unfairly treated. Members of the majority may take offense from assertions that seem to question their decency and good faith. Members of minorities may feel that their predicament has not been fully and accurately described, but they keep silent out of reluctance to be put in the position of seeming to speak for their entire group.

These reactions may not only fail to promote understanding but even make matters worse. To minimize such outcomes, all instructors who take up material on diversity might benefit from prior training on how to deal successfully with the kinds of misunderstandings that can arise in teaching these sensitive subjects. As with group learning, however, if faculty members are obliged to undergo special training, far fewer of them are likely to agree to introduce such material into their courses.

As one would expect when the topic is so complicated and sensitive, efforts to evaluate the impact of diversity courses, like those focused only on race, have come to varying conclusions. Overall, however, the findings have been positive and have identified a wide range of benefits far beyond improvements in attitudes toward diversity. In their comprehensive review of one thousand studies of undergraduate education on the effects of going to college published from 2002 to 2012 (carrying forward the work of previous volumes by Ernest Pascarella and Patrick Terenzini), Matthew Mayhew and his colleagues conclude that courses on diversity have a surprising variety of positive effects.

> The burgeoning literature on diversity-related coursework suggests that this experience increases academic ability, writing ability, racial identity development, drive to achieve, intellectual self-confidence, well-being, personal and social development, civic attitudes and behaviors, and positive diversity attitudes. Diversity courses may also bolster cognitive and moral growth, but these findings are inconclusive.[41]*

Apparently, the tendency of such courses to challenge students to examine their opinions, explain their positions, and adjust their views in the light of new evidence and arguments helps to improve a variety of attitudes and intellectual skills. In summing up their review of these studies, Professor Mayhew and his colleagues observe that "we were struck by the consistency in the evidence that . . . quality engagement with peers of diverse racial and ethnic backgrounds, social classes, world views, and sexualities inspires positive attitudes in ways that few other interventions have the power to do."[42]

---

* A recent study has concluded that "diversity courses, as an aspect of the undergraduate curriculum, are likely to yield a profound positive influence on students' moral discernment by the end of the college." Eugene I. Parker III, Cassie L. Barnhart, Ernest T. Pascarella and Jarvis A. McCowin, "The Impact of Diversity Courses on Students' Moral Development," *Journal of College Student Development* 57 (2016), p. 895.

CHAPTER SEVEN

Improving Intrapersonal Skills

Although few, if any, of the so-called noncognitive skills have no connection at all with other people, a number of them are connected weakly enough that they are often classified as *intra*-personal. One of these, conscientiousness, has already been discussed in chapter 4. Three others—creativity, lifelong learning, and resilience—are sufficiently important to warrant separate treatment here.

CREATIVITY

The fifteenth edition of the *Encyclopaedia Britannica* defines creativity broadly to include "the ability to make or otherwise bring into existence something new, whether a new solution to a problem, a new method or device, or a new artistic object or form."[1] In educational circles, however, one form of creativity has tended to overshadow the others. For a long time, the term was used primarily by teachers of art and literature, and efforts to encourage students to do creative work were largely confined to these fields. In contrast, the recent upsurge of interest in fostering creativity has come primarily from the business sector. The definitions most often used today are more practical, referring to "an ability to discover something useful—a concept, a process, or an artifact—that is both useful and novel in solving a problem or meeting a need."[2] The recent pressure on colleges to nurture creativity of this kind has come most often from corporate sources, such as the Business Roundtable or the Council on Competitiveness, or from government entities concerned with economic growth, such as the Organisation for Economic Co-operation and Development (OECD).

Several trends in the modern economy have contributed to the growing concern with creativity in business. Companies competing here and abroad look to creativity to supply new ideas for lowering costs, boosting sales, and opening new markets. Government officials have come to appreciate the vital role of innovation in stimulating economic growth. Meanwhile, many students have cast an envious eye on entrepreneurial college graduates and dropouts such as Bill Gates and Mark Zuckerberg and dream of following in their footsteps by conjuring up a new idea and using it to make a fortune. Other students may appreciate the value of creative talent in offering protection from being displaced by robots and computers as well as its usefulness in solving a variety of problems that arise in everyday life. Recent surveys reveal that 78 percent of college graduate professionals consider creativity important in their work, while an equal percentage wish that they were more creative.[3]

The shift in focus to more practical, commercial innovation has been accompanied by a heightened interest in teaching students to become more creative.[4] While research on this subject dates back at least to the 1950s, the number of articles on the subject has grown especially rapidly in the past twenty years. Investigators distinguish between several qualities of mind that enter into a creative discovery. One is a capacity for divergent thinking—the ability to imagine a variety of possibilities for approaching a problem. Another is a willingness to question conventional assumptions rather than take them for granted. A third is the ability to suspend judgment and tolerate uncertainty in order to keep one's mind open to new possibilities. Still another is an eagerness to keep trying new ideas and, if they do not succeed, to look upon failure not as a cause for discouragement but as a source of additional insight for solving complicated problems. Finally, creative individuals are said to engage more frequently in meta-cognition—analyzing one's own thinking in order to discover flaws, overlooked clues, or new strategies of inquiry.

As with many of the other soft skills, most researchers now agree that creativity is not a fixed quality but a malleable capability that can be nurtured and developed at least through early adulthood.[5] Disagreement remains, however, over whether creativity is transferable from one field of endeavor to another—for example, whether creative musicians will also be creative in seeking a cheaper way to market a new product. What seems most likely is that individuals need to have ample background knowledge in order to arrive at creative solutions to the specific type of problem they are trying to solve. Once this knowledge is acquired, however, the qualities of mind needed to succeed may be similar to those required for creativity in other fields of activity. If this explanation is correct, it should be possible to teach students a way of thinking that, combined with thorough subject matter knowledge, will help them arrive at creative solutions to a wide variety of problems.

The efforts of researchers to discover how to foster this kind of thinking have been hampered by difficulties and disagreements over how to measure creativity in order to test instructional methods and discover whether those methods succeed.* Differences of opinion abound, but most scholars agree that several methods of teaching commonly used both in schools and in college tend to discourage the very habits of mind that are needed for original thought.[6] In traditional classrooms, the emphasis is often on covering material rather than coaching students to be more imaginative and allowing them sufficient time to think of new solutions. The incentives given to students when they are asked to solve a problem frequently take the form of extrinsic rewards, such as outdoing competitors or obtaining a good grade, that many researchers believe discourage creativity rather than increase it. Critical thinking is usually favored over speculative and unconventional approaches. The questions asked in class may have a single correct answer, and students who stray from the appropriate path by asking unexpected questions or raising novel, seemingly unfruitful possibilities are discouraged in order to keep the discussion "on track" and under the control of the teacher. Tests are often of the short-answer variety so that the questions asked have only one correct answer. According to experts, these practices can stifle students' latent capacity for creativity. Tales are frequently told

---

*For example, some tests measure only one or two skills, such as divergent thinking, among the several qualities of mind involved in creativity. According to one prominent researcher, Adrian Furnham of the University of London, "The crucial issue that is holding researchers back from doing good research is the lack of a valid, reliable, and multi-dimensional measurement of creativity." Furnham, "From Fascination to Research: Problems and Progress in Creativity Research," in Robert J. Sternberg and James C. Kaufman, eds., *The Nature of Human Creativity* (2018), p. 861; see also Arthur J. Cropley, "Defining and Measuring Creativity: Are Creativity Tests Worth Using?" *Roeper Review* 23 (2000), p. 72.

of brilliant, imaginative thinkers such as Albert Einstein who were frustrated in school and did not do well, although they managed to display remarkable creativity in later life.[7]

There is no one method for teaching creativity that has been reliably proven to be successful. Based on what we now know, however, several steps appear to hold promise. To begin with, teachers can convince their students that creativity is not an immutable quality that is fixed at birth but a capability that can be improved with practice. They can encourage divergent thinking by conducting brainstorming exercises in which members of the class try to come up with as many solutions as possible to a problem. Students can also be taught to identify the assumptions underlying their initial responses to a given problem and to examine each assumption to discover whether it is accurate or imperfect in ways that block more creative solutions to a problem. In addition, teachers can try to persuade students not to become discouraged if their initial solutions to a problem prove to be wrong but to regard such failures as useful lessons from which they can learn to do better. Finally, instructors can find ways of rewarding creativity when students display it in classroom discussions or homework assignments.[8]

In recent years, business consultants have developed a similar way to help individuals and companies become more creative through design thinking, a process briefly discussed in chapter 5.[9] By practicing a series of simple steps, they claim, most people can train themselves to unleash their creative potential. Once again, the essential first step is to convince oneself that creativity is not a rare talent that few people possess but a skill that many can develop through conscious effort. The way to begin, according to design thinkers, is to search for a problem requiring an innovative solution. To do this well, one must put oneself in the shoes of other people, such as customers, and summon the empathy to understand what they need or would like to possess. Armed with such insight, one can then conjure up a variety of possible ways to meet the need, taking care to resist the tendency to discard ideas prematurely as far-fetched or impractical. The next step is to test the ideas, at least the ones that are not impossible on their face. In carrying out these tests, one must conquer the instinctive fear of failure and use the opportunity it provides to learn more about how to find a successful solution. Above all, it is important not to lose heart and give up but to persevere until success is eventually achieved.

Although proponents of this method are enthusiastic about its potential, the evidence they cite tends to be anecdotal, prompting some critics to dismiss the approach as a fad dressed up with "floating balloons of jargon."[10] Most design thinkers, however, do not merely prescribe a way for individuals to train themselves to become creative. In fact, they firmly reject the common tendency to regard great creative insights as the work of lonely inventors. Instead, they cite many examples of well-known innovators, such as Thomas Edison and the Wright Brothers, whose breakthroughs resulted from the cooperative efforts and contributions of several people. Accordingly, design thinkers usually advise their corporate clients to form teams of employees with diverse skills to work together to produce innovative solutions to problems through a process of collaboration akin to that described in chapter 6.

A number of universities have sought to encourage creativity of this kind by providing "innovation laboratories" where students receive tools, materials, and coaching to try out their ideas for novel products.[11] Stanford University has gone further and established the Hasso Plattner Institute of Design, a non-degree-granting program to assist any part of the university wishing to foster creativity and innovation through the use of design thinking.[12] One example of the kind of experience this program makes possible is a trip to a less developed country by groups of students to examine a problem identified by local nonprofit organizations and work together to understand the need and produce an innovative solution.

It is not yet clear how much group learning of this kind can help individuals to become more creative. What *is* clear is that effective collaboration, by pooling the diverse talents of a group of people, can increase the likelihood of producing imaginative solutions to practical problems. For this reason, many companies and other organizations increasingly use collaborative teams to stimulate innovation.

As we learned in chapter 6, success in teaching students through group learning depends on having instructors who are proficient in the use of this technique. Under the guidance of competent teachers, the method can be employed in many different courses to teach students basic skills for creative teamwork that can prove useful in working for a wide variety of organizations. The principal challenge is persuading faculty members to take the time to master the technique of teaching students to collaborate successfully.

LIFELONG LEARNING

There is much talk in educational circles today about the importance of "lifelong learning," or what some researchers refer to as "a continuing desire to engage in effortful cognitive activity."[13] The latter definition makes clear that this quality of mind encompasses both the motivation and the ability to keep on learning new things.

What accounts for the growing interest in lifelong learning? Part of the reason, surely, is the pervasive sense that technology is forcing employees in many companies to make more frequent changes in their knowledge and skills in order to remain effective. In addition, as lifetime employment in the same institution has become increasingly rare, young people today must expect to change jobs and learn new skills more frequently than their parents and grandparents did. Outside the workplace, technological change requires consumers to learn to use a succession of new and complicated products such as computers, smartphones, and the like. Understanding income tax requirements, choosing the most appropriate health-care plan, and many other familiar adult tasks also seem to have become more complex, forcing users to exert greater intellectual effort to respond effectively. Finally, the average life expectancy has increased dramatically over the past century, so that young people today must anticipate many additional years in which they can enliven their retirement by exploring new subjects and pursuing new intellectual interests.

A few investigators have studied the continuing desire to learn, or what such scholars call the "need for cognition" (NFC). They generally agree that NFC is a disposition that is capable of being nurtured and enhanced.[14] It is connected to one of the "Big Five" personality traits, "openness" to new experiences and ideas, which in turn is partly genetic but partly capable of change during early adulthood. According to some researchers, NFC is a quality of mind that can be developed in college students regardless of characteristics such as their parents' level of education or their high school grade point average.[15]

Although educators often talk about kindling a desire for lifelong learning, there is little settled knowledge of how to do so. Students seem to acquire an appetite of this kind simply by going to college. According to the latest massive volume reviewing a decade of research about the effects of undergraduate education: "College attendance appear[s] not only to increase the capacity for life-long learning but it also crystallize[s] the predisposition to engage in life-long learning and intellectual development with a greater inclination to seek out learning opportunities."[16] This conclusion is supported by findings that college graduates are much more likely than adults with only a high school education to attend cultural events, borrow books from public libraries, and enroll in massive open online courses (MOOCs) on a variety of challenging subjects.

Few studies contain reliable evidence of specific policies and practices in colleges that help to develop a continuing need for cognition. As two authors recently observed, "The need for cognition has been traditionally studied as a stable enduring dispositional characteristic and as such, has been treated as an explanatory variable rather than as an outcome itself."[17] The bits and scraps of empirical evidence that do exist offer only general hints. One scholar has found that differences in residential living arrangements in college account for a small but significant percentage of the variation among undergraduates in their capacity for lifelong learning.[18] Other authors point to the influence of first-year seminars and positive interactions among students of different races and backgrounds.[19] According to two other researchers, "certain clusters of activities and environmental factors influence the disposition for lifelong learning, including students' overall satisfaction with college, the amount of effort they devote to classroom activities, the amount of effort they devote to science and technology, and an institutional environment that values critical, evaluative, and analytical performance."[20]

Although there is much yet to be discovered about nurturing the desire to continue learning, common sense suggests a number of ways in which existing courses can help to achieve this result. Certain competencies taught in college can open intellectual doors that enable students to explore entire fields of knowledge in later life. For example, gaining a basic grasp of statistics and calculus enables students to continue reading scholarly works about important subjects such as economics, political science, and sociology. Other skills that can be acquired in college through courses in the humanities, such as the ability to read, see, and listen with greater perceptiveness and understanding, may increase the motivation to continue learning by heightening the satisfaction gained from exploring works of literature, art, and music. Success during college in mastering difficult skills and bodies of knowledge can increase students' confidence in their ability to pursue new and challenging subjects after they graduate. Acquiring habits of thinking, such as metacognition (the ability to analyze one's own thought processes), can facilitate subsequent efforts to tackle a wide variety of complicated subjects.

These examples suggest that increasing the motivation to learn has little to do with creating special courses for lifelong learning and much more to do with teaching existing classes in ways that give students a greater appreciation of the satisfaction gained from continuing to pursue new subjects and master new skills. An inspiring teacher who lectures to a passive student audience can awaken latent interest in a new subject. More often, however, dry lectures delivered by highly specialized professors fail to accomplish this result. Active teaching that makes material interesting, offers opportunities to master new skills that facilitate future learning, and demonstrates the link between these capabilities and issues that matter to students is more likely to awaken a continuing desire to keep on learning.

PERSEVERANCE AND RESILIENCE (AND GRIT?)

The film *The Sound of Music* has one memorable scene in which a young nun asks her abbess whether she should remain in the convent or leave it to pursue her dream of marrying the handsome Count von Trapp with his seven attractive children. The abbess responds quite unexpectedly by bursting into song with the now-familiar words: "Climb every mountain, ford every stream, follow every rainbow, 'till you find your dream." This refrain echoes a widespread belief in the

United States that we can all achieve success in life with enough pluck, persistence, and good old-fashioned hard work.

Psychologists, especially education psychologists, refer to persistence in pursuit of one's longer-term goals as "perseverance," and the capacity to overcome obstacles, recover from setbacks, and keep on trying as "resilience."* These qualities have attracted much attention from colleges in recent years because of concern over the growing mental health conditions of undergraduates and the toll that these problems can take on academic performance and graduation rates. By 2010, the percentages of college students suffering from severe stress, anxiety, and depression had reached levels above any previously recorded. Since then, the incidence of these afflictions has risen even more. According to the 2017 report from the American College Health Association, during the preceding twelve months the share of students receiving a diagnosis and/or treatment by a health professional reached 17 percent for anxiety, 21 percent for depression, and 13.5 percent for both anxiety and depression.[21] Some observers report rates as high as one-third or even one-half of students experiencing afflictions of this kind during college.[22] Such emotional fragility does not bode well for coping with stresses and difficulties in later life and indicates a need to help students acquire ways to overcome adversity and persevere in trying to achieve their goals.

Students try to cope with stress and anxiety in different ways—with prayer or meditation, by seeking help from support groups such as family or friends, or by avoidance tactics such as resorting to alcohol, marijuana, or video games. Self-help measures are sometimes helpful, but they can also be ineffective or downright harmful. In that event, colleges can provide much needed assistance.

Since most college officials are anxious to keep students from dropping out and policymakers worry about the sluggish growth of graduation rates, educators have every reason to seek ways of enabling undergraduates to deal with the psychological pressures that can produce distress and cause them to perform poorly in their classes and

* Some observers have popularized another term, "grit," to describe perseverance combined with "consistency of effort"—the ability to maintain one's objectives over substantial periods of time. Several researchers have found, however, that adding consistency of effort does not increase the ability to achieve goals beyond what is accomplished by perseverance alone.

abandon college prematurely. Many colleges are already teaching students how to improve their study skills by setting goals and time schedules for achieving them, avoiding distractions that interfere with preparing for class, such as social media, and adopting specific methods of study that have been shown to assist learning. Interventions of this kind are often useful, but the lessons they teach have more to do with helping students avoid behaviors that interfere with learning than with developing the resilience and perseverance that will serve them well in coping with the inevitable pressures and difficulties they will face after they graduate.

Other measures seek to help undergraduates acquire greater confidence in their ability to succeed. Researchers have found that simply persuading students that their mental capabilities are not immutable but can be improved through persistent effort can improve academic performance, at least slightly.[23] Instructors have tried several ways to overcome the "stereotype threats" that can lead women and minorities to underperform on tests or tasks that they think may confirm their fear that members of their sex or race are inferior intellectually.[24]

During the past twenty-five years, mental health practitioners and psychologists have experimented with a variety of different methods to help individuals cope with situations or events that cause them acute anxiety and mental distress. One of the most common interventions is cognitive reappraisal—"modifying one's appraisal of a situation in order to alter its emotional impact."[25] By reflecting on an experience that is causing them distress, students can often recognize that they are overreacting or misinterpreting events and learn to discard irrational worries by reinterpreting the experience in a more positive light.[26]

Many studies have been conducted to test the effectiveness of cognitive reappraisal, and most have found that it does yield positive results of at least small or moderate size.[27] However, the quality of this research is often weak. The number of subjects is frequently small, and the evidence of effectiveness may consist entirely of self-reports of questionable reliability. All too often, the results of the intervention are not well described, and efforts are seldom made to conduct follow-up studies to determine how long the positive effects endure.[28]

Critics have expressed greater doubts about helping students deal with adversity and increase perseverance than about attempts to develop other soft skills.[29] According to one recent study, many people who attempt cognitive reappraisal find that it does no good and may even make their situation worse, either because they are not sufficiently skillful in applying the techniques or because the type of problem they are trying to reappraise does not lend itself to this method.[30] Other critics observe that some people are trying to cope with genuinely distressing problems that should not be "reappraised" and brushed aside. As one investigator has pointed out, "Reappraisal can also be maladaptive when it is used in ways that lead to heightened risk taking and decreased sensitivity to potential losses."[31]

While few educators worry much about attempts to make young people *too* conscientious, *too* creative, or *too* adept at relating to other people or collaborating effectively in teams, one can easily think of situations in which students can become too perseverant.* For example, some students may simply be unable to achieve the goals they set for themselves. In real life, few aspiring novelists are talented enough to succeed, and most graduates of architecture programs never have an opportunity to design a building of their own. Almost half of all first-string Division IA football players appear to believe that they will have successful careers in the National Football League; even though experience shows that only a tiny fraction of these athletes will ever play so much as a single professional game, after having neglected their education at college in their single-minded pursuit of success on the field. For all these students, encouraging "grit" and telling them to "never give up" may simply bring greater frustration and disappointment.

---

*This is not to say that it is impossible to be too conscientious or too creative. For example, while attending an inauguration ceremony at MIT, I was struck by the fact that the new president devoted most of his speech to urging students to take full advantage of the social and cultural opportunities at MIT and the surrounding metropolis. When I expressed my surprise at his remarks over lunch, he replied: "You see, here at MIT, one major problem with our students is that they try to take *too many* courses." In a study of the influence of extracurricular activities on the academic success of Harvard undergraduates, we discovered that although some students who performed below their expected level spent too much time on extracurriculars, an even larger number of underperformers were students who engaged in no extracurricular activities and seemed to devote almost all their waking hours to their studies.

According to a recent report issued by the US Department of Education: "Persevering to accomplish goals that are extrinsically motivated, unimportant to the student, or in some way inappropriate for the student can induce stress, anxiety, and distraction, and have detrimental impacts on a student's long-term retention, conceptual learning, and psychological well-being."[32] As the authors of the report point out, however, "little research has examined this to date."[33]

In some cases, of course, colleges can be reasonably sure that their efforts to help undergraduates persevere will be beneficial. For example, officials in selective colleges can be quite confident that the students they have admitted are capable of graduating and that they will benefit from help in overcoming initial apprehensions and insecurities that could cause them to become discouraged and drop out. Interventions to help these undergraduates adjust to college by such measures as making first-generation students feel welcome or giving advice about study skills to freshmen who are struggling in class seem clearly beneficial. According to one experienced team of educators:

> When students feel a sense of belonging in an academic community, believe that effort will increase ability and competence, believe that success is possible and within their control, and see work as interesting or relevant to their lives, students are much more likely to persist at academic tasks and to exhibit the kinds of academic behaviors that lead to school success. Conversely, when students feel as though they do not belong, are not smart enough, will not be able to succeed, or cannot find relevance to the work at hand, they are much more likely to give up and withdraw from academic work and demonstrate poor academic behaviors.[34]

With other students, however, efforts to change their attitudes so that they habitually interpret adverse events in a positive fashion or come to believe that hard work and perseverance will invariably bring success could eventually backfire and cause even greater disappointment and distress. Thus, the challenge for instructors who try to increase resilience and perseverance is not merely knowing enough about how to teach these qualities, but knowing enough to avoid doing students harm.

THE BOTTOM LINE

The skills discussed in this chapter and chapter 6 are important enough to undergraduates in their careers and personal lives to deserve a place among the goals of a college education. Each of these skills appears to be changeable enough to be nurtured and improved. Each can be of value to graduates both in the workplace and outside it. The question for educators, then, is not whether these capabilities are appropriate subjects for colleges to teach, but whether enough is yet known about how to teach them to warrant their inclusion among the goals of a college education.*

Efforts to teach these skills and qualities of mind have thus far had mixed results. Most colleges seem to have made at least modest progress in helping undergraduates learn to interact successfully with diverse groups of people. With more experience, instructors should gradually do even better. Colleges appear to succeed in fostering a disposition among their students to continue learning after they graduate, although research has not yet fully explained how this quality can be developed. Teachers have also begun to make promising efforts to foster teamwork and interpersonal skills by having groups of students work collaboratively to solve problems, and further progress seems well within reach as instructors become more practiced in these methods. On the other hand, although creativity is undoubtedly a valuable quality of mind, colleges are just beginning to experiment with ways to help individual students develop their creative imagination, and the prospects for improvement remain uncertain. Finally, while some success has been achieved in increasing perseverance and resilience, the results are still

---

*One way by which some selective colleges try to overcome the problems associated with teaching soft skills is to require applicants for admission to submit the results of tests of such skills along with their SAT and ACT scores. However, there are reasons why this course of action is inadvisable. For one thing, since many of the existing tests of soft skills take the form of questions asking students about their capabilities, applicants may be able to inflate their scores by giving the desired answers. Even if this hurdle is overcome, using the admissions process to improve the soft skills of the entering class does not solve the underlying problem but simply shifts it from selective institutions to other colleges.

quite modest; here the need is not merely to discover how to nurture these capabilities but to know when it would be wise not to try.

The challenge of infusing the whole of undergraduate education with the teaching of soft skills is further inhibited by a difficulty similar to the problem encountered in improving critical thinking and the skills of collaborating with others. Some of these capabilities may not be best developed by offering special classes. Instead, colleges may accomplish more by introducing appropriate methods of instruction into existing courses. To do that, however, colleges will have to persuade a lot of faculty members to alter their teaching significantly. Accomplishing this task is likely to be difficult.

Problems such as those just described suggest that success in teaching soft skills will not come quickly. Although some significant improvements have already been made, much remains to be discovered through a patient process of research and experimentation. Future progress will depend in no small measure on the importance that universities and their patrons choose to place upon this task.

CHAPTER EIGHT

Unconventional Methods of Teaching

Two new ways of training the mind—meditation and positive psychology—have recently gained a following both in colleges and universities and with the general public. Unlike more traditional forms of teaching and learning, these methods are not primarily intended to convey useful information or to teach students workplace skills. Rather, they are practices designed to change the way people perceive the world and their relationship to it. By doing so, according to proponents, these techniques can help colleges achieve a surprising number of the goals discussed in previous chapters.

MEDITATION

Meditation had already been practiced for centuries by Buddhist monks before it began to reach the American public during the 1950s. In this country, however, the practice has been kept largely free of any religious purpose or content. Its use has steadily increased over the years, fueled by the desire of countless individuals to improve their powers of concentration and ease the pressures of modern life.[1] A nationwide survey in 2007 counted over 20 million Americans practicing meditation on a weekly basis, and the figure is probably considerably higher today. According to one national survey, one out of every six undergraduates claims to meditate several times per week.[2]

Some companies are now recommending such exercises for their executives. Hospitals are experimenting with meditation to lower blood pressure and treat depression. In England, up to 370 schools are introducing meditation in an effort to improve students' mental health by teaching them to regulate their emotions. Sports teams such as the Seattle Seahawks and the New York Knicks have utilized such exercises in the hope of boosting the performance of their players. One of the in-flight entertainments offered by Air France is a televised lecture on meditation delivered in several languages. Even the US Army has experimented with practices of this kind to help soldiers cope with the emotional strain of combat. The rapid spread of the "meditation movement" has been sufficiently remarkable to merit a *Time* magazine cover story on the subject.

Although there are different types of meditation, what most have in common are breathing exercises to develop an ability to concentrate, often referred to as "mindfulness"—becoming aware, without judgment, of one's thoughts, feelings, and sensations as they come and go in any given situation or moment.[3] To achieve this state of mind, students of meditation are usually asked to practice an hour each day for at least eight weeks, although accomplished practitioners believe that some beneficial effects of meditation require several years of regular practice.[4]

Drawing upon the many hundreds of separate studies that have now been published on the effects of meditation, researchers point to a wide assortment of results that could be helpful to undergraduates. Among the most frequently studied effects is the alleviation of stress, anxiety, and depression, conditions that have reached epidemic proportions among college students.[5] Some investigators have found that meditation can help people cope with these afflictions by actually changing the structure of the brain to shrink the amygdala—the part of the brain responsible for fear and anxiety in the face of danger—while strengthening the prefrontal cortex, which is the source of more deliberate, thoughtful responses to threatening stimuli.[6] Meditation can thus increase resilience by inhibiting negative reactions to stressful or troubling events and encouraging more constructive responses.

In place of stress and anxiety, meditation produces a feeling of equanimity that can benefit undergraduates in a number of ways. According to the authors of one large-scale longitudinal study, equanimity is associated with higher grade point averages, greater advances in critical thinking, and increased appreciation of college.[7] Apparently, breathing exercises also improve the power of concentration in listening, reading, and observing while encouraging metacognition, the ability to reflect on one's own thought processes. Thus, instructors who introduce meditation into their teaching argue that practice in cultivating mindfulness and concentration does not interfere with more traditional ways of learning but enhances these efforts.

Other research findings are even more intriguing. For example, some investigators have reported that meditation can increase creativity by opening the mind to new perspectives, new information, and new ways of thinking about familiar subjects.[8] Researchers also assert that meditation makes individuals more alert to the sufferings of others and thereby encourages acts of kindness and other forms of helping activity.[9] Investigators have even claimed that meditation can improve interpersonal relations and ethical behavior by increasing awareness of the effects of one's actions on the feelings of others.[10]

Taken together, these findings suggest that the practice of meditation could help students develop a remarkable number of the skills and qualities valued by employers and educators alike. One might therefore have anticipated a determined effort on the part of academic leaders to encourage their faculties to introduce meditation into a wide variety of courses and programs. Instead, most colleges have responded passively by simply allowing instructors who wish to use meditation in their classes to do so. By now, hundreds of professors have introduced meditation exercises, not only in humanities courses but in the sciences as well, and not merely in colleges but in schools of law, business, and medicine. Supporters have created a national Center for Contemplative Mind in Society, which has provided over 150 fellowships for faculty members wishing to employ meditation exercises in their teaching. In a few universities, enterprising faculty members have persuaded a dean or provost to authorize a new center on mindfulness. For example, Stanford's Center for Compassion and Altruism Research and Education offers an eight-week course on compassion cultivation training using meditation methods. Many campus health services have incorporated meditation into their repertoire of treatments for the flood of students suffering from anxiety, stress, and depression.

However helpful these initiatives have been, they have reached only a tiny fraction of faculty members in the country and have hardly achieved the level of institutional effort that could help colleges everywhere meet the growing array of demands on them from the outside world. What accounts for this limited response? One answer, surely, is that there is no powerful constituency demanding the use of meditation in the curriculum or extra-curriculum. Another contributing factor is the reluctance of most faculty members to undergo the extensive training needed to introduce meditation methods into their classes. The most persuasive reason for this cautious response, however, is that the research supporting the practice of meditation, though interesting, is not yet compelling enough to warrant a widespread commitment on the part of colleges and universities to expand its use.[11]

Several researchers have found that the positive effects of meditation, while varied in nature, are relatively small. For example, a meta-analysis of the many tests on the impact of mindfulness exercises on persons suffering from depression found that the results were generally positive, but no more so than the beneficial effects of other commonly used treatments, such as talk therapy, cognitive reappraisal, or even regular exercise.[12] One recent experiment has even found that the positive effects of meditation in relieving stress and improving concentration are frequently offset by a decline in motivation to complete required tasks.[13] These findings do not rule out the possibility that some students may gain a lot from meditation, although there is little careful research to help identify who these students are.

The quality of meditation research to date has also been criticized for being insufficiently rigorous to inspire great confidence in the results. Many studies use too few subjects to yield reliable findings, and the type of meditation exercises employed is frequently unclear. The amount and nature of previous meditation training by the students involved in the study and how conscientiously they performed the necessary exercises are often either not described or derived from self-reports of uncertain reliability. The duration of the positive effects is typically brief or not specified. Because of deficiencies of this kind, one meta-analysis by investigators who examined more than sixteen hundred citations to meditation studies could find only forty-seven trials that satisfied their requirements for reliability.[14] According to critics, the quality of the research has improved very little in recent years.[15]

It is only fair to add that it is quite hard and often very expensive to perform rigorous experiments on meditation. Truly double-blind, random assignment trials are not feasible, since there is no way to keep the members of the control group from knowing that they are not receiving the treatment. Longitudinal studies over long periods of time tend to be prohibitively expensive. Thus, according to Richard Davidson, a highly respected researcher of meditation practices who discovered how compassion meditation affects the activity of the brain: "It is important for both the research community and the policy-makers to understand that although there is much excitement about this area, there are still very few methodologically rigorous studies that demonstrate the efficacy of mindfulness-based interventions in either the treatment of specific diseases or in the promotion of well-being."[16] Given our present state of knowledge, then, meditation remains an intriguing but still insufficiently proven method for helping to meet the new demands on undergraduate education.

POSITIVE PSYCHOLOGY

The field of study known as positive psychology was not formally introduced in the United States until the year 2000, although a number of its insights had already appeared in the writings of thinkers dating back as far as Aristotle. In essence, what this body of thought stresses is the importance of identifying and building upon people's strengths instead of focusing primarily on their weaknesses and pathologies. Although positive psychologists have written about a variety of subjects—from methods for increasing resilience and avoiding depression to the almost mystical feeling of becoming totally absorbed in one's work (or "flow," to use the author's term)—it is the use of positive psychology to achieve happiness that will be examined here. College courses that use this method typically differ from the courses on happiness described in chapter 5. They do not merely discuss the results of research concerning the effects of various experiences and behaviors on feelings of well-being but prescribe specific exercises for students to use in order to *become* happier.[17]

Proponents of this new school of thought recommend that individuals who wish to improve their well-being begin by identifying their "signature strengths" from a lengthy list of positive attributes, such as integrity, curiosity, judgment, gratitude, and teamwork. Having done so, they can perform regular exercises to increase their strengths by finding new ways to use them—for example, by seeking additional opportunities to assist others, or to express gratitude to persons who have been of help to them in the past, or simply by writing down good things that happen each day. Such exercises can allegedly help to bring about more positive attitudes toward life. For example, according to Professor Sonja Lyubomirsky, a well-known investigator and proponent of positive psychology, research suggests that "working on how to become happier . . . will not only make a person feel better but will also boost his or her energy, creativity, and immune system, foster better relationships, fuel higher productivity at work, and even lead to a longer life."[18]

On closer reading, some of the recommended exercises are more complicated than they might initially appear to be. For example, in Professor Lyubomirsky's popular book *The How of Happiness*, she encourages readers to practice expressions of gratitude and acts of kindness toward others, but cautions that using these methods too often can dissipate their effects on well-being.[19] Instead, it is better to vary the nature of these acts and to choose a particular day or two in the week to practice them rather than do them every day. Self-reflection is helpful, but excessive use can lead to overthinking problems, which in turn can result in negative thoughts and loss of happiness.[20] Overall, she reminds her readers, "it takes a great deal of effort and determination to become happier."[21]

From this brief description, skeptical readers might conclude that positive psychology is just another example of so-called positive thinking, in the tradition of Norman Vincent Peale. Yet positive psychology differs from books such as Peale's in several respects. First, the theory and practice of positive psychology have been developed through much experimentation by reputable researchers such as Martin Seligman, a professor at the University of Pennsylvania, cofounder of positive psychology, and past president of the American Psychological Association. Seligman has repeatedly emphasized the need to build the principles of positive psychology on a foundation of solid research. The suggested exercises for developing signature strengths have been tested by researchers to document their effects on well-being. The results have satisfied proponents that the six basic virtues and twenty-four strengths they have identified and the practices they describe for strengthening them do not merely reflect wishful thinking but constitute a scientifically tested method of achieving authentic happiness that can overcome common afflictions such as depression, anxiety, and stress and provide satisfaction through helping others and abiding by high ethical standards.

Professor Seligman further differentiates his theory from superficial "feel good" prescriptions by stressing that mere hedonism, or the pursuit of pleasure, brings only an illusory happiness and that authentic well-being must be guided by proven virtues of universal validity, such as truthfulness, promise-keeping, and respect for the rights of others. In keeping with his commitment to building a science rather than merely asserting beliefs, he has undertaken extensive research to show that the virtues he emphasizes are not simply matters of faith or personal opinion but embody principles of behavior that have proven to be essential in all major religions and societies.[22] In this way, he argues, his research provides an "escape from the value-laden, blame-accruing, religiously inspired, class oppressing notion of character" that has been built upon "social convention, peculiar to the time and place of the beholder." Instead, he claims to offer a vision of virtuous behavior derived from scientific observation.[23]

Seligman and like-minded scholars are not so naive as to promise unlimited well-being to anyone who adopts the exercises they suggest. They recognize that the degree of happiness and satisfaction with life that one can achieve is influenced partly by genetic factors, which no exercises can overcome, and by life circumstances that are largely beyond one's power to control, such as poverty or illness. Still, they insist—and many scholars would agree—that a substantial part of an individual's perceived well-being can be changed through deliberate, persistent effort.[24]

The teachings of positive psychology have attracted a lot of interest during the years since this school of thought was formally announced to the world. The National Institutes of Health have awarded large amounts of money for research on the subject. The US Army has given a huge grant to launch an effort to train soldiers in positive psychology in the hope of mitigating the effects of combat, such as post-traumatic stress disorder. Books explaining the methods of positive psychology, such as *The How of Happiness*, have been translated into many languages and sold many thousands of copies. Schools in Britain and Australia have introduced programs of positive psychology into their classrooms.

Like meditation, positive psychology has attracted enthusiastic supporters in a number of colleges. Advocates for this approach, like those who favor meditation, have urged the use of Professor Seligman's theories in pursuing several of the college goals discussed in earlier chapters, including civic education, improved people skills, multicultural competence, effective collaboration, resilience, and the choice of a purposeful, meaningful, and satisfying life. If positive psychology is as successful as its proponents claim, it could be an exceptionally versatile tool for increasing the value of undergraduate education.

It is hard to argue with some of the uses of positive psychology. For example, few would take issue with the suggestion that college teachers and advisers should take care to recognize and support the strong qualities of student work as well as calling attention to its shortcomings. Advocates, however, see a much larger role for positive psychology. In addition to its use in the classroom, supporters look upon this method as a way of improving remedial education, mental health services, student advising, and even athletic programs by developing students' strengths instead of emphasizing ways to overcome their weaknesses.[25]

The University of New Mexico exemplifies the ambitious use of positive psychology in the curriculum.[26] At least three courses offered by the Psychology Department are based on this approach. The first of these offers a basic introduction to positive psychology to help students learn how to live a successful and satisfying life. In addition, undergraduates who want to go further in exploring and applying positive psychology can take a seminar for this purpose. Finally, a course for first-year, first-generation students teaches the principles and practices of positive psychology to help them succeed in college, using upperclassmen from the advanced seminar to mentor individual members of the class.

Not everyone is enthusiastic about positive psychology, and critics have raised a number of objections to its teachings. Some of the carping seems insubstantial, reflecting the scorn that scholars often heap on colleagues who write books for the general public that sell large numbers of copies. For example, Alistair Miller dismisses the writings of Seligman and like-minded professors by asserting that "the model of mental health depicted by positive psychology turns out to be little more than a caricature of an extravert—a bland, shallow, goal-driven careerist."[27] Such characterizations seem too facile and give too little credit to the research and analysis that underpin the theory.

Another common complaint from left-leaning critics is that by concentrating on authentic happiness and the steps one can take to achieve it, positive psychologists divert attention from the privations and injustices of the world that produce a great deal of "authentic suffering." Thus, Micki McGee observes that "the flourishing of positive psychology is an example of how neoliberalism helps maintain the political and social status quo in part by emphasizing individualistic efforts rather than communitarian or political ones."[28] This criticism also seems extreme, since one could make the same complaint about the work of cookbook authors, fitness coaches, music teachers, and countless others. What McGee overlooks is that learning to enjoy life and joining the fight against injustice in society are not incompatible aims. Pursuing one goal does not necessarily detract from the other. Not surprisingly, prominent spokespersons for happiness studies and positive psychology come from both sides of the political spectrum, while the happiest countries of the world tend to be northern European nations with extensive social welfare programs.

Another criticism sometimes made about positive psychology is that its precepts are much more feasible for individuals with comfortable incomes than for those mired in poverty, handicapped by discrimination, and trapped in high-crime neighborhoods and low-paid menial jobs. To people in such dire circumstances, upbeat statements such as "positivity can change your life" or pronouncements that only 10 percent of happiness is determined by one's life circumstances can hardly seem persuasive. Even so, this objection seems too sweeping. Books that offer help to substantial segments of the population are not worthless merely because they may not work for everyone.

A more legitimate criticism of positive psychology is that its emphasis on thinking positively can overlook the frequent usefulness of negative thoughts. Feelings of guilt and self-doubt may lead to worthwhile changes of behavior. Pessimism is sometimes warranted, and looking too hard for silver linings may cause one to persevere in an unproductive or even harmful course of action. Like perseverance, therefore, one can have too much "positivity" as well as too little. For example, some positive psychologists appear to believe in the value of illusions, such as overlooking the faults of a spouse in order to make one's marriage seem better than it actually is. Yet much needless suffering has often ensued for those who realized too late that the problems in their relationship were too serious to be ignored or papered over.[29]

There is also something disingenuous about expressing gratitude or performing acts of kindness not out of actual concern for other people but to make oneself feel happier. It may be true that one can act with both motives in mind, but helping others to increase one's own happiness makes generous actions seem less authentic.

Finally, just as with meditation, questions have been raised about the body of research on which the field of positive psychology rests.[30] One criticism is that the favorable effects confirmed by the experiments conducted thus far tend to be quite small.[31] For example, the multimillion-dollar program conducted for the US Army under Professor Seligman's supervision found that among soldiers receiving the training, only 1.6 percent did less "catastrophizing" (worrying that disasters will occur) than those who received no training; only 1.3 percent were better at developing "coping skills," only 1.36 percent were more "emotionally fit," and only 1.1 percent became more adaptable to changing circumstances.[32] These results may have been uniformly positive, but the benefits achieved seem more modest than some of the writings by positive psychologists might lead one to believe.

In the past decade, a rapidly growing number of studies have tested the effects of interventions that seek to develop subjects' strengths in order to increase their happiness. The results have generally been encouraging, but they leave many questions unanswered. There is strong evidence for some findings, such as the proposition that increasing the propensity to behave in positive ways, such as being generous, can increase feelings of well-being. But some psychologists have concluded that more evidence is needed to confirm the effectiveness of other acts such as listing what one is grateful for or thanking people for past acts of kindness.[33]

Some studies also rely on self-reports of questionable validity, while others are only correlational and do not prove causation. Further research is likewise required to determine whether and why some interventions work for some people but not everyone, or in some situations but not others. Unsettled questions such as these raise doubts about the sufficiency of the evidence cited in popular books by psychology professors who claim that, "if you crave more in your life, this book is for you," or who offer a "list of fundamental ingredients that make up the delicious dish of happiness."[34]

Many books of this kind can seem superficial. As Nobelist Daniel Kahneman has observed, "The word happiness does not have a simple meaning and should not be used as if it does."[35] Moreover, in writing books for the general public on how to achieve happiness or incorporating such teachings into courses used in schools and universities, proponents may convey an impression that one can learn to live a flourishing and happy life without having to grapple with the conflicting values, ethical dilemmas, and competing philosophies of life that have preoccupied thinkers for centuries.

Amid these critiques and differences of opinion, Professor Kristjan Kristjannson from the University of Iceland has offered a careful but balanced appraisal of the positive psychology movement and its relevance to undergraduate education:

> At this moment, I can say only that many people seem to be heading already in the direction of positive education but that not enough is yet known to ascertain if the good in it is new and the new in it is good. At the same time, only a pouty spoilsport would reject in advance the hope that something new and good will eventually come of it.[36]

DO MEDITATION AND POSITIVE PSYCHOLOGY BELONG IN THE CURRICULUM?

In light of the existing evidence about meditation and positive psychology, should courses that utilize these methods receive academic credit? Should colleges offer more teaching of this kind? At present, most campus leaders leave these questions to the academic departments involved. Since professors have traditionally enjoyed wide discretion in choosing which methods of instruction to use, those who wish to introduce meditation or happiness exercises into their courses are usually free to do so. Accrediting organizations and policymakers have generally refrained from interfering with these decisions.

Some critics, however, will question the appropriateness of awarding academic credit for courses that have students practice deep breathing meditation or engage in building their "signature strengths" by performing frequent acts of gratitude and kindness toward others. Such activities seem more akin to therapies administered by the campus health services or recommended by academic counseling offices than they do to credit-bearing courses.

On the other hand, if tenured faculty insist on lectures and seminar discussions as prerequisites for college credit, they risk looking like a guild trying to preserve the customary practices of their profession rather than educators dedicated to maintaining the quality of teaching. The purpose of undergraduate education is to provide students with the knowledge and skills to meet their legitimate needs as well as those of society and the economy. If instructors believe (as some researchers claim) that meditation and positive psychology can contribute to the development of valuable qualities of mind, why shouldn't courses that make heavy use of these methods receive college credit?

Past experience gives no clear answer to this question. The closest precedent is the recent decision of the Department of Education to begin authorizing payments to colleges that award credit not only for time spent in courses and classrooms but also for skills acquired in very different ways at work or during military service. If students can earn college credits by acquiring relevant skills without ever being enrolled in college or attending a class, why shouldn't they receive credit for working toward legitimate educational goals by receiving unconventional forms of instruction?

On closer scrutiny, however, the action of the Department of Education does not provide clear guidance for colleges in deciding whether to grant credit to courses making extensive use of teaching methods of uncertain efficacy. Students who seek course credit for skills learned at a previous job must at least demonstrate in some accepted way that they possess the skills in question. Can a college provide comparable assurance about the effects of meditation or positive psychology?

In considering how to treat the use of unconventional methods, one might begin by recalling the aims that colleges should seek to achieve and the values they need to reconcile. On the one hand, colleges should certainly welcome the discovery of new and better ways of helping students acquire valuable knowledge, skills, and qualities of mind. At the same time, they also need to protect students from spending time in courses and other learning activities that are of little or no educational use.

Applying these principles to the practice of meditation and positive psychology, colleges should not *require* undergraduates to take courses that make extensive use of these methods until more reliable evidence of their efficacy becomes available. Yet there is clearly enough promise in these methods to warrant a deliberate effort to experiment with their use and evaluate the results in hopes of finding new and more effective ways to teach. To avoid inhibiting innovation, therefore, faculties should permit, and even encourage, instructors to try these methods, provided that adequate steps are taken to protect unwary or unwilling undergraduates. Specifically, students should be put on notice at or before the beginning of such courses that instructors will be making extensive use of techniques whose educational value is not yet proven. Colleges should also take steps to ensure that instructors are properly trained or otherwise qualified to use these methods. Finally, campus authorities should endeavor to work with participating instructors to evaluate the experimental techniques in order to determine whether they improve on existing methods of instruction. If the innovations are successful enough, colleges can try to make technical assistance available and supply funding, where needed, to encourage their use.

Some members of the faculty may object to these guidelines on the grounds that they interfere too much with the traditional autonomy of professors to teach their material in whatever way they choose. Most faculties have at least a few professors who keep on giving courses year after year despite being known to be very poor teachers. Even so, they are allowed to continue because the risk of inadequate teaching is thought to be outweighed by the danger involved in having the administration pass judgment on the competence of instructors. Why should instructors who wish to experiment with promising methods of teaching be forced to meet more exacting tests?

In response, it is true that most colleges are extremely reluctant to interfere with the way individual instructors teach their classes. Yet this reluctance is hardly a precedent worth extending to the use of unconventional teaching methods. After all, students can at least make use of the ubiquitous course evaluations to avoid ineffective teachers. They are much less able to judge whether or not to enroll in classes that use experimental methods of unproven usefulness. If professors fear the possibility of arbitrary judgments by college administrators, procedures can easily be devised to have faculty representatives participate in reaching a decision.

Implicit in the approach recommended here is the suggestion that academic leaders take more initiative in working with their faculties to encourage and assess attempts to develop new and improved methods of teaching. Until now, most campus authorities have left the process of innovation to individual instructors who choose to try new methods of teaching and to researchers who happen to evaluate the new techniques. This laissez-faire approach has never been particularly efficient or expeditious. If universities make no effort to support educational research and evaluate the results, much time may elapse before investigators develop enough reliable evidence to establish the effectiveness of innovative methods.

The reluctance of colleges to take a more active part in promoting and evaluating innovative teaching is unfortunate in the best of times. It is especially regrettable at times like the present when new and challenging goals are being urged upon colleges that may require methods of instruction quite different from the traditional lecture and seminar. Corporations, government agencies, and other large organizations typically engage in much research and development to improve the quality of the goods and services they provide. Colleges, at least those in universities with extensive research capabilities, should do the same. Now more than ever, academic leaders and their faculties need to work together to improve the search for new and better ways to educate their students.

CHAPTER NINE

Prospects for Change

Imagine an America in which much larger numbers of college graduates could analyze problems successfully; adapt readily to changing conditions and new challenges; collaborate effectively with others in producing creative solutions to novel problems; meet their commitments conscientiously; and interact easily and harmoniously with others from different races, socioeconomic backgrounds, and cultures. Suppose further that larger percentages of college graduates voted regularly in elections, participated in cooperative efforts to improve their communities, and welcomed opportunities to join with others to address needs and solve problems, either local, national, or global, through public service, political activity, or membership in nonprofit citizen organizations. Imagine, lastly, that many more graduates left college with stronger ethical principles, greater empathy for the problems of others, and a clearer sense of the purpose and values to guide their lives.

Although this vision is optimistic, it is not mere fantasy. All of the behaviors just listed involved habits, skills, and qualities of mind that might be improved through effort guided by capable instruction. Neuroscientists and psychologists have even found that some of these qualities develop most during the years of early adulthood, when the majority of undergraduates go to college.

Colleges are already helping their students acquire a number of valuable capabilities. The most rigorous efforts to measure the average gains by college seniors over their four years as undergraduates have found that proficiency in critical thinking increases substantially. Most seniors also appear to graduate with considerably more competence than they had as freshmen in writing, moral reasoning, problem-solving, subject matter knowledge, reflective judgment, and, at least for many students, quantitative skills. Once out of college, they vote in far greater numbers and are much more active in their communities than adults of the same age with only a high school education. A majority of college seniors believe that they have acquired a greater capacity to get along with others and to interact successfully with different kinds of people. They also claim to have a clearer sense of the purpose and direction of their lives than they possessed when they entered as freshmen.

Although these improvements seem impressive, a variety of critics have challenged them. Many employers feel that most of the college-educated employees they hire are deficient in critical thinking, teamwork, oral and written communication, and other skills and behaviors that are needed for success in the workplace.[1] Commission after commission has called attention to the neglect of civic education, but with little observable response from the nation's colleges apart from providing more opportunities for community service. Commentators deplore the lack of attention paid by most colleges to developing the character of their students and helping them accept responsibility for choosing the values and direction for their lives. Moreover, even though researchers find that undergraduates improve in a number of important respects, most of the gains are quite modest in size, and well below the progress students *think* they have made.[2]

THE ASSOCIATION OF AMERICAN COLLEGES AND UNIVERSITIES PROGRAM

As pointed out in chapter 1, the AAC&U, which represents more than 1,400 member institutions drawn from all segments of higher education, has responded to these criticisms by mounting an unprecedented effort to review and reform undergraduate education. This project has produced an ambitious set of "essential learning outcomes" identified through a multiyear effort to solicit the opinions of students, faculty members, employers, and public officials. Detailed descriptions of what graduates ought to know and be able to do have been developed with the help of hundreds of academic leaders and faculty members. These outcomes include virtually all of the qualities of mind and behavior discussed in previous chapters of this book.

Why the AAC&U Report Should Be Taken Seriously

There is a lot to like about the AAC&U program and the way the association went about creating it. The extensive consultation with employers, public officials, and faculty make its recommendations the closest approximation we have to a consensus among the interested groups in our society on what college graduates should know and be able to do. The time and effort devoted to soliciting such a wide range of views represent a refreshing change from the customary practice of assembling a commission of notables who meet a few times and eventually issue a report largely written by an anonymous staff.

The AAC&U's elaborate consultations revealed an unanticipated amount of agreement among the several interested parties on the goals of undergraduate education. In hiring college graduates, corporate CEOs turned out to attach great importance to a number of capabilities that have long been central to a liberal education, such as critical thinking, written and oral communication, and ethical judgment. Employers highly valued several other qualities shared by the AAC&U and its member colleges, such as adaptability, lifelong learning, teamwork, and the ability to interact well with people of other races and cultural backgrounds. The goals adopted by the AAC&U, however, go beyond meeting workplace needs. They include such broader aims as preparing active and informed citizens and helping students develop the personal values they will need to live purposeful and meaningful lives—or, in the words of the AAC&U report, enabling students not just to know "how to get things done" but to recognize "what is most worth doing."

Another strength of the AAC&U's proposal is the fact that hundreds of academic leaders and faculty members helped to choose the goals and provide detailed descriptions for each of the skills and qualities of mind included in the association's essential learning outcomes. This extensive involvement lends credibility to the AAC&U's proposals and guarantees that its program can count on committed supporters in a wide variety of colleges.

Possible Objections

At the same time, not everyone will be enthusiastic about the AAC&U's proposals. Some critics will argue that the skills and qualities of mind identified by the association are excessively vocational and insufficiently rigorous to be appropriate subjects for a liberal education. Professors in research-oriented universities may complain that they are not trained to teach skills and capabilities such as teamwork or resilience or leadership and that asking them to learn how to do so will take too much time from their research.

On close scrutiny, neither of these arguments is persuasive. The objection that the recommended skills and behaviors are too vocational is clearly spurious. The vast majority of colleges already offer vocational majors in a host of fields ranging from arts administration to zookeeping. Moreover, most of the skills and behaviors recommended by the association are not merely useful for students' careers; qualities such as creativity, conscientiousness, and empathy will be of obvious value to graduates in their personal lives outside the workplace.

It is true that many professors have not been trained to help students develop several of the proposed qualities of mind, but the same could have also been said prior to the adoption of many new teaching programs that colleges have created over the years. Moreover, it would be most unwise to define the proper scope of undergraduate education by restricting it to the subjects and skills that existing faculty already know how to teach. No profession can insist on such a static and self-serving definition of its mission. Instead, the choice of what to include in a college curriculum should be determined primarily by the needs of students and those of society, provided that the desired skills and knowledge are teachable. If new needs arise and faculty members are unable or unwilling to provide the necessary instruction, they should not object to attempts by their college to find or train instructors capable of doing what is needed.

There is also little substance to the claim that the new material will be less rigorously taught than the more traditional subjects in a liberal arts education. Insufficient rigor is not a condition unique to the teaching of so-called noncognitive skills but a problem that can afflict every segment of the curriculum. Almost all of the capabilities and qualities discussed in this book can be taught with substantial home-work assignments, vigorous discussion, challenging questions to ponder, and strict grading. If individual faculty members wish to teach courses that make heavy use of unusual methods such as meditation or cognitive reappraisal, the classes can be offered on an experimental basis, with or without awarding academic credit.

There is likewise little substance to the claim that teaching new behaviors and qualities of mind will force professors to take too much time from their important research activities. In theory, academic leaders could create such a problem if they tried to order members of their faculty to spend a great many days and hours adapting their teaching to embrace new and complicated methods of instruction. As a practical matter, however, this problem is unlikely to arise. If the administration of a research university attempted to impose such demands, the faculty would surely protest and issue a vote of no confidence in the leadership. If academic leaders still persisted in their efforts, the better researchers would depart before long for greener pastures. Not surprisingly, therefore, few if any cases have arisen in which presidents or deans of research universities used such tactics. Instead, academic leaders have hired additional instructors to teach the new subjects.

Finally, critics may argue that the AAC&U proposal contains so many goals that colleges could end up doing a little about everything but nothing especially well. This criticism has some validity, and colleges need to bear it in mind as they think about pursuing additional aims. At this early stage, however, it is impossible to determine how much of the AAC&U agenda a college can adopt without overloading the circuits. Most colleges can meet some of the goals, such as strengthening civic education, by simply improving what they are already doing. Increasing students' collaborative skills can largely be accomplished in existing courses by including more group projects. Still other qualities, such as resilience, may be nurtured by members of the support staff, such as student affairs officers and health services personnel, without imposing burdens on the faculty. Some desired attributes will not impose an immediate burden because no one yet knows how to teach them. If a college is still unable to adopt all of the AAC&U's reforms, it can at least attend to as many as it can.

In the end, there is no escaping the responsibility of colleges and universities to do what they can to develop the competencies and qualities of mind and behavior that will help their students to live successful, responsible, and fulfilling lives. Colleges are the dominant institutions for teaching and nurturing young people during four critical years in which they are capable of growth not only in their intellects but in other qualities of personality and behavior that can help them succeed and flourish after they graduate. For most of these capabilities, there is no satisfactory alternative to college for providing the necessary instruction.

It is perhaps for this reason that in the absence of any organized effort by college faculties to teach these subjects, classes for such purposes have been cropping up. Some are taught by venturesome faculty members, but most are being given by members of the supporting staff, such as student affairs officers, career services personnel, and psychologists in the health services. These efforts are commendable but random and fragmented, and they often do not receive the assistance that many colleges give to innovative courses taught by members of the faculty. Since the teaching required is challenging and often experimental, it suffers from the lack of encouragement and quality control available for courses in the formal curriculum. This situation will continue so long as colleges fail to treat these experimental efforts as important steps toward improving their undergraduate teaching program.

Practical Difficulties

The AAC&U's reports, while comprehensive, overlook several more serious problems that are likely to arise when colleges attempt to implement its program. Although one report discusses how to avoid what it describes as "potholes" on the road to reform, the analysis deals almost entirely with the procedural mistakes that have often been made in the course of past efforts to make minor changes in the general education program; it does not recognize the more fundamental problems that are bound to arise in trying to implement the association's more ambitious proposals.[3]

A threshold difficulty is that no one yet knows how to achieve several of the "essential learning outcomes." Educators understand a lot about improving critical thinking, moral reasoning, oral communication, writing, and quantitative skills. They are also learning a good deal about teaching students to collaborate in teams and will doubtless learn more in time. But they know much less than they need to know about helping students to acquire some of the other skills and qualities of mind endorsed by the plan, such as creativity and resilience. They know even less about teaching students to act ethically and have yet to evaluate with care the various methods proposed for helping students discover a purpose and meaning for their lives. These gaps in existing knowledge will clearly require more experimentation and research before colleges are in a position to provide effective instruction.

The new material required to achieve many of the goals recommended by the AAC&U must also be fitted into a curriculum that is often already crowded with courses. The most likely way to find the necessary space will be to reduce the number of electives, which typically account for up to a full year's worth of courses. Such a step, however, may well encounter opposition from students who cherish the ample freedom they enjoy under existing curricula to pick and choose which courses to take.

More potent objections are likely to arise from within the faculty as specific plans are proposed for implementing the desired reforms. Most professors are not opposed in principle to the new goals sought by the AAC&U proposals. In fact, large majorities of the faculty either "agree" or "strongly agree" that colleges should help students prepare themselves for employment, acquire strong personal values, develop emotionally, and strengthen their moral character.[4] But agreement in principle is not the same as a willingness to take the concrete steps required to achieve these goals.

Several of the recommended skills and qualities of mind do not need entirely new courses. Instead, they call for different methods of teaching and the integration of new subject matter into existing courses. Political science professors may be urged to incorporate material about global problems or about current issues of democratic governance and the forces that impede its performance. Scientists may be asked to discuss the relevance of their subject to major contemporary problems such as climate change and to introduce more opportunities for group problem-solving in their classes. Humanists may be pressed to consider how their courses can be taught in ways that will help students become more creative, develop greater empathy for the needs of others, or consider larger questions about how to live their lives. Faculty in all departments may be strongly encouraged to abandon lecturing in favor of active forms of instruction that do more to foster deep learning, critical thinking, and problem-solving.

All of these pressures will chip away at the long-standing freedom of instructors to determine the content of their courses and their methods of teaching. Most professors regard their autonomy in the classroom as one of the most treasured aspects of academic life. They are not likely to give it up easily. Nor will they readily embrace new assessment methods that, however artfully constructed, will exert additional pressure on their traditional freedom to teach their classes in the manner they think best.

Finally, some faculty members may be concerned by the lack of attention in the AAC&U's program to the substantive knowledge that students will need to acquire in addition to the various skills and qualities of mind that are described in such painstaking detail. The essential learning outcomes merely refer briefly to a need for "knowledge of Human Cultures and the Physical and Natural World [through] study of the sciences and mathematics, social sciences, humanities, histories, languages, and the arts." Nowhere is there a detailed discussion of what students need to know and how this knowledge could help them to achieve the goals of their college education.

Perhaps the kinds of knowledge needed seemed too numerous and varied too much from one student to another to be easily summarized. Even so, the AAC&U might have provided some apt examples. For instance, in view of the declining student interest in the humanities, it would have been reassuring to include at least a brief discussion of the relevance of literature, history, philosophy, and related subjects to the achievement of goals such as becoming an engaged citizen, acquiring strong ethical principles and the empathy to act on them, developing personal values and lifelong interests, and understanding and respecting others of different races, cultures, sexual orientation, and socioeconomic background. The lack of such discussion is likely to trouble faculty members who rightly regard imparting knowledge as an important part of their role as educators.

The likely opposition of tenured faculty and students threatens to arouse an internal resistance to the AAC&U program that will set it apart from earlier periods of major reform in undergraduate education. In the decades following the Civil War, the classical curriculum gave way to discipline-based education, majors, and extensive student choice. In the late 1960s and early 1970s, colleges introduced ethnic and gender studies, abandoned most parietal rules, and accommodated a massive shift of students from liberal arts to vocational majors. In each of these transitions, students and faculties either welcomed the changes or did not feel that their essential freedoms were endangered. The AAC&U's ambitious program is unlikely to enjoy such a trouble-free reception.

THE OUTLOOK FOR REFORM

Given the points of contention detailed here, what are the prospects for adopting changes of the kind advocated by the AAC&U and affirmed by influential groups in society? Will the approval of powerful outside groups and the support of the many academic leaders and professors who helped develop the proposals be enough to achieve significant reform? Or will colleges react to objections from faculty members and students by making only token changes?

In 1956, the prominent sociologist David Riesman published a slim volume, *Constraint and Variety in American Education*, in which he likened reform in higher education to "a snake-like process with a turning and twisting head and an imperceptibly moving and elongated tail."[5] As he described it, changes usually began in the most selective, private institutions and the great public flagship universities and proceeded by emulation down the hierarchy of institutions, with the weakest segments being the last to adapt.

However accurate this account may have been when Riesman's book was published, it no longer describes the likely pattern for the kind of comprehensive improvement envisaged by the AAC&U. Instead of a series of changes starting from the top and moving to the bottom of the academic pyramid, different types of colleges are likely to respond to today's pressures for reform in different ways and in a much less orderly and predictable sequence.

Research Universities

The colleges of the great public and private research universities that initiated most of the reforms in Riesman's model continue to occupy the highest rungs on the ladder of prestige in American higher education. Their prominence, if anything, has been augmented in recent decades by the appearance of national rankings of the kind published annually by *US News & World Report*. These colleges regularly attract the best students, hire the most highly esteemed professors, and receive the most money from the federal government, private philanthropy, and alumni. They are consequently in the best position of any group of colleges to lead the search to discover effective ways of teaching students to master new skills and habits of mind. They have the most power to inspire emulation by other colleges and can most easily pay the cost of implementing ambitious reforms such as those proposed by the AAC&U.

The culture of these institutions and the nature of their priorities, however, threaten to create impediments to the AAC&U's reforms that could exceed the resistance in other kinds of academic institutions. Most members of prestigious faculties are more interested in research than in teaching undergraduates. They are normally hired, promoted, and paid primarily for the quality of their publications rather than their ability in the classroom. The reputation they acquire among their fellow scholars and beyond is based almost entirely on their published work. Their rewards from the outside world—whether from government grants and summer salaries, attractive job offers, opportunities to travel and consult, or success in winning prizes and other forms of recognition—come almost entirely from their research.

Despite much external criticism to the contrary, the prevailing incentives do not regularly cause professors to neglect their students. Most members of the faculty in research universities are conscientious teachers. When classes are in session, they devote far more of their time to their courses than they do to their research.[6] Professors who publish a lot receive student ratings that are just as high as those of their colleagues who publish little.[7] At the same time, however carefully they prepare for class and revise their courses to keep them up to date, they are likely to balk at making the kinds of changes that require sufficient time and effort to interfere significantly with their research. Because they know that the great majority of their students will go on to graduate and professional schools and receive further opportunities to acquire valuable skills, they may feel even less urgency to make fundamental changes.

The leaders of prominent research universities are also likely to be slow in launching efforts to implement fundamental reforms such as those championed by the AAC&U. Their faculties are more powerful than those of colleges lower in the academic hierarchy because they are harder to replace and chiefly responsible for their college's reputation and for the amount of outside funding it receives. Campus leaders may conclude that they will put the reputation of their university at risk and lose whatever political capital they possess if they push too hard to get their faculties to agree to teaching reforms that many professors oppose.

Presidents of leading universities will also see little tangible benefit from pressing for such reforms even if they personally favor the recommended changes. Their colleges are not likely to attract more students by doing so, and in any case, they already have far more qualified applicants than they can possibly admit. Reform will not improve their rating in *US News & World Report*, since the rankings have little to do with the quality of a college's curriculum or how much its students learn. The results from any progress made in introducing reforms will often be hard to measure, depriving leaders of the satisfaction they can derive from more tangible accomplishments.

These inhibitions do not block all efforts at educational reform. In response to mounting criticism about the quality of undergraduate education, interest in teaching has grown on many research university campuses. Academic leaders are doing more to encourage their faculty members to experiment by publicizing innovations in teaching and offering small grants and technical assistance to teachers who wish to try new methods of instruction. Many professors have embraced new uses of technology in their classes. In fact, there is probably more experimentation in teaching undergraduates today than there has been in decades.*

Initiatives of this kind can gradually improve the quality of instruction and increase the amount of innovation in pedagogy. But offering incentives to interest individual professors in changing how they teach is much easier than getting a large faculty composed of busy, independent-minded teachers and scholars to agree on a new curriculum, especially one like the plan proposed by the AAC&U, which would require substantial changes in the content and methods of instruction.

For all these reasons, great research universities are unlikely to play the role described in Professor Riesman's book by leading a nationwide effort to introduce a comprehensive reform of undergraduate education. They may have more individual professors than other colleges who discover innovative teaching methods to help students acquire the new skills and qualities of mind discussed in earlier chapters. But they are less likely to succeed in persuading their entire faculty to agree to the ambitious list of reforms required to implement the AAC&U program.

---

* The new initiatives launched by my own institution within the past ten years illustrate some of the efforts beginning to be made even by large universities; I summarize them here not because Harvard is exceptional but simply to suggest the kinds of activities that are under way in numerous colleges around the country. To build a useful database, Harvard has been gathering precollege facts for its students, extensive material about their undergraduate experience, and information about their subsequent careers and recollections of Harvard— all to gather insights about the strengths and weaknesses of existing programs and practices. In addition, more than one hundred grants have been given during the past five years to support innovations in teaching and learning; these projects range from improving feedback to students and creating new experiential programs to trying innovative ways of teaching teamwork and developing cases for use in problem-based courses. A variety of methods have been introduced to describe interesting innovations in teaching and disseminate this information within Harvard and to other universities. Graduate seminars are now being offered to teach PhD students how to design new courses. The History Department has experimented with a project to partner tech-savvy graduate students with professors interested in using technology in their classes, and the practice is now being expanded for use in other departments. In still another venture, 75 undergraduates have volunteered to work with instructors who are trying new methods of teaching and to offer feedback and suggestions for improvement. In 2017–2018, the Center for Teaching and Learning offered 22 seminars on teaching, provided workshops for more than 50 new faculty members, attracted 737 graduate students to programs on teaching, and worked with 324 faculty members, including more than 100 full professors. As one would expect, some of these initiatives have worked better than others. Together, however, they represent a large increase in the faculty's interest in improving teaching compared with the situation thirty years ago when I retired as Harvard's president or even fifteen years later when I returned as interim president.

Comprehensive Universities

The large regional and comprehensive universities enroll several million students. Most of these institutions are public. They tend to graduate few PhDs but award many professional master's degrees along with a multitude of BAs. They place less emphasis on research than the flagship state universities, while paying more attention to the needs of the regional employers that hire many of their graduates.

Some of these institutions have resisted the siren song of rankings and research and work harder than many more prominent universities at improving their teaching programs. Nevertheless, comprehensive universities are inhibited in several ways from initiating changes of the kind promoted by the AAC&U. Because they receive substantially less funding from their state and local governments than research universities and have far less success in raising money from the private sector, they often lack the resources to finance a comprehensive program of educational reform. Their leaders normally serve for shorter terms than their counterparts in research universities and may therefore hesitate to launch initiatives to improve undergraduate education that could take many years to implement. To save money, they rely more than research universities on part-time, non-tenure-track (NTT) instructors who, because they are often poorly paid, overworked, and hired year-to-year, are unlikely to participate in a major effort to overhaul the curriculum or adopt new methods of instruction.

Occasionally, comprehensive or regional public universities choose exceptional presidents who serve for long periods, care about teaching and learning, and accomplish great things. The example of Freeman Hrabowski at the University of Maryland–Baltimore County comes to mind. But these successes are quite rare, and even some exemplary leaders may choose to build on their achievements by moving up the ladder of conventional prestige and emphasizing research rather than attempt the kinds of comprehensive reform advocated by the AAC&U.

Community Colleges

Community colleges make up still another important segment of higher education, accounting for more than one-third of the entire undergraduate population. Their response to large-scale educational reform may resemble that of many regional and comprehensive universities, with whom they often cooperate to devise clearer paths for students who wish to transfer and complete their studies for a BA degree. Because they educate the least academically prepared students and dropout rates are high, community college leaders tend to direct much of their time and energy to balancing the budget and increasing the percentage of students who graduate.

Community colleges are also seriously hampered by the conditions under which they operate. They receive the least funding from all sources of any segment of higher education. To save money, they hire the largest percentage of part-time adjunct instructors, who typically lack the time or the motivation to engage in ambitious reform efforts. Moreover, according to an Aspen Institute survey of search firms with extensive experience in recruiting community college presidents, trustees rarely look for candidates who are interested in educational reform; instead, they favor leaders who can raise money, balance the budget, and avoid controversy.[8]

Once again, exceptions do exist, and some community colleges have resourceful leaders who accomplish a lot. Yet even these enterprising presidents are likely to devote most of their attention to increasing their graduation rate and launching new programs geared toward local employer needs. With only two full years of college to work with, accomplishing the full range of "essential learning outcomes" often seems impossible on these campuses. Goals such as building character and interesting students in global problems will usually have a lower priority, if indeed they are given any priority at all. The chronic lack of resources and the large number of adjunct instructors on short-term appointments will often make comprehensive curricular reform seem even further beyond the realm of possibility.

Independent Colleges

In the end, the most promising sector of nonprofit higher education for instituting a comprehensive reform of undergraduate education may be the several hundred small, private four-year colleges. Because these institutions are less likely to have strong ambitions to excel in research, their professors are more open to educational reforms that require a lot of time and effort to implement. Faculties at these colleges are much more cohesive, with many fewer adjunct instructors and other non-tenure-track faculty than the other institutions of higher education considered here. Their very justification for existing and attracting students in spite of their high tuitions rests on their claim to offer better teaching, more dedicated professors, and closer attention to the needs of individual students than most universities. Last but not least, their small size makes agreement on a curriculum far easier to achieve than it is in institutions with much larger, more heterogeneous faculties.

At the same time, small independent colleges have problems of their own that can inhibit ambitious reform. Money is often a constant preoccupation. Many of their presidents are consumed by the urgent necessity to find the resources and attract enough students to keep their doors open. In some small colleges, faculty resistance, inability to agree, or weak leadership can all undermine reform efforts. Still, the smaller size and greater cohesiveness of these institutions, coupled with their motivated faculties and leaders, seem more conducive to comprehensive changes in goals and methods of instruction than the conditions that prevail at other kinds of colleges.

Ironically, the very strengths that advantage small, independent colleges limit their power to serve as agents of change. Because of their small size, these institutions, although numbering in the hundreds, collectively educate less than 5 percent of the total undergraduate population. When they do succeed in improving the quality of their educational programs, they typically lack the visibility to allow them to receive much publicity or inspire much emulation. Thus, their impact on reform throughout the whole of higher education promises to be more limited than it would be if the same innovative success were achieved by prominent research universities.

In sum, the implementation of comprehensive educational reform today is unlikely to bear much resemblance to the serpentine movement described by David Riesman. There will be success stories, but they will be more widely scattered throughout the hierarchy of colleges than Riesman's model would predict, and less common among the most prestigious institutions. The boldest innovations by large research universities will probably either be the work of individual

professors or involve new ventures that do not ask a great deal of their
faculties, such as the initiatives in online education that the University
of Massachusetts and Purdue have introduced, or the massive expansion of undergraduate enrollments that has taken place at Arizona State
and the University of Central Florida. Faculties at leading universities
will be slow to make a collective commitment to the comprehensive
changes in teaching and curriculum envisioned by the AAC&U. If these
reforms ever spread widely through the whole of higher education, they
are likely to do so gradually and in a more piecemeal fashion than they
would under the Riesman model.

THE PROGRESS THUS FAR

The fact that attempts to adopt the entire AAC&U program could encounter strong headwinds does not mean that meaningful progress
cannot occur. Many colleges will find some useful items on the initiative's ample menu of reform, especially items that can be put in place
at no great expense or without substantially changing the way instructors teach their courses. Improvements of that kind have already been
introduced on many campuses during the decade or more since the
AAC&U proposal was first unveiled. The results are documented in a
survey published in 2016, which was sent to 1,001 AAC&U member
institutions by Hart Research Associates to ascertain the progress made
from 2008 to 2015 in implementing the AAC&U plan.[9]

With the help of prodding accreditors, the share of survey respond-
ers who claimed that their institution had adopted a set of learning
goals (though not necessarily those of the AAC&U) increased from
78 percent to 85 percent over the eight-year period.[10] The percentage
of colleges in which all departments had defined specific learning outcomes also rose, albeit slightly, from 65 to 67 percent.[11] While a growing share of institutions endorsed the essential learning outcomes recommended by the AAC&U, the increases tended to be quite small. The
percentages claiming to have adopted several of these goals did not
increase at all, and for a few of the outcomes, including civic engagement and competence in oral communication, the percentage of adopt-
ers actually declined slightly.[12]

The survey also found progress since 2008 in the general education programs of the surveyed institutions. The percentage of respondents claiming to have installed methods for assessing student achievement of essential learning outcomes rose from 49 percent to 68 percent; the percentage with course requirements linked to learning outcomes rose from 62 percent to 66 percent; and the share reporting the adoption of a coherent sequence of general education courses increased from 35 percent to 44 percent.[13] The effects of these reforms on student learning remain unclear.

Modest increases were also reported by the responding colleges in the percentages that made changes in their general education programs and were using specific subjects and practices recommended by the AAC&U:[14]

Educational Practice	Percent Using	
	2008	2015
Includes global culture courses	60	70
Includes first-year seminars	58	63
Includes diversity courses	56	60
Includes interdisciplinary courses	51	55
Includes service learning opportunities	38	46
Includes civic learning or engagement	38	42

Evidence provided in 2017 by the National Survey of Student Engagement also reveals some progress since 2013 in the use of several of the high-impact educational practices (HIPs) endorsed by the AAC&U, especially capstone projects by college seniors.[15] However, most of the institutions responding to the Hart survey reported that they required only three or fewer of the six high-impact practices recommended by the AAC&U.[16] Moreover, in contrast with the previous survey, NSSE data also show little or no progress in adopting several recommended practices, such as the use of active teaching methods (rather than lectures), student discussions with diverse peers, and interaction between students and faculty.[17]

Finally, in responding to another national survey conducted by the National Institute for Learning Outcomes Assessment in 2017, a substantial number of institutions reported adopting AAC&U recommendations in their regular evaluations of student learning. Twenty-eight percent claimed to be using the essential learning outcomes to define their educational goals, while 44 percent reported using the AAC&U's rubrics describing the stages through which students pass before reaching the desired outcomes.[18]

THE BOTTOM LINE

How, then, can we summarize the progress thus far toward making the kinds of improvements in instruction and curriculum recommended by the AAC&U? On the positive side, colleges are clearly paying more attention today than they have in many decades to improving teaching and the quality of undergraduate education. Almost all colleges have now defined their goals for what their students need to learn. That is an essential first step toward focusing faculty effort and ascertaining how much progress students are actually making. Large majorities of faculties nationwide also claim that they endorse ambitious goals for their students such as emotional development, building character, and fostering tolerance and understanding of other races and cultures. More colleges are encouraging their faculty members to attend workshops to learn new methods of instruction and many are offering support to professors who seek to use more active forms of teaching in their classes. Much greater quantities of information are being collected about the performance of students in order to measure gains in learning and identify weaknesses in need of improvement.

This progress is not trivial. Although most of the goals discussed in this book are far from being achieved, that is hardly a surprise. The list of useful things to do is very long, and some of the necessary steps are formidably difficult. No one has yet discovered all that colleges will need to know to accomplish everything the AAC&U proposal requires. Implementing the full agenda is not a task to be completed in a few years but a project that will require a generation or more.

At the same time, the progress to date has been slow and could slow even further as colleges have to cope with the havoc wrought by COVID-19 before they begin to consider changes in the curriculum and the way courses are taught. Even then, three obstacles threaten to impede the pace of reform and cause colleges to stop well short of the complete agenda recommended by the AAC&U.

Educational Research

The first impediment is the lack of rigorous research to discover new and better methods for helping students learn all they will need to know to develop the skills and qualities of mind described in previous chapters. Part of the problem is a lack of funding. Of every $100 that the federal government allocates to research, only an estimated 43 cents is directed to improving education, and most of that sum goes to fund studies involving public schools and preschool programs. Various foundations support research to improve undergraduate teaching and learning, but the amounts provided, even when added to government funding, fall far short of the totals made available for research in fields such as medicine, public health, and national defense.

Universities, especially the more prominent institutions, share responsibility for the weaknesses of educational research. Academic leaders have never paid much attention to identifying and testing new ideas for improving the quality of the education they provide. Even the best-endowed universities have not devoted anything like the effort and resources to research and development typical of large companies. The most obvious reason for not doing more is that research to improve the quality of education does not promise the financial rewards that result from successful innovations in business.*

---

*To illustrate this point, one need only compare the behavior of universities in developing new and more effective methods of instruction with how they reacted to the prospect of obtaining patents and earning royalties from discoveries in their laboratories. When Congress enacted legislation allowing universities to patent discoveries by their scientists from research financed by government grants, academic leaders responded immediately by creating technology transfer offices to comb through their laboratories in search of discoveries that could be patented and licensed to private corporations. Scores of research universities continue to maintain such offices in the hope of striking it rich even though more than 80 percent of them do not collect enough money from royalties to pay for their own operating costs. See Matthew Wisnioski and Lee Vinsel, "The Campus Innovation Myth," *Chronicle of Higher Education* (June 21, 2019), p. 36.

Despite the lack of attention and funding, researchers continue to investigate teaching and learning. Hundreds of papers on these subjects are published every year. The quality and rigor of most of the studies, however, tend to be weak. For instance, as mentioned earlier, a meta-analysis based on over sixteen hundred citations to papers on meditation could find only forty-seven studies that were of sufficient quality to merit inclusion in the study.[19] Another review of the research on the effectiveness of online courses found no studies rigorous enough to yield reliable results.[20] Seldom do educational researchers undertake expensive, large-scale studies using randomly assigned control groups or longitudinal methods to determine whether innovative methods actually cause the desired changes or to reveal how long the changes last.

Lack of Leadership

The second obstacle that can impede educational innovation and reform is the reluctance of academic leaders to devote much of their time and energy to the task. Amid the many duties that crowd the calendars of presidents and deans, the prospect of launching a campaign to make major changes in their institution's curriculum and teaching methods can hardly seem very attractive. Despite the criticism from sources outside the university, neither students nor faculty are clamoring for reform. Such efforts can consume enormous amounts of time, take years to complete, and often result in only token changes. Unlike the launch of new programs, the construction of additional buildings, or the completion of a successful fund drive, educational reforms rarely bring immediate, tangible satisfaction. The value of changes to the curriculum and teaching methods will usually become evident, if ever, only years after they were introduced.

It is hardly surprising, then, that according to a recent survey of how public university presidents spend their time, "academic affairs" (which presumably include many matters besides curricular reform) ranked no higher than thirteenth on a list of twenty typical activities. Private university presidents devoted more of their time to educational matters, yet academic affairs still ranked only fifth in importance. Leaders of private independent colleges ranked academic matters even lower (in eighth place) among their regular activities.[21]

Faculty Resistance

The third impediment to educational reform is the difficulty of persuading the faculty to agree to important changes in the curriculum, especially those that require professors to alter the way they teach or the content of their courses. This resistance is partly explained by the fear on the part of professors in research universities that implementing reforms will steal valuable time from the laboratory and library. But large-scale improvements in undergraduate education can meet with faculty resistance in all kinds of colleges. Most professors, wherever they are employed, are conscientious instructors who care a lot about their efforts to educate young people and believe that they are succeeding. Reforms that seek to change the way they teach seem to call into question their efforts over many years to expand the minds and imagination of their students. Since the vast majority of professors consider themselves above-average teachers, they will often dismiss such changes as unnecessary and unwise.

The obstacles just mentioned are not peculiar to the AAC&U proposals. They are impediments that are likely to interfere with any serious effort to satisfy the current demands on undergraduate education. If colleges are to respond effectively to the new opportunities before them, they must somehow overcome the roadblocks that inhibit progress. Finding practical ways to accomplish this result is the subject of the next and final chapter of this book.

CHAPTER TEN

Encouraging Reform

The slow pace of reform described in the preceding chapter is not unique to this era, nor to improvements of the kind described in this book. To cite but one example, Harvard president Charles W. Eliot, in his inaugural address in 1869, gave one of the most vivid explanations ever uttered about the disadvantages of the lecture method: "The lecturer pumps laboriously into sieves. The water may be wholesome, but it runs through. A mind must work to grow."[1] Yet almost 150 years later, in 2012, after the National Science Foundation had spent millions of dollars to demonstrate the value of more active methods of instruction, the Council of Advisors on Science and Technology acknowledged that "scientifically validated methods of improving the teaching of science and math simply have not found widespread adoption at American colleges."[2] Today fully half of all college professors still lecture extensively in their classes.*

Not all examples are that extreme. Nevertheless, the most comprehensive study ever made of innovation in higher education concluded that new ideas of all kinds have tended to take at least three times as long to work their way through the ranks of colleges and universities as the average length of time that innovative ideas take to spread through

---

*Recent research not only finds that active teaching tends to result in more student learning than lecturing but throws added light on why lecturing continues to be extensively used; see Louis Deslauriers et al., "Measuring Actual Learning Versus Feeling of Learning in Response to Being Actively Engaged in the Classroom," *Proceedings of the National Academy of Sciences in the United States of America* (September 24, 2019), https://doi.org/10.1073/pnas.1821936116. This study, using randomly assigned student groups, showed that students in a physics class using active learning methods learned more than students in a control group using traditional lectures, but that students in the lecture course *thought* that they had learned more than students taught with active discussion methods. These results indicate that students will often prefer lectures and resist active methods unless professors explain at the outset why active methods are usually more effective.

companies in the private sector.[3] If colleges are to proceed more ex-
peditiously to carry out the reforms discussed in this book, they will
have to discover ways to overcome the three impediments to reform
mentioned at the end of the previous chapter: the weakness of educational research, the reluctance of academic leaders to seek major reforms of undergraduate education, and the tendency of the tenured
faculty to resist basic changes in the curriculum or the methods of
instruction.

IMPROVING EDUCATIONAL RESEARCH

As previously mentioned, the federal government spends very little
money on improving undergraduate education compared with what
it spends on research and development in other fields of importance
to the nation. To take full advantage of the current opportunities for
innovation and improvement in higher education, additional resources
will be needed to fund the creation of large databases to support a variety of valuable studies, the greater use of longitudinal methods, and
much additional research employing randomly assigned control groups
to evaluate new ways to develop the skills and qualities of mind discussed in previous chapters. Additional support will be needed to discover more accurate methods for measuring the results of efforts to
foster these new capabilities. Without adequate means of measurement,
it will remain difficult for colleges to identify weaknesses in their educational program or to learn through trial and error how to help students make greater progress.

Fortunately, the sums required are quite modest—an increase of tens
of millions of dollars per year rather than billions. If undergraduate
education contributes only a fraction of what economists estimate it
does to increase economic growth and opportunity, this additional
support will prove to be an eminently sound investment.

Increased federal funding will not suffice by itself to meet the needs
for better educational research. Major universities will have to do
more to encourage the kind of studies that are required. It is neither
necessary nor desirable to interfere with the traditional methods by

which individual professors obtain outside support for their research. Instead, academic leaders should work with their faculty to agree on ways to evaluate their teaching programs to discover weaknesses and identify promising new ideas that deserve research and experimentation. They should then enlist interested professors or hire competent investigators for their own staff who are capable of carrying out the necessary studies to review current programs and evaluate promising new methods of instruction. Finally, they can seek the help of capable reviewers to examine proposals for university-funded studies and make sure that they are adequately designed to yield reliable results.

Foundations and accrediting agencies can help to encourage research universities to implement the changes just described. Foundations, of course, have far fewer resources than the government. They cannot be expected to pay for everything that major universities need to do to evaluate existing programs and test new methods of teaching. What they could do, however, is offer funding for a limited period to a handful of universities with the most promising plans for expanding and improving their educational research program. The examples set by these institutions could then inspire other universities to strengthen their own research efforts.

Accreditors could likewise begin to pay attention to the institutional research conducted by major universities and suggest improvements, taking care not to pressure academic leaders to accept them. This modest step would require accrediting organizations to recruit qualified researchers for their staffs or their inspection teams. If properly done, however, this adjustment could reinforce the attempts by government and foundations to lift the quality of research and development in leading universities to a level somewhat closer to that of other large and successful organizations.

These proposals for improving the quality of research will seldom require much additional effort on the part of the faculty and thus are unlikely to provoke internal resistance. Of the three obstacles to reforming undergraduate education, therefore, the anemic effort to discover how to provide more effective instruction should be the easiest to overcome, given the will to do so.

ENCOURAGING REFORM-MINDED LEADERS

Every study of successful reform in colleges and universities emphasizes the importance of able and committed leadership. At present,
however, the incentives for presidents and chief academic officers to
initiate reforms are quite weak. Attempts by governments to create
stronger incentives—either by offering rewards in the form of increased
funding for colleges that meet agreed-on educational goals or by bringing market pressure to bear on underperforming institutions by pub-
lishing information comparing the learning gains of their students with
those of other colleges—have failed to produce the hoped-for results.[4]
There are better ways, however, in which interested parties could encourage academic leaders to engage in serious efforts to improve their
educational programs.

Primary responsibility for providing such encouragement rests
with the trustees, who have the responsibility for choosing presidents
and monitoring their performance. Members of the board could start
by placing more emphasis on educational reform when they choose
new leaders. Thereafter, they could help to sustain a focus on improving undergraduate teaching by asking presidents to provide detailed
information about student learning and scheduling periodic discussions of the results. A board chair could begin by requesting evidence
of how much students are improving their writing skills or their critical thinking or moral reasoning abilities. If the response seems un-
convincing, presidents could be asked for concrete proposals to bring
about better results. Boards could also give strong support when a president does decide to launch a substantial effort at curricular reform,
thus serving notice to faculty and students that the president is not
acting alone but has the backing and encouragement of the trustees.

Foundations could also play a useful role in stimulating reform. Philanthropy cannot assume the cost of revising curricula and improving
instructional methods throughout the whole of undergraduate education. What foundations might do, however, is seek out and support a
few colleges that have developed thoughtful plans for improvement with
the cooperation of their faculties. Such assistance could contribute to

successful reform initiatives that might inspire other colleges to follow suit. The Lilly Foundation project that funded college efforts to help students develop a clearer and more meaningful purpose for their lives (described in chapter 5) exemplifies such an initiative.

Accrediting organizations could also encourage educational reform. Accreditors have already made important progress in persuading almost all colleges to define their learning goals and adopt methods of assessment to measure progress toward their objectives. But they have rarely evaluated the goals and assessment methods of the colleges they inspect in order to point out weaknesses and suggest alternatives that have already led to successful results at other comparable institutions. Of course, when accreditors do have these discussions, they should be careful not to try to impose their preferred methods on the colleges they inspect. Attempts to pressure colleges into accepting specific reforms will only provoke resistance and turn constructive dialogue into adversarial encounters in which colleges try to hide their weaknesses and impress accreditors with their accomplishments rather than talking candidly about their problems.

In order to engage in useful discussions that command the respectful attention of college authorities, accreditation organizations will have to strengthen their existing capabilities. Evaluating a college's goals, scrutinizing its efforts to improve, and calling attention to promising reforms at other institutions all require more specialized knowledge than most inspection teams currently possess. Accreditation organizations must either include members with the requisite knowledge and experience on their inspection teams or, if that is not possible, recruit knowledgeable individuals for their own staffs. Without capable inspectors, efforts to evaluate the progress of colleges toward self-improvement are likely not only to fail but to weaken the respect accorded to the accreditation process.

If taken individually, none of the actions suggested above are likely to succeed in convincing academic leaders to launch the kind of far-reaching reform proposed by the AAC&U. Together, however, they could lift the sights of campus leaders and let them know that they will not be left exposed and alone if they launch an ambitious and potentially contentious effort to improve their undergraduate program.

PERSUADING FACULTIES TO
ACCEPT SERIOUS REFORM

While trustees, foundations, and accreditors can help to lay the groundwork for genuine reform, more will be needed to persuade tenured
faculty members to make substantial changes in the established curriculum and their familiar methods of teaching. In some colleges, faculties may have already been persuaded. In fact, large majorities of the
nation's full-time instructors already "agree" or "strongly agree" that
colleges should help students develop their moral character, meet their
emotional needs, define their personal values, and acquire appreciation and respect for other racial-ethnic groups.[5] But agreeing on the
purposes of undergraduate education is one thing; accepting the part
that individual faculty members must play to achieve these goals is
another. In most institutions, many tenured professors are not yet prepared to participate in carrying out the kind of comprehensive reforms
proposed by the AAC&U. To convince them that changes of this magnitude are necessary, academic leaders must first persuade them that
current methods are not working as well as many professors assume.

Accomplishing this feat of persuasion is no simple matter. Now that
most colleges and their professors have defined their goals for student
learning, academic leaders need to work with their faculties to agree
on appropriate ways of measuring students' progress toward achieving these goals. Without such prior agreement, faculties may ignore
findings that students are not learning as much as they could, or as
much as most professors think they are.

Even these findings may not immediately persuade faculties to embrace far-reaching reforms. Nevertheless, most professors, including
those heavily engaged in research, believe that they are above-average
teachers devoted to helping their students learn and develop. Once they
come to recognize that their efforts are not yielding as much improvement as they had assumed, they are likely to experience discomfort.
They may initially seize upon various rationalizations to persuade
themselves that basic changes are unnecessary. Eventually, however, the
discrepancy between what they thought their students were learning
and the results revealed by the evidence should bring them to accept

the need for basic reform. However, because this process is uncertain and may take a long time to bear fruit, reform-minded academic leaders need to take additional steps that can hasten the process of change.

The Influence of the Tenure-Track Faculty

Reformers must begin by recognizing the effects of granting virtually complete power to the tenure-track faculty to determine the content of the undergraduate curriculum and how it is taught. Of course, tenured professors are responsible for most of the achievements of our colleges and universities and deserve much praise for what they have accomplished. However, like most human beings who have such extensive power over the content and methods of their work, they have fashioned a curriculum and a set of teaching duties that are often shaped to suit their own training and professional interests rather than serve the needs of their students.

The basic curricular structure adopted in most colleges by 1915—the major, a distribution requirement, and student electives—still remains in place a century later, in large part because it allows most professors to teach what they want. Meanwhile, teaching loads have diminished, and more and more of the less agreeable work of teaching undergraduates has been shifted to others. Elementary courses in mathematics, foreign languages, and expository writing are usually left to non-tenure-track instructors of one kind or another. Most of the drudgery of grading papers and exams has been transferred to graduate student assistants. More and more teaching of lower-division general education courses is now done by full- or part-time NTT instructors who are often hired hastily on short-term contracts and paid much less than their tenured colleagues. Efforts to meet emerging student needs of the kind discussed in previous chapters are frequently left to student affairs personnel, career counseling offices, and health services personnel. As a result, tenure-track faculty now make up fewer than one-third of all those who teach undergraduates.

There is something to be said for these developments. It makes good sense to have highly trained scientists and scholars spend as many of their working hours as possible performing tasks that require their special talents and expertise rather than devoting their time to duties that others can do as well. At the same time, the resulting arrangements are so congenial to the tenured faculty that many professors are reluctant to modify them, even when there are persuasive reasons for doing so.

During the periodic faculty reviews of the undergraduate curriculum, consideration is seldom given to issues that might disturb the status quo and its advantages for tenure-track professors. Rarely do faculties discuss whether liberal arts majors need as much space in the curriculum as they typically receive in order to ensure the desired "depth" of study, or whether the typical distribution system that makes undergraduates take two or three courses each from existing offerings in the sciences, social sciences, and humanities is the best way to help them gain the hoped-for "breadth" of education. Topics such as whether to teach resilience, conscientiousness, creativity, and other new competencies, and even such familiar questions as how to prepare students as citizens or strengthen their character, are seldom debated at all.

Today many tenured professors do not even attend faculty meetings to discuss revisions to the curriculum, and those who do attend often come primarily to defend the interest of their department in preserving ample opportunities to attract enough students to justify its full complement of tenure positions. The limitations that faculties impose on the scope of the discussion have been strong enough to maintain the basic structure of the curriculum for more than one hundred years despite a series of reports from commissions, foundations, and even associations of colleges that have harshly criticized the status quo. Major reforms may never occur without changing existing procedures. In order to improve upon current practice and embrace the opportunities discussed in previous chapters, colleges will need to add fresh voices to faculty debates about the undergraduate curriculum.

Placing relevant findings from research on the agenda for discussion at faculty meetings is one way to introduce new perspectives. Experience suggests, however, that new ideas will have their greatest impact if they are expressed by voices within the institution. Suggestions for achieving this result take up the remainder of this chapter. The following proposals deliberately avoid such drastic remedies as giving seats at the table to public officials and employers. These steps would create serious risks and meet with justifiable opposition from all sectors of higher education. However, there are other ways to broaden campus discussions of undergraduate education that are less likely to provoke resistance from the tenure-track faculty or to threaten the important contributions to society brought about by their research. The following suggestions are designed with these considerations in mind.

Creating a Teaching Faculty

The first step would be to gradually transform the present cadres of full-time and part-time non-tenure-track instructors into a better-trained and better-treated teaching faculty. The numbers of NTT faculty have steadily grown over the years; to such a point that up to 70 percent of college instructors are not on the tenure track. More than half of these teachers are employed on a part-time basis and are frequently hired haphazardly without the careful vetting that normally precedes the appointment of a tenure-track professor.* They typically receive very low salaries, work on short-term appointments, and often do not have access to computers, telephones, or even offices on campus. In most colleges, they have no voice or vote in faculty meetings, although they do much of the undergraduate teaching.

The present condition of many NTT instructors seems untenable for the long run. The treatment they frequently receive amounts to ex-

---

*A substantial percentage of NTT instructors are hired on a full-time basis, and many of them receive salaries and benefits approaching those of tenure-track professors; most NTT instructors, however, are hired on a one-year basis and enjoy much less job security as a result. College authorities now employ increasing percentages of part-time NTT instructors for at least three reasons—they can be paid far less than professors; they can be hired without an expensive, time-consuming search; and their presence gives the college greater flexibility, since NTT instructors can be hired or let go very quickly in response to fluctuations in student demand. Part-time NTT instructors typically have little say in the choice of syllabi or texts for the classes they teach and usually play no part in governance. Often, they are hired so near the beginning of the semester that they have little opportunity to prepare and are let go so late that they have insufficient time to look for another appointment. As one would expect, they tend to be less satisfied than tenure-track faculty or full-time NTT instructors with their compensation, working conditions, status in the university, and prospects for advancement. See, generally, Adrianna Kezar and Cecile Sam, "Non-Tenure-Track Faculty in Higher Education: Theories and Tensions," *ASHE [Association for the Study of Higher Education] Higher Education Report* (special issue) 36 (2010).

ploitation of a kind that makes an increasing number of their tenured colleagues feel uncomfortable. The casual way in which they are often hired suggests an embarrassing lack of concern on the part of college officials for the quality of education. Evidence is also accumulating that the use of part-time NTT instructors may have adverse effects on graduation rates and contribute to grade inflation.[6] Some researchers have found that NTT instructors spend less time than tenured faculty preparing for class and talking with students.[7] Meanwhile, unionization is spreading and beginning to erode the financial benefits that colleges derive from the meager compensation they give to part-time faculty. Under these circumstances, it is only prudent to start imagining a better alternative.

The situation just described provides an opportunity to improve the process of educational reform as well as the quality and conditions of work for both the non-tenure-track faculty and their tenured and tenure-track colleagues. The optimum outcome would be to create a carefully selected, full-time teaching faculty primarily for the first two years of college. Contracts for non-tenure-track faculty members might provide an appointment that begins with a probationary period of several years followed by longer terms of service, together with enforceable guarantees of academic freedom and of substantial advance notice if the contract is not going to be renewed. NTT faculty would receive ample opportunities for professional development and encouragement to use them in order to become more knowledgeable and proficient teachers. They would not be expected to conduct traditional research but instead would teach more hours per week than the tenured faculty. In return, they would receive improved salaries, benefits, and access to facilities, and they would participate as full voting members in deliberations about undergraduate education (though not in matters involving research and the appointment and promotion of tenure-track professors).

A full-time teaching faculty created along these lines would be likely to devote more time and effort to improving the quality of the first two years of college than is the case today on most college campuses. Since the salary and status of these instructors would depend primarily on their contribution to the educational program, they would also pay more attention than most of their tenured colleagues in research-oriented colleges to new developments in teaching and curriculum and spend more time experimenting with innovative methods of instruction, learning to teach in different or more effective ways, and incorporating new material into their courses. They would consequently tend to be more receptive to new ideas for improving the curriculum and the methods of instruction.

Tenured professors would lose little and even gain advantages from the arrangement just described. Those with a flair for teaching general education courses would still be free to do so if they wished. Such professors can be found on every campus. They add a great deal to the quality of the college experience, and their participation in undergraduate teaching should be welcomed. Many of their colleagues, however, prefer to concentrate on mentoring graduate (PhD) students and teaching advanced undergraduate courses and seminars in their field while reserving sufficient time to pursue their research. A university with a corps of full-time instructors devoted entirely to teaching introductory and general education courses would give these faculty members more freedom to teach and conduct research according to their own preferences. In addition, granting higher status and participation in governance to NTT instructors would relieve tenured professors of some of the administrative and housekeeping functions that have grown more burdensome in many colleges as the ranks of tenured professors have dwindled and retiring faculty have been replaced by cheaper part-time NTT instructors who seldom engage in governance or administrative activities.

The creation of a teaching faculty for lower-division courses is not a new idea. It was tried at one time by a number of graduate programs with foundation support but was abandoned because few doctoral students preferred what was widely regarded then as a second-class role.[8] Today, however, college teaching has become more challenging and important than it was once thought to be, and more graduate students claim to be interested in positions primarily devoted to that function. The possibilities for discovering new and better methods of teaching have never been brighter. Besides, the existence of a teaching faculty is already an established fact on almost every campus; the only open questions have to do with the terms and conditions of employment provided for its members. At the very least, the reforms described here would represent a marked improvement over the status quo.

The ultimate question that bears upon the potential success of a teaching faculty is whether college authorities will engage the members of the new faculty as active participants in a search for new and better ways of teaching undergraduates. To achieve this goal, college authorities will need to create conditions for the teaching faculty that make their work more meaningful and absorbing. Members of this faculty should be encouraged from the outset to experiment with new methods of instruction and given opportunities for professional development that will prepare them to do so. They should be invited to work with the administration to develop appropriate forms of evaluation to determine whether experimental teaching methods are successful. And finally, their achievements in improving and expanding the teaching of undergraduates should receive the recognition they deserve, not only to show appreciation for their innovative work but also to inform the faculties at other universities of their discoveries. If these steps are implemented, members of the teaching faculty may realize that the search for better methods of instruction can be as absorbing as the quest for new discoveries and insights in the laboratory and the library.

The obvious difficulty with this plan is the added expense of giving adequate salaries to the NTT teaching faculty. This problem may put the proposal out of the reach of community colleges, many of which are chronically starved for funds. But hundreds of research universities and public regional universities may find the plan feasible in time. The cost per hour of instruction will be substantially less than it would be for teaching done entirely by tenure-track professors, since members of the teaching faculty might not receive as high a salary and would have a heavier teaching load.* Moreover, rather than replacing all NTT instructors immediately, colleges could carry out the shift in stages, starting with a limited number of instructors selected for their

---

*Some readers may ask why NTT faculty with higher teaching loads should earn less than tenured professors. As a practical matter, universities must respond to the realities of the marketplace. Faculty members with solid publication records normally command higher salaries than their colleagues who do not publish, just as professors of computer science and economics typically earn higher salaries than professors of social work and religious studies. Universities that do not respect these differences will soon find themselves unable to compete for the scientists and scholars they might wish to recruit for their faculty.

demonstrated talents in teaching undergraduates. Such a process would have the added advantage of instantly offering to all NTT instructors the chance to compete for a higher position with better pay and amenities in return for successful performance in the classroom.

Some academic leaders and tenured faculty may resist giving NTT teachers better benefits and privileges. They may welcome the casual and less cumbersome methods of hiring part-time instructors and appreciate the ease of arranging their departure when their services are no longer required. Yet recent surveys of tenured professors, deans, provosts, and even trustees suggest that majorities of each group will approve of the policies suggested here.[9] The American Association of University Professors has formally recommended granting voting rights to NTT faculty when issues of educational policy are under consideration.[10] A number of college faculties have already agreed to some of these changes. If the reforms are debated openly, and with knowledge of the facts, it will be difficult for anyone to argue publicly that the current treatment of NTT faculty should be continued merely for the sake of administrative convenience.

Improving Graduate Education

More than one hundred years ago, William James complained about the state of graduate education by asking: "Will anyone pretend for a moment that the doctor's degree is a guarantee that its possessor will be successful as a teacher?"[11] A century later, this question continues to be relevant. While the situation has improved considerably, the improvements are not sufficient and the consequences have become more serious than ever.

As previously mentioned, graduate students now have opportunities to teach small sections of large lecture courses, although they often receive limited, if any, supervision and advice from the professor in charge of the course. In addition, most universities have created teaching and learning centers that offer orientation programs for new graduate students, individual coaching and critique for section leaders, an occasional workshop on new methods of instruction, and, in some graduate schools, even a special course or two on pedagogy. Nevertheless, while these opportunities are clearly helpful, they are typically optional, and not all graduate students who plan on academic careers take advantage of them. Moreover, they do not fully dispel the message conveyed by many tenured faculty mentors that research is what really matters and that teaching is merely a skill that young instructors can grasp and develop on their own through practical experience in the classroom.

Whether or not this advice was ever sound, it is surely misleading today. Over the past half-century, a vast literature has accumulated on the quality of undergraduate education and the multitude of proposals to improve it. Advances in technology have brought forth new ways of teaching that college instructors need to master. Thousands of studies have been conducted on the effectiveness of different methods of instruction. Becoming a proficient teacher and a knowledgeable contributor to departmental and faculty deliberations can no longer be left to practical experience; it is a competence requiring study and preparation. Neglecting such preparation seems especially unwise in the present era when so many new PhDs will not obtain tenure-track jobs in research universities but instead will occupy positions whose primary responsibility is classroom teaching.

The importance of helping graduate students become teachers as well as scholars is heightened by the growing body of research evaluating the effects of classroom practice on the amount that students learn. In the words of the authors of the most recent volume analyzing the many studies on student progress in college: "Good teaching matters: It *really* matters. Across all outcomes reviewed in this volume, . . . results confirmed that good teaching is the primary means through which institutions affect students."[12]

Departments cannot be expected to provide all the instruction that graduate students need to prepare them as teachers and educators. Professors of physics or English literature are unlikely to know much about cognitive psychology and its relation to teaching and learning, or the uses of technology in the classroom, or the possibilities and limitations of assessment methods for ascertaining student progress. If academic leaders simply leave reform for departments to deal with, the current deficiencies may never be overcome. Only deans and provosts are in a position to recruit qualified teachers from other parts of the university who can offer the needed instruction. The changes involved will not require much additional effort on the part of tenured professors. If a department is truly concerned about the deteriorating job market for its graduate students, it should welcome opportunities to enhance their teaching skills rather than resist them.*

Improving the preparation of graduate students will not have an immediate impact on the reform of undergraduate education. Nor will it threaten the primacy of research in PhD-granting departments; the prevailing incentives, both within and outside academe, are much too powerful for that. However, if new members of the faculty, both tenure-track and non-tenure-track, arrive already acquainted with the best of the literature on higher education and its evolving needs, they are likely to be more open to new ideas for improving existing practices and more knowledgeable about the possibilities and problems in proposals for reform. With appropriate support and encouragement, they should be more willing to experiment with new approaches that will improve their teaching and more aware of new ideas and useful information to enrich discussions about undergraduate education. Over time, as their numbers increase, their influence will grow.

The Extra-Curriculum

In the past, the extracurricular life of the college has seldom been considered an integral part of undergraduate education. The dozens of student organizations, the athletic programs, and the arrangements for undergraduate housing have long been looked upon both as a periodic headache for the administration when a scandal occurs and as a useful source of school spirit and a necessary means of providing suitable opportunities for diversion and enjoyment. Support activities,

---

* Some PhD candidates, especially in the sciences, plan to seek careers as researchers in industry or government, not as teachers, and courses about pedagogy or educational reform may be unnecessary for them. But doctoral students who do expect to seek teaching positions in a college or university should receive ample opportunities to study additional subjects such as the uses of technology, the relevance of cognitive psychology, current research on the effectiveness of different instructional methods, and debates about the demands that are now being made on the undergraduate curriculum. Even graduate students who plan to pursue alternative careers need at least *some* initial preparation if they wish to serve as teaching assistants in undergraduate lecture courses.

such as health clinics, placement offices, and student counseling, have generally been treated by the faculty as necessary auxiliary services rather than integral parts of undergraduate education.

In recent decades, one can detect a growing interest in the extra-curriculum as a significant force in helping to achieve the academic purposes of the college. Of the 168 hours in the week, students typically spend no more than 26 to 28 on classes and homework. The remaining hours are too numerous and valuable to be devoted entirely to eating, sleeping, and recreation.

One of the most striking conclusions to draw from this book is that several of the educational needs that society is now asking colleges to meet are already being attended to on many campuses by members of the support staff, such as career counselors, health service personnel, and student affairs professionals, or through extracurricular activities such as student government, athletics, and community service. Extra-curricular activities and support services can also be useful in helping students develop soft skills such as interpersonal relations; the ability to understand and respect people of different races, backgrounds, genders, and beliefs; and the qualities of leadership, civic engagement, and teamwork.

Not only do employers value these skills, but they also often look more to job applicants' extracurricular activities than to their grade point averages for evidence of such qualities. Lauren Rivera has vividly illustrated this point in her firsthand account of the methods used by the hiring partners of much sought-after employers, such as investment banks and management consulting firms.[13] These enterprises need a quick and easy method to reduce to a manageable number the swarms of applicants responding to announcements of job openings. The firms that Rivera studied sought to solve this problem by the arbitrary method of first eliminating the graduates of all but the most selective colleges on the grounds that admission committees of such prestigious institutions could be trusted to identify the applicants with the highest intelligence and best work habits. Having reduced the applicant pool in this manner, the partners reviewed the records of the remaining candidates by looking more closely at their extracurricular activities rather than their college grade point averages. They gave particular weight

to activities that demanded a high degree of teamwork, perseverance, and self-discipline (such as membership on athletic teams) and
to positions of leadership and responsibility (as in student government), which signaled interpersonal and communication skills. With
the help of these clues, the hiring partners narrowed the list of applicants to a select group to be interviewed and evaluated more
carefully.

The potential contribution of the extra-curriculum to the development of important skills and qualities of mind may call for a shift in
the oversight of these activities. For example, colleges that are not in
thrall to the demands of a high-powered athletic program may find it
useful to hire coaches not only, or even primarily, for their ability to
compile a winning record but also for their capacity to develop qualities such as teamwork, resilience, concern for other team members,
leadership, and respect for rules and fair play.* Student government
could be given more prominence and responsibility because of the contributions it makes to the civic education, interpersonal skills, and
leadership abilities of its members. Colleges and universities could do
more to link community service activities with related coursework in
view of what we know about the way in which this combination stim-
ulates the development of empathy, intercultural competence, and
civic engagement.†

By making adjustments in the organization of their staff to improve
their oversight over the extra-curriculum, campus leaders may be able
to better coordinate the multitude of existing activities and strengthen

---

* Having read many essays by Harvard athletes on their experience in college, I am
struck by how many emphasize the contribution of athletics and the influence of coaches to
their own growth in resilience, perseverance, time management skills, conscientiousness,
and other valuable behaviors.

† Other extracurricular activities may not be so readily incorporated into efforts to reform undergraduate education. Opportunities for friendship and peer support available at
fraternities, sororities, and Third World centers can enhance students' interpersonal skills,
help them overcome feelings of loneliness and isolation, and improve the college's retention
and graduation rates. But the membership policies of these organizations can also undermine efforts to draw upon a diverse student body to increase racial understanding and
sensitivity to other kinds of cultural and class differences. Skillful administrative oversight
may be necessary to guide these organizations to emphasize the most fruitful experiences
for their members. Even the methods used in making roommate assignments in other undergraduate living units can have significant effects on the interpersonal skills of student
residents and the integration of undergraduates into the life of the college.

their role in achieving some of the learning goals of today's colleges, including the lengthening list of skills and qualities of mind that they are now being asked to nurture.

In addition, colleges could consider steps to give key staff members involved in extracurricular programs a greater voice in the academic planning of the college. The views of student affairs counselors and career services personnel deserve more attention in light of the insights they derive from their work and the multiple contributions they make to student development through their contact with individual undergraduates and the courses they teach. Staff members in the health services gain valuable insights from their talks with many students about the stresses and strains of their lives at college. Student affairs professionals come to understand a lot about the concerns and beliefs of undergraduates by teaching courses on the search for a meaningful life. Academic counselors learn from working with students individually or in groups about the difficulties they are encountering in their coursework.* As Professor Mayhew and his colleagues have observed in their comprehensive review of research on undergraduate education: "Co-curricular educators have their finger on the pulse of issues facing students and can bring that knowledge and expertise to educate faculty."[14]

On many campuses, support staff have few established channels through which to contribute their ideas. It is not necessary to have every member of a college's burgeoning bureaucracy join in faculty debates over educational policy. What could be useful would be to allow sufficient representation to ensure that the knowledge and experience gained in this sector of the institution are brought to bear on discussions within the faculty and administration about improving efforts to meet today's demands on the nation's colleges.

---

* In writing this book, I have been struck by the number of articles and books I have read that cite with approval the writings of William Perry on the development of students' thinking during college. Although Perry was for many years the director of Harvard's Bureau of Study Counsel, I cannot recall ever seeing him present during discussions of the college curriculum, let alone being asked to contribute his views on subjects in which he was far more knowledgeable than members of our faculty.

A LESSON FROM THE PAST

Some readers may regard the proposals put forth in this chapter as extreme. In fact, however, they are not unprecedented. During the nineteenth century, while college presidents continued to play the dominant role in educational policy, their faculties gradually changed. The young college graduates who offered instruction for a few years before moving on gave way to longer-serving professors who were trained in European universities or in the newly formed graduate schools in the United States. Many of these faculty members had acquired the ideas, methods, and knowledge required to replace the classical curriculum with an education more attuned to the needs of students and society in an industrializing America. Meanwhile, college presidents were becoming more and more preoccupied with fund-raising and administration and had less time to spend on teaching and the educational policies of their institution. In recognition of these developments, responsibility for the curriculum and the methods of instruction gradually moved to the faculty.

This process proved to be appropriate and beneficial because it allowed the locus of power and responsibility over undergraduate education to gravitate into the hands of those most able to decide how to serve the needs of students. Today colleges are again encountering new demands and new opportunities for the education of undergraduates. Many of these challenges, however, are outside the training and experience of most tenure-track professors. The steps recommended in this chapter could help to remedy this deficiency. By proceeding on this path, colleges will be adapting, much as they did a century ago, to align the decision-making body for undergraduate education to conform more closely with an expanded range of desirable goals and opportunities.

The time is surely ripe for another change in the locus of decision-making for the content and quality of undergraduate education. The tenure-track faculty continue to make immense contributions to society through the quality of their research and their success in training new generations of productive scientists and scholars. Despite much criticism to the contrary, many tenured professors are inspiring teachers, and most work hard at carrying out their responsibilities in the classroom. At the same time, they have not performed well in exercising their collective responsibility for determining the policies and practices of undergraduate education. All too frequently, they have failed to address important educational problems appropriately, preferring instead either to ignore these issues or to settle for an ineffective or self-serving response.

- For over a century, they have failed to take adequate steps to prepare their graduate students for their role as teachers and educators.
- Although the average number of hours per week that students spend studying for their classes has decreased by approximately 40 percent over the past fifty years, faculties have not only failed to reverse this decline; they have given higher grades to their students on most campuses over the same time period.[15]
- Instructors have continued to make excessive use of classroom lectures despite an impressive body of evidence that active methods of teaching and learning are usually more effective, especially in courses on science, mathematics, and engineering.
- Faculties have done very little to consider long-standing questions about the content of general education programs, such as the continued use of distribution requirements as the preferred means of achieving the desired "breadth" of learning and the lack of attention paid on most campuses to such familiar aims of college as preparing citizens and providing moral education.
- Professors have often failed to devise effective procedures for dealing with cheating and plagiarism. Instead, they frequently ignore the existing rules and procedures, preferring to deal with such cases in their own way. Meanwhile, studies consistently find that a majority of students admit to having cheated during their college years.
- Faculties have shown little collective interest in helping students learn many new and important skills and qualities of mind that will serve them well in meeting the challenges of the twenty-first century.
- Finally, they have done little to resist the growing use of non-tenure-track instructors, who are often hired hastily and without careful quality controls, while receiving compensation, supervision, and conditions of employment that have been repeatedly criticized as inadequate.

The intent of the changes proposed in this chapter is not to deny the role of tenured professors in determining the content of undergraduate education but simply to supplement faculty debates on the subject with contributions from individuals who are capable of supplying new ideas and insights about teaching that are relevant to the challenges facing America's colleges. Thus, the reforms suggested here are not only "precedented"; they represent important steps toward enabling colleges to meet the present needs of students and society.

Reflections on the Future

Over its long history, undergraduate education has gradually evolved from its early years when colleges offered an exacting study of classical texts to the tiny segment of America's young men destined for careers as ministers, teachers, and civic leaders. Once the United States began to industrialize during the nineteenth century, the demand for graduates with practical skills increased and led eventually to the demise of the classical curriculum to make way for more useful and contemporary subjects. In the decades following World War II, the gross domestic product grew rapidly, and the need for competent managers and professionals grew with it. In response, vocational programs expanded in size and variety as never before to accommodate the surge in the number of young men and women seeking a college education.

Today the undergraduate curriculum may be entering a new phase. The needs of an increasingly sophisticated economy, coupled with advances in the cognitive sciences, have given rise to intriguing possibilities for helping students acquire additional competencies and qualities of mind that will enable them to live more successful, useful, and satisfying lives. The political apathy and ignorance of so many young people today, together with a growing recognition of the vulnerabilities of our democracy, point to an urgent need to pay greater attention to the familiar but neglected goal of civic education. The rising levels of mental health problems among undergraduates and the difficulties that recent graduates experience in making the important decisions of adulthood raise new concerns about how to help students develop a meaningful purpose for their lives.

It is not yet clear how successful educators will be in meeting these needs or in nurturing such sought-after qualities as conscientiousness, creativity, collaboration, and character. Neuroscientists and psychologists have already learned much about the nature of behaviors such as these, and greater understanding will undoubtedly come in time. As yet, however, it is impossible to predict just how much will be discovered and how effectively colleges can adapt the new knowledge for educational purposes.

The stronger research efforts recommended in chapter 10 should increase our understanding of these subjects. The addition of new voices to campus discussions of undergraduate education should stimulate thinking about how to weave this new knowledge into the teaching of undergraduates. In the past, however, colleges and universities have typically been slow to alter their curriculum or their methods of teaching unless the proposed changes will help them enroll more students or unless voices within the institution have pressed for reform. The innovations discussed in these pages do not have a strong internal constituency and offer no immediate prospect for attracting students, thus making the outlook for reform all the more uncertain.

One thing, however, is clear. No matter how promising the new discoveries may be and how eloquent new voices become, the tenure-track faculty and their leaders will have a decisive role in determining what will be done. College and university presidents may recognize the value of developing the sought-after skills and qualities, or they may prefer to concentrate on more immediate, tangible goals. Tenured professors can either embrace new aims or resist such efforts on the grounds that the qualities of mind involved are not academic enough to deserve a place among the purposes of undergraduate education.

In considering which course to pursue, campus leaders and their faculties need to bear in mind the many benefits and advantages of broadening their goals. Cognitive science has discovered possibilities for student growth that could conceivably increase the value of a college education to an extent not seen for more than one hundred years. Success in this endeavor will improve the economy, the society, and, most important of all, the future lives of undergraduates. The necessary reforms do not seem prohibitively expensive. The only step that could call for substantial funds is the transition from part-time, non-tenure-track instructors to a full-time teaching faculty, and even that change can be accomplished in stages, as economic conditions permit. Moreover, most of the new forms of education discussed in these pages are not subject to displacement by technology in the foreseeable future. It is possible to imagine lectures and class discussions being conducted with distant audiences via the videodisc and the internet, or subjects such as statistics and mathematics being taught effectively with the aid of adaptive technology. It is much more difficult to conceive of teaching collaborative skills, building character and resilience, or helping students discover a purpose for their lives without the presence of a live audience and a capable instructor.

However academic leaders and their faculties choose to respond, attempts to satisfy the expanded set of needs discussed in these chapters are bound to come about sooner or later. The potential benefits are too important to the lives and careers of students to be postponed indefinitely by token changes. Significant initiatives may emerge from any of a number of sources—from entrepreneurial universities such as Arizona State and Southern New Hampshire, from for-profit colleges, or even from new commercial ventures created to equip students with capabilities not included in college curricula.

In the end, however, the improvements are likely to be more successful and spread more rapidly if they are based on competent research and experimentation carried out by universities with the active participation of their tenured faculties. They will be integrated more fully into the entire undergraduate curriculum if they are adopted by colleges experienced in offering a broad liberal arts education. What a poor reflection it would be on our colleges and universities if they ignored the challenge and waited for other providers to make the improvements that now seem possible.

As I approach my ninetieth birthday, I view the outlook for higher education from the perspective of seven decades of involvement with issues of teaching and learning—from studying as an undergraduate in the late 1940s to serving as a young professor, a dean, and a university president for more than twenty years, and finally, to writing books about colleges and universities in my retirement.

My first two decades, beginning in college and extending well beyond, were years of great progress for higher education. Colleges and universities grew rapidly to accommodate an ever-increasing number of high school graduates seeking higher degrees. Faculties made strenuous efforts to internationalize their curricula and increase their scholarly contributions. Aided by ample federal support, universities created a research capability of unrivaled quality. Throughout this period, educational leaders forged an alliance with federal and state governments to pursue a set of common purposes of vital importance to the nation. American higher education became a source of national pride and a model that the rest of the world sought to emulate.

Toward the end of the 1960s, a different and more troubled period began, and angry student protests over race and the Vietnam War took a toll on the trust and goodwill built up over the preceding decades. Government funding began to fluctuate, and higher education had to compete with more and more government programs, both domestic and international. In the 1980s, a series of critical books appeared by authors from both sides of the political spectrum containing a litany of complaints about the policies of universities and the behavior of their professors. The ensuing decades brought mounting concerns over rising tuitions and the growth of student debt.

In the wake of these developments, public opinion has gradually shifted to reflect growing doubts about the work of colleges and universities. Employers have complained that many college graduates are not adequately prepared for employment in the modern economy. Parents are increasingly dismayed by the cost of sending their children to college and wonder whether a degree is any longer worth the price. Conservatives insist that universities are too liberal, while liberals maintain that selective colleges are exacerbating inequality. Amid these discontents, a survey in 2019 revealed that more than half of all Democrats and over 70 percent of Republicans believe that higher education is moving in the wrong direction.

Some of the harshest criticisms leveled against colleges are not entirely fair. Although tuition has risen steadily, much of the resulting pain stems from the stagnant incomes of most Americans over the past thirty-five years. Public funding for state universities has also severely declined. Although student debt has risen to forbidding levels, much of it is held by graduate students preparing for well-compensated careers, by undergraduates who drop out without attaining a degree, and by students enrolled in for-profit institutions that charge substantial tuition but do not deliver the jobs they promised students when they entered.

Rightly or wrongly, however, the gradual loss of public trust has encouraged governments to intervene more and more into the affairs of colleges and universities. For the first time, Congress has taxed the endowments of the wealthiest universities. Title IX of the Higher Education Act has now been interpreted to regulate college disciplinary procedures for claims of sexual assault. The president has signed an executive order denying federal funds to universities that fail to protect free speech on campus. Meanwhile, several states have already intervened in the admissions procedures of colleges and universities by prohibiting the use of race, and growing complaints about the way selective colleges decide which applicants to admit could result in yet more regulation of the process.

Further worsening of public attitudes toward higher education is bound to provoke new efforts to increase government supervision over colleges and universities. Some commentators recommend "communication strategies" to avoid these dangers and counter the continuing stream of negative articles about problems on campuses involving sexual assaults, admissions practices, racial conflicts, and college athletic programs. Nothing in my experience, however, suggests that skillful public relations and repeated reminders of the greatness of America's universities will do much to solve the problem. To regain the public trust, colleges and universities must improve the narrative by undertaking new and successful efforts to meet the current needs of students and society.

Against this background, colleges would be ill advised to dismiss the reforms discussed in this book as merely another set of demands being urged on colleges with no additional funding to pay for them. Instead, they should be seen as a welcome opportunity to rebuild the confidence of the public through determined efforts to increase the value of a college education, both to students and to society. How colleges respond to this opportunity could easily become the most important question facing academic leaders and their faculties over the next few decades, as well as the most consequential issue for the future lives of their students. What better chance could higher education have to demonstrate its value to the nation?

Notes

CHAPTER ONE.
A BRIEF HISTORY OF THE COLLEGE CURRICULUM
FROM 1636 TO THE PRESENT

1. Report of the Committee of the Corporation to the full Corporation of Yale College, reprinted in David B. Potts, ed., *Liberal Education for a Land of Colleges: Yale's Report of 1828* (2010), p. 7.

2. Laurence Veysey, "Stability and Experiment in the American Undergraduate Curriculum," in Carl Kaysen, ed., *Content and Context: Essays on College Education* (1973), p. 3.

3. Quoted in Frederick Rudolph, *Curriculum: A History of the American Undergraduate Course of Study Since 1636* (1977), p. 127.

4. Edward Thorndike, *Educational Psychology* (1903).

5. Rudolph, p. 95.

6. Rudolph, p. 289.

7. Steven Brint, Mark Riddle, Lori Turk-Bicakci, and Charles S. Levy, "From the Liberal to the Practical Arts in American Colleges and Universities: Organizational Analysis and Curricular Change," *Journal of Higher Education* 76 (2005), p. 151.

8. Carnegie Foundation for the Advancement of Teaching, *Missions of the College Curriculum: A Contemporary Review with Suggestions* (1977).

9. Carnegie Council on Policy Studies in Higher Education, *Three Thousand Futures: The Next Twenty Years for Higher Education* (1980).

10. National Governors' Association, Center for Policy Research and Analysis, *Time for Results* (1986).

11. National Commission on Excellence in Education, *A Nation at Risk: The Imperative for Education Reform* (1983).

12. See, for example, Roger Kimball, *Tenured Radicals: How Politics Has Corrupted Our Higher Education* (1990).

13. See, for example, Charles J. Sykes, *Profscam: Professors and the Demise of Higher Education* (1988); Martin Anderson, *Imposters in the Temple: American Intellectuals Are Destroying Our Universities and Cheating Our Students of Their Future* (1992).

14. Allan Bloom, *The Closing of the American Mind: How Higher Education Has Failed Democracy and Impoverished the Souls of Today's Students* (1987).

15. Lynne L. Cheney, *50 Hours: A Core Curriculum for College Students* (1989), p. 1. See also Cheney, *Tyrannical Machines: A Report on Educational Practices Gone Wrong and Our Best Hopes for Setting Them Right* (1990).

16. William J. Bennett, *To Reclaim a Legacy: A Report on the Humanities in Higher Education* (1984), p. 30.

17. Barbara Herrnstein Smith, "Cult-lit: Hirsch, Literacy, and the 'National Culture,'" in Darryl J. Gless and Barbara Herrnstein Smith, eds., *The Politics of Liberal Education* (1992), p. 75.

18. Stanley Fish, "The Common Touch, or, One Size Fits All," in Gless and Smith, p. 241.

19. Henry A. Giroux, "Liberal Arts Education and the Struggle for Public Life: Dreaming About Democracy," in Gless and Smith, p. 119.

20. Ernest L. Boyer, *College: The Undergraduate Experience in America* (1987).

21. Association of American Colleges, *Integrity in the College Curriculum: A Report to the Academic Community* (1985).

22. Boyer, p. 2.

23. Association of American Colleges, p. 2.

24. Association of American Colleges, p. 28.

25. Association of American Colleges, p. 11.

26. Association of American Colleges, pp. 7, 14.

27. Jerry G. Gaff, "General Education at Decade's End: The Need for a Second Wave of Reform," *Change* 21 (July/August 1989), p. 11.

28. Damon Kent Johnson, James L. Ratcliff, and Jerry G. Gaff, "A Decade of Change in General Education," *New Directions for Higher Education* 125 (2004), pp. 9, 18.

29. Association of American Colleges and Universities, *College Learning for the New Global Century* (2007), p. 3.

30. Association of American Colleges and Universities, p. 13.

31. Terrel L. Rhodes, *Assessing Outcomes and Improving Achievement: Tips and Tools for Using Rubrics* (2010), pp. 22–51.

32. The AAC&U set forth these "guided pathways" in a report by Andrea Leskes and Ross Miller, *Purposeful Pathways: Helping Students Achieve Key Learning Outcomes* (2006).

33. See George Kuh, *High-Impact Educational Practices: What They Are, Who Has Access to Them, and Why They Matter* (2008).

34. Paul L. Gaston and Jerry G. Gaff, *Revising General Education—and Avoiding the Potholes* (2009).

35. Rhodes, *Assessing Outcomes and Improving Achievement*, pp. 25, 39.

CHAPTER TWO.
EDUCATING CITIZENS

1. Michael X. Delli-Carpini and Scott Keeter, *What Americans Know About Politics and Why It Matters* (1996).

2. US Department of Education, National Center for Education Statistics, *The Nation's Report Card: Civics 2010: National Assessment of Educational Progress at Grades 4, 8, and 12* (May 2011).

3. American Political Science Association Task Force on Civic Education in the Next Century, "Expanded Articulation Statement: A Call for Reactions and Contributions," *PS: Political Science and Politics* 31 (1987), pp. 636–37.

4. Christian Smith, with Kari Christoffersen, Hilary Davidson, and Patricia Snell Herzog, *Lost in Transition: The Dark Side of Emerging Adulthood* (2011), pp. 214, 225.

5. Amy K. Syvertsen, Laura Wray-Lake, Constance A. Flanagan, D. Wayne Osgood, and Laine Briddell, "Thirty Year Trends in US Adolescents' Civic Engage-

ment: A Story of Changing Participation and Educational Differences," *Journal of Research on Adolescence* 21 (2011), p. 586; Jean M. Twenge, *I-Gen: Why Today's Super-Connected Kids Are Growing Up Less Rebellious, More Tolerant, Less Happy—and Completely Unprepared for Adulthood* (2017), pp. 278–81.

6. Quoted in Derek Bok, *The Trouble with Government* (2001), p. 405.

7. See, for example, John R. Hibbing and Elizabeth Theiss-Morse, "Civics Is Not Enough: Teaching Barbarics in L-12," *PS: Political Science and Politics* 29 (1996), p. 57; Keith Melville, John Dedrick, and Elizabeth Gish, "Preparing Students for Democratic Life: The Rediscovery of Education's Civic Purpose," *Journal of General Education* 62 (2013), p. 258.

8. Kathleen Hall Jamieson, "The Challenges Facing Civic Education in the 21st Century," *Daedalus* (Spring 2013), p. 65; National Center for Education Statistics, *The Nation's Report Card: Civics 2010.*

9. Quoted in William Talcott, "Modern Universities, Absent Citizenship? Historical Perspectives," Center for Information & Research on Civic Learning & Engagement (CIRCLE) Working Paper 39 (September 2005), p. 2.

10. Stanley Fish, "Citizen Formation Is Not Our Job," *Chronicle of Higher Education* (January 17, 2017), p. B13.

11. Carol Geary Schneider, "Educational Missions and Civic Responsibility: Toward the Engaged Academy," in Thomas Ehrlich, ed., *Civic Responsibility and Higher Education* (2000), pp. 98, 120.

12. Jonathan Haidt, "Why Do They Vote That Way?" (2018), from Haidt, *The Righteous Mind: Why Good People Are Divided by Politics and Religion* (2012).

13. See, for example, Bruce Maxwell, "The Debiasing Agenda in Ethics Teaching: An Overview and Appraisal of the Behavioral Ethics Perspective," *Teaching Ethics* 16 (2016), p. 1; Lawrence Blum, "Political Identity and Moral Education: A Response to Jonathan Haidt's *The Righteous Mind*," *Journal of Moral Education* 42, no. 3 (2013), p. 298; Jeanette Kennett and Cordelia Fine, "Will the Real Moral Judgment Please Stand Up?," *Ethical Theory and Moral Practice* 12 (2009), p. 77; Cordelia Fine, "Is the Emotional Dog Wagging Its Rational Tail or Chasing It? Reason in Moral Judgment," *Philosophical Explorations* 9 (2006), p. 83.

14. Ernest T. Pascarella and Patrick T. Terenzini, *How College Affects Students,* vol. 2: *A Third Decade of Research* (2005), p. 156.

15. Pascarella and Terenzini, *How College Affects Students,* vol. 2, p. 342.

16. Ashley Finley, "Civic Learning and Democratic Engagements: A Review of the Literature on Civic Engagement in Post-Secondary Education," paper prepared for the US Department of Education (May 24, 2011).

17. Pascarella and Terenzini, *How College Affects Students,* vol. 2, p. 129; Richard Arum and Josipa Roksa, *Academically Adrift: Limited Learning on College Campuses* (2011).

18. Center for Information & Research on Civic Learning & Engagement, "All Together Now: Collaboration and Innovation for Youth Engagement: The Report of the Commission on Youth Voting and Civic Knowledge" (2013), p. 11.

19. Jason Schnittker and Jere R. Behrman, "Learning to Do Well or Learning to Do Good? Estimating the Effects of Schooling on Civic Engagement, Social Cohesion, and Labor Market Outcomes in the Presence of Endowments," *Social Science Research* 41 (2012), p. 306.

20. See, for example, Paul W. Kingston, "Failing at Citizenry," *Change: The Magazine of Higher Learning* 48 (2016), p. 20; Terry T. Ishitani and Sean A. McKitrick, "The Effects of Academic Programs and Institutional Characteristics on Post-Graduate Civic Engagement Behavior," *Journal of College Student Development* 54 (2013), p. 379.

21. Syvertsen et al., "Thirty Year Trends in US Adolescents' Civic Engagement," p. 586.

22. See, for example, Norman Nie and D. Sunshine Hillygus, "Education and Democratic Citizenship," in Diane Ravitch and Joseph Viteritti, eds., *Making Good Citizens: Education and Civil Society* (2001), p. 30.

23. Delli-Carpini and Keeter, *What Americans Know About Politics*, p. 105, note 1.

24. Eric L. Dey, Mary Antonaros, Molly C. Ott, Cassie L. Barnhardt, and Matthew A. Holsapple, "Developing a Moral Compass: What Is the Campus Climate for Learning?," Association of American Colleges and Universities (2009), p. ix.

25. Dey et al., p. 3.

26. Dey et al., p. 10.

27. Ibid.

28. See, for example, Lion F. Gardiner, *Redesigning Higher Education: Producing Dramatic Gains in Student Learning* (1994), p. 46.

29. Winston Churchill, statement to the House of Commons, November 11, 1947.

30. Pascarella and Terenzini, *How College Affects Students*, vol. 2, p. 156.

31. These findings are reported in Thomas R. Bailey, Shanna S. Jaggars, and David Jenkins, *Redesigning America's Community Colleges: A Clearer Path to Success* (2015), pp. 85–86.

32. John M. Braxton, "Selectivity and Rigor in Research Universities," *Journal of Higher Education* 64 (1993), p. 657.

33. Ellen Bara Stolzenberg et al., *Undergraduate Teaching Faculty: The HERI [Higher Education Research Institute] Faculty Survey, 2016–2017* (2019), p. 33.

34. See, for example, Lindsay Beyerstein, "Can News Literacy Grow Up? After a Decade, the Movement Tries to Prove Its Worth," *Columbia Journalism Review* (September/October 2014), p. 45; Renée Loth, "What's Black and White and Retweeted All Over? Teaching News Literacy in the Digital Age," Discussion Paper D-71, Harvard University, Shorenstein Center (February 2012); John Dyer, "Can News Literacy Be Taught?," *Nieman Reports* (Spring 2017).

35. See, for example, James Klurfeld and Howard Schneider, *News Literacy: Teaching the Internet Generation to Make Reliable Information Choices*, Brookings Institution, Center for Effective Public Management (June 2014).

36. Finley, "Civic Learning and Democratic Engagements," p. 7, note 16.

37. Elizabeth F. Farrell and Eric Hoover, "Many Colleges Fall Short on Registering Student Voters: A Third Have Not Complied with New Requirements, a *Chronicle* Survey Finds," *Chronicle of Higher Education* 51 (September 17, 2004), p. A1.

38. Sidney Verba, Kay Lehman Schlozman, and Henry E. Brady, *Voice and Equality: Civic Voluntarism in American Politics* (1995), p. 438.

39. See, for example, Adam J. Berinsky and Gabriel S. Lentz, "Education and Political Participation: Exploring the Causal Link," *Political Behavior* 33 (2011), p. 357; Benjamin Highton, "Revisiting the Relationship between Educational Attainment and Political Sophistication," *Journal of Politics* 71 (2009), p. 1564; Cindy D. Kam and Carl Palmer, "Reconsidering the Effects of Education on Political Participation," *Journal of Politics* 70 (2008), p. 612.

40. Matthew J. Mayhew et al., *How College Affects Students*, vol. 3: *21st Century Evidence That College Works* (2016), p. 552.

CHAPTER THREE.
PREPARING STUDENTS FOR AN
INTERDEPENDENT WORLD

1. Council on Foreign Relations and *National Geographic*, *What College-Aged Students Know about the World: A Survey on Global Literacy* (September 2016), p. 19.

2. Derek Bok, *Our Underachieving Colleges: A Candid Look at How Much Students Learn and Why They Should Be Learning More* (2006), p. 254.

3. Richard D. Lambert, "New Directions in International Education," *Annals of the American Academy of Political and Social Science* 449 (May 1980), p. 14.

4. See, for example, John K. Hudzik, *Comprehensive Internationalization: From Concept to Action* (Washington, DC: NAFSA and Association of International Educators, 2011). "Comprehensive internationalization is a commitment confirmed through action, to infuse international and comparative perspectives throughout the teaching, research, and service missions of higher education" (p. 6).

5. Sarah Balistreri, F. Tony Di Giacomo, Ivanley Noisette, and Thomas Ptak, "Global Educational Connections, Concepts, and Careers," College Board (2012), p. 4.

6. See, for example, Jocelyne Gacel-Ávila, "The Internationalisation of Higher Education: A Paradigm for Global Citizenship," *Journal of Studies in International Education* 9 (2005), p. 121; Erica E. Hartwell et al., "Breaking Down Silos: Teaching for Equity, Diversity, and Inclusion Across Disciplines," *Humboldt Journal of Social Relations* 39 (2017), p. 143.

7. See AAC&U, "Global Learning VALUE Rubric," https://www.aacu.org/value/rubrics/global-learning.

8. American Council on Education, Commission on International Education (1998), p. 272.

9. Darla K. Deardorff, "Identification and Assessment of Intercultural Competence as a Student Outcome of Internationalization," *Journal of Studies in International Education* 10 (Fall 2006), p. 241; Bill Hunter, George P. White, and Galen C. Godbey, "What Does It Mean to Be Globally Competent?," *Journal of Studies in International Education* 10 (2006), pp. 267–77.

10. Hunter et al., p. 271.

11. See, for example, Laura D. Perry and Leonie Southwell, "Developing Intercultural Understanding and Skills: Models and Approaches," *International Education* 22 (2011), pp. 453, 458.

12. Richard L. Griffith et al., "Assessing Intercultural Competence in Higher Education: Existing Research and Future Directions," Educational Testing Service (December 2016), p. 36.

13. Carol Geary Schneider, "Deepening the Connections: Liberal Education and Global Learning," *Liberal Education* (Summer/Fall 2011), p. 7.

14. On the basis of long experience in teaching Foreign Service officers, the US State Department estimates that it takes 240 hours of instruction merely to enable the average student to read a newspaper or conduct a rudimentary conversation in one of the "easy" languages, such as French or Spanish. Richard D. Lambert, *International Studies and the Undergraduate* (1989), p. 72.

15. Alexander W. Astin, *What Matters in College: Four Critical Years Revisited* (1993), p. 223. Although this study is somewhat dated, it is doubtful that the results would be any better today, since the number of colleges requiring foreign language study has declined.

16. Mark H. Salisbury, Brian P. An, and Ernest T. Pascarella, "The Effect of Study Abroad on Intercultural Competence among Undergraduate College Students," *Journal of Student Affairs Research and Practice* 50 (2013), p. 1.

17. According to a recent report, only a minority of colleges make specific programs available to integrate foreign students with the rest of the college population. Robin M. Helms, Lucia Brajkovic, and Brice Struthers, *Mapping Internationalization on US Campuses* (2017), p. 20.

18. For an online survey carried out for the AAC&U, see Hart Research Associates, *Falling Short? College Learning and Career Success* (2015), p. 5.

19. For example, Hunter et al., p. 271, note 9.

CHAPTER FOUR.
CHARACTER: CAN COLLEGES HELP STUDENTS ACQUIRE HIGHER STANDARDS OF ETHICAL BEHAVIOR AND PERSONAL RESPONSIBILITY?

1. Immanuel Kant, *Groundwork of the Metaphysics of Morals*, in *Ethical Philosophy*, trans. James W. Ellington (1983), p. 7.

2. Hart Research Associates, *Falling Short?*.

3. Josephson Institute of Ethics, *Report Card 2002: The Ethics of American Youth* (2002).

4. Smith et al., *Lost in Transition*.

5. Smith et al., p. 61.

6. David A. Hoekema, "Is There an Ethicist in the House? How Can We Tell?," in Elizabeth Kiss and J. Peter Euben, eds., *Debating Moral Education: Rethinking the Role of the Modern University* (2010), pp. 249, 251.

7. David Brooks, "The Organization Kid," *Atlantic* (April 2001).

8. Douglas Sloan, "The Teaching of Ethics in the American Undergraduate Curriculum, 1876–1976," in Daniel Callahan and Sissela Bok, eds., *Ethics Teaching in Higher Education* (1982), pp. 1–57.

9. Stolzenberg et al., *Undergraduate Teaching Faculty: The HERI Faculty Survey, 2016–2017*, p. 33.

10. Quoted in Kiss and Euben, *Debating Moral Education*, p. 4.

11. See Christopher Peterson and Martin E. P. Seligman, *Character Strengths and Virtues: A Handbook and Classification* (2014).

12. See, for example, Matthew J. Mayhew et al., "Going Deep into Mechanisms for Moral Reasoning Growth: How Deep Learning Approaches Affect Moral Reasoning Development for First-Year Students," *Research in Higher Education* 53 (2012), p. 26.

13. Haidt, *The Righteous Mind*; Dan Ariely, *The (Honest) Truth about Dishonesty* (2012); Max H. Bazerman and Ann E. Tenbrunsel, *Blind Spots: Why We Fail to Do What's Right and What to Do about It* (2011).

14. See, for example, Bruce Maxwell, "The Debiasing Agenda in Ethics Teaching: An Overview and Appraisal of the Behavioral Ethics Perspective," *Teaching Ethics* 16 (2016), p. 75; Peter Railton, "The Affective Dog and Its Rational Tale: Intuition and Attunement," *Ethics* 124 (2014), p. 813.

15. Pascarella and Terenzini, *How College Affects Students*, vol. 2, p. 179.

16. Pascarella and Terenzini, *How College Affects Students,* vol. 2, p. 367.

17. Mayhew et al., *How College Affects Students*, vol. 3, p. 344.

18. Thomas Cooper, "Learning from Ethicists, Part 2: How Ethics Is Taught at Leading Institutions in the Pacific Region," *Teaching Ethics* 17 (2017), p. 27. Fifty-five percent of professors surveyed felt that educators cannot teach students to be "better people."

19. Mayhew et al., *How College Affects Students*, vol. 3, p. 530.

20. The following discussion draws heavily on a recent book by a Stanford psychologist, Jamil Zaki, *The War for Kindness: Building Empathy in a Fractured World* (2019).

21. Mandy Savitz-Romer, Heather T. Rowan-Kenyon, and Cheri Fancsali, "Social, Emotional, and Affective Skills for College and Career Success," *Change* (September/October 2015), p. 18.

22. Sara H. Konrath, Edward H. O'Brien, and Courtney Hsing, "Changes in Dispositional Empathy in American College Students over Time: A Meta-analysis," *Personality and Social Psychology Review* 15 (2010), p. 99.

23. Alexander W. Astin, Helen S. Astin, and Jennifer A. Lindholm, *Cultivating the Spirit: How Colleges Can Enhance Students' Inner Lives* (2011).

24. Astin et al., pp. 65–73.

25. Eric L. Dey et al., "Developing a Moral Compass: What Is the Campus Climate for Ethics and Academic Integrity?," AAC&U (2010), p. 10.

26. Pascarella and Terenzini, *How College Affects Students*, vol. 2, p. 354.

27. Donald L. McCabe, Kenneth D. Butterfield, and Laura K. Treviño, *Cheating in College: Why Students Do It and What Educators Can Do about It* (2012).

28. James M. Lang, *Cheating Lessons: Learning from Academic Dishonesty* (2013), p. 172.

29. Dey et al., p. 5.

30. Dey et al., p. 6.

31. Dey et al., p. 10.

32. Dey et al.

33. Melody A. Graham et al., "Cheating at Small Colleges: An Examination of Student and Faculty Attitudes and Behaviors," *Journal of College Student Development* 35 (1994), p. 255. See also Michael Vandehey, George M. Diekhoff, and Emily E. LaBeff, "College Cheating: A Twenty-Year Follow-up and the Addition of an Honor Code," *Journal of College Student Development* 48 (2007), pp. 468, 478, 469. Vandehey and his colleagues report that only 3 percent of cheaters in their study were caught, but they cite a later study finding that 8 percent of violators were caught.

34. McCabe et al., *Cheating in College*, p. 134.

35. Alison Schneider, "Why Professors Don't Do More to Stop Students Who Cheat," *Chronicle of Higher Education* 45 (January 22, 1999), pp. A8–A10.

36. Ibid.

37. Lee S. Duemer, Sheila Delony, Kathleen Donalson, and Amani Zaier, "Behavioral Expectations of 110 Nationally Ranked Liberal Arts Colleges," *Journal of College and Character* 10 (2008), p. 1.

38. See, generally, Angela Duckworth, David R. Weir, Eli Tsukayama, and David Kwok, "Who Does Well in Life? Conscientious Adults Excel in Both Objective and Subjective Success," *Frontiers in Psychology* 3 (2012), article 356.

39. See, for example, James W. Pellegrino and Margaret L. Hilton, National Research Council, *Education for Life and Work: Developing Transferable Knowledge and Skills in the 21st Century* (2012), pp. 52, 65; David J. Deming, "The Growing Importance of Social Skills in the Labor Market," National Bureau of Economic Research Working Paper 21473 (2015).

40. Ralph Stinebrickner and Todd R. Stinebrickner, "Time-Use and College Outcomes," *Journal of Econometrics* 121 (2004), p. 243; Marcus Credé, Sylvia G. Roch, and Urszula M. Kieszczynka, "Class Attendance in College: A Meta-Analytic Review of the Relationship of Class Attendance with Grades and Student Characteristics," *Review of Educational Research* 80 (2010), p. 272.

41. Duckworth et al., p. 37.

42. Brent W. Roberts and Jordan R. Davis, "Young Adulthood Is the Crucible of Personality Development," *Emerging Adulthood* 4 (2016), p. 318.

43. Gregory S. Blimling, "New Dimensions to Psychosocial Development in Traditionally Aged College Students," *About Campus* (November/December 2013), pp. 10, 21; Roberts and Davis, p. 318.

44. David S. Yeager and Gregory M. Walton, "Social-Psychological Interventions in Education: They're Not Magic," *Review of Educational Research* 81 (2011), p. 267.

45. Brent W. Roberts et al., "What Is Conscientiousness and How Can It Be Assessed?," *Developmental Psychology* 50 (2014), p. 11.

46. Philip S. Babcock and Mindy Marks, "The Falling Time Cost of College: Evidence from Half a Century of Time Use Data," *Review of Economics and Statistics* 93 (2011), p. 468.

47. National Survey of Student Engagement, *Promoting Student Learning and Instructional Improvement: Lessons from NSSE at 13* (2012), p. 18.

48. See, for example, John Hattie and Gregory C. R. Yates, *Visible Learning and the Science of How We Learn* (2013), p. 193.

49. Lester H. Hunt, ed., *Grade Inflation: Academic Standards in Higher Education* (2008); Stuart Rojstaczer and Christopher Healy, "Where A Is Ordinary: The Evolution of American College and University Grading 1940–2009," *Teachers College Record* 114 (July 2012), p. 1.

50. Philip S. Babcock, "Real Costs of Nominal Grade Inflation? New Evidence from Student Course Evaluations," *Economic Inquiry* 48 (2010), p. 983.

51. Jeffrey Selingo, "The Rise of College Grade Forgiveness," *Atlantic* (June 29, 2018), https://www.theatlantic.com/education/archive/2018/06/college-grades-gpa /564095/.

52. Roger L. Geiger, *American Higher Education since World War II: A History* (2019), p. 342.

53. George D. Kuh and Paul D. Umbach, "College and Character: Insights from the National Survey of Student Engagement," *New Directions for Institutional Research* 122 (2004), pp. 37, 44.

54. Hart Research Associates, *Falling Short?*, p. 12.

55. Dey et al., "Developing a Moral Compass," p. 10, note 25.

56. Dey et al.

57. Dey et al., p. 5.

58. Dey et al., p. 1.

59. For a comprehensive treatment of this subject, see Thomas G. Plante and Lori G. Plante, *Graduating with Honor: Best Practices to Promote Ethics Development in College Students* (2016).

CHAPTER FIVE.
HELPING STUDENTS FIND PURPOSE AND MEANING IN LIFE

1. William Damon, *The Path to Purpose: Helping Our Children Find Their Calling in Life* (2008), p. 33.

2. Sylvia Hurtado et al., *Undergraduate Teaching Faculty: The HERI Faculty Survey, 2010–2011* (2012), p. 26.

3. Stolzenberg et al., *Undergraduate Teaching Faculty: The HERI Faculty Survey, 2016–2017*, p. 33.

4. Astin et al., *Cultivating the Spirit*, p. 31.

5. Kendall Cotton Bronk, *Purpose in Life: A Critical Component of Optimal Youth Development* (2014), pp. 55, 57, 137.

6. Astin et al., p. 9.

7. Michael J. Stebleton and Mark Franklin, "Positive Impact of Career Planning Courses: Applying Narrative Strategies to Empower Teaching and Practice," *National Career Development Association* (September 1, 2017).

8. Lola Fadulu, "Why Aren't College Students Using Career Services?," *Atlantic* (January 20, 2018).

9. See, for example, Robert J. Nash and Michele C. Murray, *Helping College Students Find Purpose: The Campus Guide to Meaning-Making* (2010); Perry L. Glanzer, Jonathan P. Hill, and Byron R. Johnson, *Cultivating the Successful Quest for Purpose on Campus: What We Learned from Students* (2017).

10. Mayhew et al., *How College Affects Students*, vol. 3, pp. 161–62.

11. Pascarella and Terenzini, *How College Affects Students*, vol. 2, p. 273.

12. Tim Clydesdale, *The Purposeful Graduate: Why Colleges Must Talk to Students about Vocation* (2015), p. 215.

13. Damon, *The Path to Purpose*, p. 60.

14. See Alexander W. Astin, "The Changing American College Student: Thirty-Year Trends, 1966–1996," *Review of Higher Education* 21 (1998), p. 365.

15. William Deresiewicz, *Excellent Sheep: The Miseducation of the American Elite and the Way to a Meaningful Life* (2014).

16. Molly Worthen, "The Anti-College Is on the Rise," *New York Times Sunday Review*, June 8, 2019, p. 1.

17. Damon, *The Path to Purpose*, p. 1.

18. Robin Marantz Henig, "What Is It about 20-Somethings? Why Are So Many People in Their Twenties Taking So Long to Grow Up?," *New York Times Magazine*, August 18, 2010.

19. Marcia B. Baxter Magolda, *Authoring Your Life: Developing an Internal Voice to Meet Life's Challenges* (2009).

20. William M. Sullivan, *Liberal Learning as a Quest for Purpose* (2016).

21. Tim Clydesdale, *The Purposeful Graduate*.

22. Clydesdale, p. 211.

23. Clydesdale, p. 122.

24. David Denby, *Great Books: My Adventures with Homer, Rousseau, Woolf, and Other Indestructible Writers of the Western World* (1996).

25. Denby, p. 461.

26. Anthony T. Kronman, *Education's End: Why Our Colleges and Universities Have Given Up on the Meaning of Life* (2007).

27. See, for example, Ed Diener and Robert Biswas-Diener, *Happiness: Unlocking the Mysteries of Psychological Wealth* (2008).

28. See the discussion in Derek Bok, *The Politics of Happiness: What Government Can Learn from the New Research on Well-being* (2010), pp. 10–16.

29. Jeffrey D. Sachs, "Restoring American Happiness," in John Helliwell et al., eds., *World Happiness Report 2017*. United Nations (2017).

30. Glanzer et al., *Cultivating the Successful Quest for Purpose*, p. 26, note 9.

31. Bill Burnett and Dave Evans, *Designing Your Life: How to Build a Well-Lived, Joyful Life* (2016).

32. Kronman, p. 242, note 26.

33. See, for example, Baxter Magolda, *Authoring Your Life*; Marcia B. Baxter Magolda, "Promoting Self-Awareness to Promote Liberal Education," *Journal of College and Character* 10 (2009), p. 1.

CHAPTER SIX.
IMPROVING INTERPERSONAL SKILLS

1. Deming, "The Growing Importance of Social Skills in the Labor Market"; Flavio Cunha and James J. Heckman, "Formulating, Identifying, and Estimating the Technology of Cognitive and Noncognitive Skill Formation," *Journal of Human Resources* 43 (2008), p. 738.

2. Patrick C. Kyllonen, "Soft Skills for the Workplace," *Change* (2013), pp. 16, 22.

3. Quoted in Jules Evans, *Philosophy for Life and Other Dangerous Situations: Ancient Philosophy for Modern Problems* (2012), pp. 83–84.

4. Deming, p. 236, note 1.

5. Pascarella and Terenzini, *How College Affects Students*, vol. 2, p. 262.

6. Mayhew et al., *How College Affects Students*, vol. 3. Studies show growth of sixteen to seventeen percentage points in social self-confidence among college students (p. 209).

7. See, for example, Nathan W. Hudson and R. Chris Fraley, "Changing for the Better? Longitudinal Associations between Volitional Personality Change and Psychological Well-being," *Personality and Social Psychology Bulletin* 42 (2016), p. 603.

8. Ibid.

9. See, for example, Travis J. Miller, Erica Baranski, William L. Dunlop, and Daniel Ozer, "Striving for Change: The Prevalence and Correlates of Personality Change," *Journal of Research in Personality* 80 (2019), p. 10.

10. Miller et al.; see also Nathan W. Hudson, Daniel A. Briley, William J. Chopik, and Jaime Derringer, "You Have to Follow Through: Attaining Behavioral Change Goals Predicts Volitional Personality Change," *Journal of Personality and Social Psychology* 117 (October 2018).

11. "Eliot against Basketball: Harvard President Says Rowing and Tennis Are the Only Clean Sports, *New York Times*, November 28, 1906, p. 1.

12. See, for example, Emily Lai, Kristen DiCerbo, and Peter Foltz, *Skills for Today: What We Know about Teaching and Assessing Collaboration* (2017). Over 80 percent of employers in one survey listed collaborative skills as very important. Hart Research Associates, *Falling Short?*, p. 12.

13. National Academy of Engineering, *The Engineer of 2020: Visions of Engineering in the New Century* (2004), p. 35.

14. Hart Research Associates, note 12.

15. David W. Johnson, Roger T. Johnson, and Karl A. Smith, "Cooperative Learning: Improving University Instruction by Basing Practice on Validated Theory," *Journal on Excellence in College Teaching* 25 (2014), pp. 85, 93.

16. Ibid., p. 96.

17. See, for example, Larry K. Michaelson and Michael Sweet, "The Essential Elements of Team-Based Learning," *New Directions for Teaching and Learning* 116 (Winter 2008), p. 7.

18. See, for example, Cynthia J. Finelli, Inger Bergom, and Vilma Mesa, "Student Teams in the Engineering Classroom and Beyond: Setting Up Students for Success," Center for Research on Learning and Teaching Occasional Paper 29, University of Michigan (2011), p. 2.

19. Mark E. Burbach, Gina S. Matkin, Kim M. Gambrell, and Heath E. Harding, "The Impact of Preparing Faculty in the Effective Use of Student Teams," *College Student Journal* 44 (2010), p. 752.

20. Kevin Eagan et al., *The Undergraduate Teaching Faculty: The HERI Faculty Survey, 2013–2014*, Higher Education Research Institute (2014), p. 6.

21. Nicholas A. Bowman, Jay W. Brandenberger, Patrick L. Hill, and Daniel K. Lapsley, "The Long-Term Effects of College Diversity Experiences: Well-being

and Social Concerns 13 Years after Graduation," *Journal of College Student Development* 52 (2011), p. 729.

22. See Ruth S. Bernstein and Paul Salipante, "Intercultural Comfort through Social Practices," *Frontiers in Education* (July 2017), pp. 1, 3.

23. See Zaki, *The War for Kindness*, pp. 61–73.

24. Joseph J. Ramirez and Hilary Zimmerman, "2016 Diverse Learning Environments," *HERI Research Brief* (July 2016), p. 1.

25. Ramirez and Zimmerman, p. 3.

26. Kathleen Wong, "Building Capacity for Inclusion by Working across Differences: An Institutional and Societal Imperative," *AAC&U Diversity and Democracy* 19 (Spring 2016).

27. Ramirez and Zimmerman, p. 1.

28. Ibid., p. 4.

29. Ibid.

30. Pascarella and Terenzini, *How College Affects Students*, vol. 2, pp. 290, 313; Nicholas A. Bowman, "Promoting Sustained Engagement with Diversity: The Reciprocal Relationships between Informal and Formal College Diversity Experiences," *Review of Higher Education* 36 (2012), p. 1.

31. See, for example, Nida Denson, "Do Curricular and Cocurricular Diversity Experiences Influence Racial Bias? A Meta-Analysis," *Review of Educational Research* 79 (2009), p. 805. Summing up her findings, Denson concludes: "This meta-analysis has clearly established that there is indeed value in implementing diversity-related activities on college campuses." Then she adds: "However, the magnitude of the effectiveness of these interventions depends on several factors, such as level of institutional support, comprehensiveness of approach, a diverse racial composition, and more important, whether or not intergroup contact is a major component of the intervention" (p. 827).

32. See, for example, Nicholas A. Bowman, "College Diversity Experiences and Cognitive Development: A Meta-analysis," *Review of Educational Research* 80 (2010), pp. 4, 20.

33. Sylvia Hurtado and Adriana Ruiz Alvarado, "Discrimination and Bias, Underrepresentation, and Sense of Belonging on Campus," *HERI Research Brief* (October 2015), p. 2.

34. William G. Bowen and Derek Bok, *The Shape of the River: Long-Term Consequences of Considering Race in College and University Admissions* (1998).

35. Bowen and Bok, p. 211.

36. Bowen and Bok, p. 212.

37. Bowen and Bok, p. 232.

38. Bowen and Bok, p. 196.

39. Bowen and Bok, p. 206.

40. On underperformance, see Bowen and Bok, pp. 72–90; for higher earnings premiums for black college graduates, see Mayhew et al., *How College Affects Students*, vol. 3, p. 472.

41. Mayhew et al., *How College Affects Students*, vol. 3, p. 550.

42. Mayhew et al., *How College Affects Students*, vol. 3, p. 598.

CHAPTER SEVEN.
IMPROVING INTRAPERSONAL SKILLS

1. *Encyclopaedia Britannica*, 15th ed., *Macropedia*, vol. 3, p. 721.

2. See, for example, Keith Sawyer, "A Call to Action: The Challenges of Creative Teaching and Learning," *Teachers College Record* 117 (2015), p. 1; Sabine Hoidn and Kiira Kärkkäinen, "Promoting Skills for Innovation in Higher Education: A Literature Review on the Effectiveness of Problem-Based Learning and of Teaching Behaviours," OECD (Organisation for Economic Co-operation and Development) Education Working Paper 100 (2014).

3. Jimmy Daly, "Why Creativity Matters in Higher Education," *EdTech: Focus on Higher Education* (November 2012), p. 3.

4. The best recent book about creativity and education is the collection of essays in Robert J. Sternberg and James C. Kaufman, eds., *The Nature of Human Creativity* (2018).

5. See, for example, Angie L. Miller and Amber D. Dumford, "Creative Cognitive Processes in Higher Education," *Journal of Creative Behavior* 50 (2014), p. 282.

6. See, for example, Sawyer, "A Call to Action," p. 2.

7. See Walter Isaacson, *Einstein: His Life and Universe* (2007).

8. See Robert J. Sternberg, *What Colleges Can Be: A New Model for Preparing Students for Active Concerned Citizenship and Ethical Leadership* (2016), pp. 44–48.

9. See, for example, Hasso Plattner, Christoph Meinel, and Larry Leifer, *Design Thinking Research: Making Design Thinking Foundational* (2016); Tom Kelley and David Kelley, *Creative Confidence: Unleashing the Creative Potential within Us All* (2013).

10. Lee Vinsel, "Design Thinking Is a Boondoggle," *Chronicle of Higher Education* 64 (May 21, 2018).

11. For a general discussion of efforts by colleges to foster creativity, see Ronald A. Beghetto and James C. Kaufman, *Nurturing Creativity in the Classroom* (2010).

12. For a description of the Stanford program, see Hoidn and Kärkkäinen, note 2.

13. John T. Cacioppo, Richard E. Petty, Jeffrey A. Feinstein, W. Blair, and G. Jarvis, "Dispositional Differences in Cognitive Motivation: The Life and Times of Individuals Varying in Need for Cognition," *Psychological Bulletin* 119 (1996), p. 1197.

14. Andrew T. Jebb, Rachel Saef, Scott Parrigon, and Sang Eun Woo, "The Need for Cognition: Key Concepts, Assessment, and Role in Educational Outcomes," in Anastasiya E. Lipnevich, Franzis Preckel, and Richard D. Roberts, eds., *Psychosocial Skills and School Systems in the 21st Century* (2016), p. 115.

15. See, for example, Cacioppo et al., note 13.

16. Mayhew et al., *How College Affects Students*, vol. 3, p. 565.

17. Jebb et al., pp. 115, 125, note 14.

18. Jody Jessup-Anger, "Examining How Residential Colleges Inspire the Life of the Mind," *Review of Higher Education* 35 (2012), p. 431.

19. Matthew J. Mayhew, Gregory C. Woliak, and Ernest T. Pascarella, "How Educational Practices Affect the Development of Lifelong Learning Orientations in Traditionally-Aged Undergraduate Students," *Research on Higher Education* 49 (2008), pp. 337, 349; Ryan D. Padgett, Jennifer R. Keup, and Ernest T. Pascarella, "The Impact of First-Year Seminars on College Students' Lifelong Learning Orientations," *Journal of Student Affairs Research and Practice* 50 (2013), p. 133.

20. John C. Hayek and George D. Kuh, "College Activities and Environmental Factors Associated with the Development of Lifelong Learning Competencies of College Seniors," paper presented at the annual meeting of the Association for Studies of Higher Education (November 1999).

21. Higher Education Research Institute, "The American Freshman: National Norms: Fall 2010," *HERI Research Brief* (January 2011).

22. American College Health Association, "National College Health Assessment II: Executive Summary" (Fall 2017); Center for Collegiate Mental Health, *2017 Annual Report* (January 2018).

23. Daniel Eisenberg, Sarah Ketchen Lipson, and Julie Posselt, "Promoting Resilience, Retention, and Mental Health," *New Directions for Student Services* (2016), p. 87.

24. See, for example, Carol S. Dweck, *Mindset: How You Can Fulfill Your Potential* (2000).

25. See Claude M. Steele and Joshua M. Aronson, "Stereotype Threat and the Intellectual Test Performance of African Americans," *Journal of Personality and Social Psychology* 69 (1995), p. 797.

26. See, for example, James J. Gross, "Emotion Regulation: Current Status and Future Prospects," *Psychological Inquiry* 26 (2015), p. 1.

27. See, for example, Cheryl Regehr, Dylan Glancy, and Annabel Pitts, "Interventions to Reduce Stress in University Students: A Review and Meta-analysis," *Journal of Affective Disorders* 148 (2012), p. 1.

28. Ibid. For a more critical view of these studies, see Aaron L. Lappin et al., "The Efficacy of Resiliency Training Programs: A Systematic Review and Meta-analysis of Randomized Trials," *PLoS ONE* 9, no. 10 (October 2014), p. 1.

29. See, for example, Sarah Forbes and Deniz Fikretoglu, "Building Resilience: The Conceptual Basis and Research Evidence for Resilience Training Programs," *Review of General Psychology* 22 (2018), p. 452.

30. See, for example, Valerie Strauss and Alfie Kohn, "Ten Concerns about the 'Let's Teach Them Grit' Fad," *Washington Post*, April 8, 2014.

31. Brett Q. Ford and Allison S. Troy, "Corrigendum: Reappraisal Considered: A Closer Look at the Costs of an Acclaimed Emotion-Regulation Strategy," *Current Directions in Psychological Science* 28 (2019), p. 285.

32. Gross, p. 17, note 26.

33. Nicole Schechtman et al., *Promoting Grit, Tenacity, and Perseverance: Critical Factors for Success in the 21st Century*, US Department of Education, Office of Educational Technology (February 2013).

34. Ibid., pp. 29, 79.

CHAPTER EIGHT.
UNCONVENTIONAL METHODS OF TEACHING

1. See, generally, Lauren Cassani David, "When Mindfulness Meets the Classroom," *Atlantic* (August 31, 2015).

2. Astin et al., *Cultivating the Spirit*, p. 54.

3. Marilee J. Bresciani Ludvik, ed., *The Neuroscience of Learning and Development: Enhancing Creativity, Compassion, Critical Thinking, and Peace in Higher Education* (2016), p. 80.

4. Norman A. S. Farb, Adam K. Anderson, Julie A. Irving, and Zindel V. Segal, "Mindfulness Interventions and Emotion Regulation," in James J. Gross, ed., *Handbook of Emotion Regulation*, 2nd ed. (2014), pp. 548, 551; Robert J. Davidson and Alfred W. Kaszniak, "Conceptual and Methodological Issues in Research on Mindfulness and Meditation," *American Psychologist* 70 (2015), pp. 581, 591.

5. See, for example, Philippe Goldin, Wiveka Rimel, and James Gross, "Mindfulness Meditation Training and Self-Referential Processing in Social Anxiety Disorder: Behavioral and Neural Effects," *Journal of Cognitive Psychology* 23 (2009), p. 242.

6. Bresciani Ludvik, *The Neuroscience of Learning and Development*, pp. 156–57.

7. Astin et al., *Cultivating the Spirit*, p. 148.

8. See, for example, Shauna L. Shapiro, Kirk Warren Brown, and John A. Astin, "Toward the Integration of Meditation into Higher Education: A Review of Research Evidence," paper prepared for the Center for the Contemplative Mind in Society (October 2008), pp. 19, 29.

9. See, for example, Hooria Jazaieri et al., "Enhancing Compassion: A Randomized Controlled Trial of a Compassion Cultivation Training Program," *Journal of Happiness Studies* 14 (August 2013), pp. 1113–26; Eric L. Stocks, David A. Lishner, and Stephanie K. Decker, "Why Does Empathy Promote Pro-Social Behavior?," *European Journal of Pro-Social Behavior* 39 (2009), p. 649.

10. James W. Carson, Kimberly M. Carson, Karen M. Gil, and Donald H. Baucom, "Mindfulness-Based Relationship Enhancement," *Behavior Therapy* 35 (2004), p. 471.

11. See, for example, Nicholas T. Van Dam et al., "Mind the Hype: A Critical Evaluation and Prescriptive Agenda for Research on Mindfulness and Meditation," *Perspectives on Psychological Science* 13 (2017), p. 36.

12. Madhav Goyal et al., "Meditation Programs for Psychological Stress and Well-being: A Systematic Review and Meta-analysis," *JAMA Internal Medicine* 174 (March 2014), p. 357; see also Peter Sedlmeier, Caroline Losse, and Lisa Christin Quasten, "Psychological Effects of Meditation for Healthy Practitioners: An Update," *Mindfulness* 2 (2018); Stefan G. Hofmann, Alice T. Sawyer, Ashley A. Witt, and Diana Oh, "The Effect of Mindfulness-Based Therapy on Anxiety and Depression: A Meta-analytic Review," *Journal of Consulting and Clinical Psychology* 78 (2010), p. 169.

13. Andrew C. Hafenbrack and Kathleen D. Vohs, "Mindfulness Meditation Impairs Task Motivation but Not Performance," *Organizational Behavior and Human Decision Processes* 147 (July 2018), p. 1.

14. Goyal et al., "Meditation Programs for Psychological Stress and Well-being"; Farb et al., "Mindfulness Interventions and Emotion Regulation," p. 598.

15. Simon B. Goldberg et al., "Is Mindfulness Research Methodology Improving over Time? A Systematic Review," *PLoS ONE* 12, no. 10, e0187298, https://doi.org/10.1371/journal.pone.0187298.

16. Richard J. Davidson and Alfred W. Kaszniak, "Conceptual and Methodological Issues in Research on Mindfulness and Meditation," *American Psychologist* 70 (2015), pp. 581, 598.

17. Martin E. P. Seligman, *Flourish: A Visionary New Understanding of Happiness and Well-being* (2011), and Seligman, *Authentic Happiness: Using the New Positive Psychology to Realize Your Potential for Lasting Fulfillment* (2002).

18. Sonja Lyubomirsky, *The How of Happiness: A Scientific Approach to Getting the Life You Want* (2007), p. 2.

19. Lyubomirsky, p. 92.

20. Lyubomirsky, p. 112.

21. Lyubomirsky, p. 276.

22. Peterson and Seligman, *Character Strengths and Virtues*.

23. Quoted in Daniel Horowitz, *Happier? The History of a Cultural Movement That Aspired to Transform America* (2018), p. 157.

24. See, for example, Lyubomirsky, note 18; John C. Wade, Lawrence I. Marks, and Roderick D. Hetzel, eds., *Positive Psychology on the College Campus* (2015), p. 9; Jeffrey J. Froh and Acacia C. Parks, *Activities for Teaching Positive Psychology: A Guide for Instructors* (2012).

25. For a collection of essays on the uses of positive psychology, see Wade et al., *Positive Psychology on the College Campus*, especially chapter 1.

26. See Bruce W. Smith, Belinda Vicuna, and Glory Emmanuel, "The Role of Positive Psychology in Fostering Spiritual Development and a Sense of Calling in College," in Wade et al., *Positive Psychology on the College Campus*, pp. 261, 270–71.

27. Alistair Miller, "A Critique of Positive Psychology—or 'The New Science of Happiness,'" *Journal of Philosophy of Education* 42 (2008), p. 600.

28. Micki McGee, "From Makeover Media to Remaking Culture: Four Directions for the Critical Study of Self-Help Culture," *Sociology Compass* 6 (2012), p. 686.

29. See, for example, Julie K. Norem, *The Positive Power of Negative Thinking: Using Defensive Pessimism to Harness Anxiety and Perform at Your Peak* (2001); Scott Lilienfeld, "Is Positive Psychology for Everyone?," *Psychology Today* (June 19, 2009); Sissela Bok, *Exploring Happiness: From Aristotle to Brain Science* (2010), p. 121.

30. See, for example, Barbara Ehrenreich, *Bright-Sided: How Positive Thinking Is Undermining America* (2009).

31. See, for example, Linda Bolier et al., "Positive Psychology Interventions: A Meta-analysis of Randomized Control Studies," *BMC Public Health* 13 (2013), p. 119.

32. Miller, "A Critique of Positive Psychology," note 27.

33. For a careful look at the state of the research on applications of positive psychology, see Jordi Quoidbach, Moïra Mikolajczak, and James J. Gross, "Positive Interventions: An Emotion Regulation Perspective," *Psychological Bulletin* (2015), http://dx.doi.org/10.1037/a0038648.

34. Diener and Biswas-Diener, *Happiness*, p. 208.

35. Quoted in Horowitz, *Happier?*, p. 174.

36. Kristján Kristjánnson, "Positive Psychology and Positive Education: Old Wine in New Bottles?," *Educational Psychologist* 47 (2012), pp. 86, 103.

CHAPTER NINE.
PROSPECTS FOR CHANGE

1. See, for example, Hart Research Associates, *Falling Short?*, p. 12.

2. Ashley Finley, "Making Progress? What We Know about the Achievement of Liberal Education Outcomes," Association of American Colleges and Universities (July 11, 2012).

3. Jerry Gaff and Paul L. Gaston, "Revising General Education—and Avoiding the Potholes: A Guide for Curricular Change," Association of American Colleges and Universities (February 20, 2009).

4. Stolzenberg et al., *Undergraduate Teaching Faculty: The HERI Faculty Survey 2016–2017*, p. 33.

5. David Riesman, *Constraint and Variety in American Education* (1956), p. 23.

6. Jack H. Schuster and Martin J. Finkelstein, *The American Faculty: The Restructuring of Academic Work and Careers* (2006), p. 469.

7. Kenneth A. Feldman, "Research Productivity and Scholarly Accomplishment of College Teachers as Related to Their Instructional Effectiveness: A Review and Exploration," *Research in Higher Education* 26 (1987), p. 227.

8. Aspen Institute and Achieving the Dream, *Crisis and Opportunity: Aligning the Community College Presidency with Student Success* (2012).

9. Hart Research Associates, "Recent Trends in General Education Designs, Learning Outcomes, and Teaching Approaches: Key Findings from a Survey among Administrators at AAC&U Member Institutions" (January 2016).

10. Hart Research Associates, p. 3, note 1.

11. Ibid., p. 4.

12. Ibid., p. 11.

13. Ibid., p. 12.

14. National Survey of Student Engagement, *NSSE 2018 Multi-Year Report*, p. 9.

15. Hart Research Associates, "Recent Trends in General Education Designs, Learning Outcomes, and Teaching Approaches," p. 5.

16. Natasha A. Jankowski, Jennifer D. Timer, Jillian Kinzie, and George D. Kuh, *Assessment That Matters: Trending toward Practices That Document Authentic Student Learning* (January 2018), p. 28.

17. NSSE, *NSSE 2018 Multi-Year Report*, p. 12.

18. Jankowski et al., p. 28.

19. Goyal et al., "Meditation Programs for Psychological Stress and Well-being," p. 357.

20. Kelly A. Lack, "Current Status of Research on Online Learning in Postsecondary Education," Ithaka S+R (April 10, 2012), https://sr.ithaka.org/publications/current-status-of-research-on-online-learning-in-postsecondary-education/.

21. Wei Song and Harold V. Hartley III, "A Study of Presidents of Independent Colleges and Universities," Council of Independent Colleges (2012).

CHAPTER TEN.
ENCOURAGING REFORM

1. Quoted in Rudolph, *Curriculum*, p. 144.

2. Paul Baskin, "Crusader for Better Science Teaching Finds Colleges Slow to Change" *Chronicle of Higher Education* (June 17, 2013), http://chronicle.com/article//Crusader-for-Better-Science/139849.

3. Malcolm Getz, John J. Siegfried, and Kathryn H. Anderson, "Adoption of Innovation in Higher Education," *Quarterly Review of Economics and Finance* 37 (1997), p. 605.

4. Derek Bok, *The Struggle to Reform Our Colleges* (2017), pp. 125–26, 129–30.

5. Stolzenberg et al., *Undergraduate Teaching Faculty: The HERI Faculty Survey 2016–2017*, p. 33.

6. Paul D. Umbach, "How Effective Are They? Exploring the Impact of Contingent Faculty on Undergraduate Education," *Review of Higher Education* 30 (Winter 2007), p. 9.

7. M. Kevin Eagan Jr. and Audrey J. Jaeger, "Closing the Gate: Part-time Faculty Instruction in Gateway Courses and First-Year Persistence," in John M. Braxton, ed., *The Role of the Classroom in College Student Performance* (2008), p. 39.

8. Stephen R. White and Mark K. McBeth, *A History of the Doctor of Arts Tradition in American Higher Education* (2003).

9. Adrianna Kezar, Daniel Maxey, and Elizabeth Holcombe, "The Professoriate Reconsidered: A Study of New Faculty Models," University of Southern California, Delphi Project on the Changing Faculty and Student Success (October 2015).

10. American Association of University Professors, "The Inclusion in Governance of Faculty Members Holding Contingent Appointments: Recommendations" (2012; updated 2014), https://www.aaup.org/report/inclusion-governance-faculty-members-holding-contingent-appointments.

11. William James, *The PhD Octopus* (1903).

12. Mayhew et al., *How College Affects Students*, vol. 3, p. 133.

13. Lauren A. Rivera, "Ivies, Extracurriculars, and Exclusion: Elite Employers' Use of Educational Credentials," *Research in Social Stratification and Mobility* 29 (2011), p. 7.

14. Mayhew et al., *How College Affects Students*, vol. 3, p. 599.

15. See Bok, *The Struggle to Reform Our Colleges*, pp. 21–42.

Acknowledgments

Several people have helped me write this book. My research assistant, Meredith Krause, used her thorough knowledge of higher education and her talent as a researcher to discover all sorts of relevant articles and monographs that I could never have found by myself. Carol Geary Schneider, past president of the Association of American Colleges and Universities, read an early draft of the entire manuscript and gave me many valuable suggestions. My good friends Howard Gardner and Dick Light read later drafts and offered numerous helpful comments. Erin Driver-Linn and Henry Rosovsky kindly examined the last two chapters and supplied me with useful thoughts to consider. Once again, my editor at Princeton University Press, Peter Dougherty, offered encouragement and helpful advice while finding knowledgeable outside readers to comment on my manuscript. Cindy Buck, my copyeditor, did much to improve the final version. My stalwart assistant for more than twenty-five years, Connie Higgins, gave me invaluable assistance in finding books and articles, while preparing innumerable drafts of chapters. And finally, Sissela, my wonderful wife of sixty-five years, read the entire manuscript more than once and contributed many ideas to deepen my analysis. To all these friends, advisers, and helpmates, I owe a great debt of gratitude.

Index

CPSIA information can be obtained
at www.ICGtesting.com
Printed in the USA
LVHW030434260322
714338LV00003B/3